WHEN YOU PLACE A CHILD....

WHEN YOU PLACE A CHILD....

By

ERWIN H. PLUMER, A.C.S.W.

Youth Services Associates
Durham, North Carolina

CHARLES C THOMAS • PUBLISHER
Springfield • Illinois • U.S.A.

Published and Distributed Throughout the World by

CHARLES C THOMAS • PUBLISHER
2600 South First Street
Springfield, Illinois 62794-9265

© *1992 by* CHARLES C THOMAS • PUBLISHER

ISBN 0-398-05770-2

Library of Congress Catalog Card Number: 91-32425

With THOMAS BOOKS *careful attention is given to all details of manufacturing
and design. It is the Publisher's desire to present books that are satisfactory as to
their physical qualities and artistic possibilities and appropriate for their particular
use.* THOMAS BOOKS *will be true to those laws of quality that assure a good
name and good will.*

Printed in the United States of America
SC-R-3

Library of Congress Cataloging-in-Publication Data

Plumer, Erwin H.
    When you place a child— / by Erwin H. Plumer.
      p. cm.
    Includes bibliographical references.
    ISBN 0-398-05770-2 (cloth)
    1. Foster home care—United States.   I. Title.
HV881.P55 1992
362.7'33'0973—dc20   91-32425
                                                        CIP

Dedicated to Two Teachers:

Richard M. Eastman, Ph.D., inspired and inspiring Professor of English. He taught excellence in English and, by his example, excellence in teaching.

Hazel K. Boss, Social Worker. A consummate worker with children, she sensitized her students to the pain of children who had to undergo separation.

PREFACE

The child's sob in the silence
curses deeper than the strong man
in his wrath.

Elizabeth B. Browning

This book is intended especially for the beginning worker and for the worker who has never placed a child. It may also be helpful for the worker who has been so busy that she has never had time to reflect on what placement really means and for the worker who has placed children so frequently that it has become routine. Placement may become routine for the worker; it never becomes routine for the child.

Separation of a child from his family is the most devastating thing that can happen to a child. Separation and placement in alternate care are traumatic for the child irrespective of the nature of his family life, which may have included neglect or abuse. Separation wounds both the child and the family, and the wounds caused by separation are the more insidious for being invisible.

Legally, separation is a simple operation: a court order can take the child out of the family. No effort, skill, or wishes, however, can take the family out of the child. The family is a permanent part of the child; any circumstances or conditions which cause the child and family to be separated interfere with, but cannot dissolve, the bond which links child to parents.

Placement of a child in alternate care is a process, not an act. When it is necessary to separate a child from his family, a carefully planned process must take place. The placing worker who orchestrates the placement process must work with exquisite sensitivity to the needs of both child and parents, for she is in a unique position to help determine the future of the child and the fate of the family.

If the child and his family are supported, counseled, and nurtured through the placement experience, if their right to self determination, in accordance with their capacity, is upheld, and if emotional stability and maturation are encouraged and preserved, the likelihood that the child will turn out to be a self respecting, self disciplined, responsible adult is enhanced, the child and his family may for the first time develop a viable relationship with each other, and the possibility of family reunion is increased.

If, on the other hand, the child is moved arbitrarily, capriciously, repeatedly, and/or without awareness of the inner needs of both child and parent and without due regard for the indissoluble connection between child and family, it is likely that the child will develop into an ineffectual adult, engaged in a lifelong search to have his needs met, always dependent upon outside sources of support and guidance. Concomitantly, the family may be permanently estranged from the child and from sources of help for themselves. In crass terms, the social worker will help to determine whether the child turns out to be a tax payer or tax consumer.

The basic task of the placing worker is to "get inside the skin" of the child and his family, insofar as this is possible, to see their world as they see it, to feel their world as they feel it, with all of the pressures, hostility, frustrations, sense of hopelessness, exhaustion, or apathy which is theirs. What logic says they should see and feel is irrelevant; what they may be able to see, understand, feel, or be able to do six months later, with sensitive help of the worker, is still a dream. The worker never stops working or dreaming, but her work is rooted in reality, and the reality is what the parents and child see, feel, and are able to do today. The worker must use the classic social work dictum, "Start where the client is."

The following considerations will be determined in large part by the sensitive handling of the child and his family when placement in alternate care appears to be necessary:

- Will the process of separation and placement have ingredients of healing for child and family?
- Will the family and child be supported and assisted in moving through the experience at a rate to which they can adjust?
- Will this child have some sense of his own identity and know to whom he belongs?
- Will this child feel himself to have intrinsic worth?
- Will the family members feel themselves to be accorded the dignity of individuals?
- Will the family's continuing right to make decisions be honored in accordance with their capacity?

• Will the family have a continuing role in the life of their child? If not, why not?

• Will this child spend his growing-up years in alternate care?

• Is the child/family connection strengthened or weakened by the worker's involvement?

BASIC RULES

Three basic rules obtain in work with the child and his family:

• Feelings before facts. If feelings are attended to, more often than not the facts will take care of themselves.

• All behavior has meaning. The worker may or may not be able to ferret out the reasons for the behavior, but she needs to remember that behavior does not just "happen." Behavior is the natural consequence of antecedent circumstances or conditions.

• Listen to the kids. In our society, too frequently children are given short shrift. Adults talk to them, but tend not to listen to them. Kids have something to say that is worth listening to; their thoughts, feelings, and reactions are valid. The worker is a different kind of adult, or should be: she listens.

PHILOSOPHY OF PLACEMENT

The philosophy of services to children and their families on which this book is based is as follows:

• The family is a psychological unit which can be conceived of and treated as a whole.

• The child's needs or pathology cannot be separated from the needs or pathology of the family; no attempt is made to perceive or treat the child as separate from the family, or, conversely, to see or treat other members of the family as separate from the child.

• A change in one part of the family may result in changes in other parts and in the whole.[1]

• Families belong together.

• When problems exist within a member of a family or among members of a family, services to attempt to relieve or to solve that problem should first be brought into the family home to prevent the need for placement of a child.

• Prevention of placement is most effective when services for the family are introduced at or near the beginning of the problem.

---

[1]Moss, Sidney Z.: Integration of the Family into the Child Placement Process. *Children*, 219, Nov–Dec 1968.

- Preventive services must reach out to families, for families at risk characteristically are unable to seek help until disaster has taken place.
- If a child must be separated from his family, he should be placed in the least restrictive environment that can be found.
- The placement resource should be within reasonable proximity to the family home.
- The goal of any placement for the child is maturation and continuous involvement with adults who have meaning to him.
- If there is any reason to believe that reunification of the family may be possible, services to the family must continue while the child is in placement.
- If reunification of the family is determined to be highly unlikely, either at the time of placement or within approximately eighteen months thereafter, permanent alternative living arrangements should be made for the child, and parental rights should be terminated, with some differential in accordance with the age of the child.
- Services to the child and his family must continue after the placement experience of the child.

Cases vary widely, as do caseloads. No formula for placement can be articulated which will serve for all cases; there is no simple "how to." The worker must use her ingenuity and creative imagination to develop an appropriate approach to each case, but if she adheres to established principles, she will likely stay out of major trouble with her cases and will have at least a fighting chance at making some progress.

This book is intended to serve as a mind-stretcher for practitioners. It is intended to be used as a measuring stick against which current practice is assessed. Caseloads in most public agencies are so large that time and energy for study are limited. For those who are interested in and have time to acquire more profound insights, a list of suggested readings is appended.

Placement is a sobering task for any worker. It is also one of the most challenging and exciting areas of practice, for here the worker has an opportunity to make a difference.

E.H.P.

CONTENTS

WHEN YOU PLACE A CHILD . . .

PART ONE
SEPARATION

Chapter 1

EARLY CHILDHOOD

The very early months and years of life constitute the most important period for the development of personality. The reason for this has been a matter of conjecture, in which the old argument between heredity and environment has played a part. It is likely that that argument never will be resolved definitively, for science continues to push back the boundaries of knowledge.

We have not yet been able to change the effects of heredity, although that may be possible in the future. We can do something about environment, however. At the very least, those who work with children, and especially those who have the task of placing children in out-of-home care, must have some specific awareness of early childhood growth and development and the implications of that process for placement.

The worker must have a framework for growth and development, some theoretical formulation which will explain to her satisfaction the process by which the infant eventually develops into an adult. Many theories of growth and development are available; the specific theory she chooses is largely immaterial, so long as it makes sense to her. She needs such a theory for two basic reasons:

• The worker must be able to identify the functional age of the children with whom she works, whether or not placement is a necessity. The placement resource chosen for the sixteen-year-old who functions as a sixteen-year-old will be different from the placement resource chosen for a sixteen-year-old who functions on the level of a twelve-year-old.

• The worker must be able to identify behavior that is normal for a particular age. This is crucial for the worker's approach to the child; it is equally crucial for the worker's interaction with the family. Normal behavior may vex the parents and try their patience, but that is a parental problem, not a child problem, and the worker's focus will be directed accordingly.

EARLY EXPERIMENTS

Research and experimentation in early childhood development is hardly new. In the thirteenth century, Emperor Frederick II conducted an experiment in which babies were deliberately subjected to institution-like experiences, being raised by nurses and foster mothers who were not permitted to speak to them.

The emperor's purpose was to find out which language the child would speak if given no biases by adults. In the absence of adult influence, would the children naturally speak Greek, Latin, or the language of their parents? In order to make that determination, he instructed the foster mothers and nurses to feed, bathe, and care for the children, but never to speak to them.

The experiment failed, however, because all of the children died. Even with adequate physical care, they could not live without stimulation and responsiveness and without loving words and normal interchange with their foster mothers.[1]

This gives us some clues as to the impact of the external environment on the early days of life.

EARLY DEVELOPMENT

The very early days, months, and years are formative in the development of the child. The reasons for this are not hard to find.

At birth the child is thrust into an environment which is totally different from the one he has known. *In utero,* he lived in a liquid environment of constant temperature where all of his needs were met, where he was warm and safe, and where he knew no needs. For nine months he enjoyed a life of ease and comfort with no responsibility or effort on his part.

The birth process propels him violently into an environment of air where he is expected to breathe on his own, where temperature changes, where he must ingest his own food, eliminate his own wastes, where he has needs, where he must signal for assistance when assistance is needed, and, most importantly, where having his needs met requires a volitional act of someone more mature than he.

Nothing is more helpless than the human infant; the infant is dependent upon others just for survival. Just as important, however, a child needs others in order to become human, as was demonstrated in the emperor's experiment. Contact with other people is needed to become aware of himself as a separate being, endowed with capacities which are both similar to and different from other individuals. Others perceive him and provide feedback on their perceptions, and he begins to see himself as he is.

The child's early attitudes and feelings toward this new world, which proceed from the response of the world to his early needs and cries, form the basis from which the child views and interprets later events; they lay the foundation for his later life.

If the child's needs are met with reasonable speed and adequacy, if the people who attend him are reasonably solicitous, if he is handled with reasonable gentleness—in other words, if his first impressions of this strange new world are reasonably positive, he concludes that this is a friendly, safe place to be.

The child who has been consistently fed, diapered, and made comfortable as an infant, who later was given time to experiment and learn at his own pace, and who, in the learning process, had his efforts recognized and validated, tends to see the world as generally benign, predictable, and supportive. These experiences form the basis for later perceptions and the child acquires a tendency to interpret the world in a generally positive way. He is free from any lingering fear or apprehension which would divert his energy and attention from his basic task of growing and learning.

On the other hand, if he cries and gets no response, if he is handled harshly or not handled at all, or if the response is long delayed, he concludes that this new world is a hostile and dangerous place, and he will react accordingly.

In learning to respond to a hostile—or even unpredictable—world, he may become impulsive, aggressive, withdrawn, or he may acquire other qualities which are problematic for those around him and, ultimately, for himself. If he suspects others of hostile intent against him, he must always assume a defensive posture. If others are seen as enemies, it is quite appropriate to attack in apparent self defense. He may strike out at the world with rage and destruction, or, alternatively, he may become a fearful and withdrawn child, feeling impotent and helpless.

A child growing up in our society has a very complex set of behaviors to learn in order to survive.

He must deny his natural inclinations to eat, sleep, and eliminate as it suits him; he must adhere to the established patterns of society. Later on, school is held within prescribed hours, and the limits of permissible behavior are preset. In the world at large, laws provide for the orderly conduct of society, sometimes at the cost of limiting individual preferences. None of these limitations has any obvious meaning for the child.

To learn to delay gratification, to eat and eliminate in designated ways and at appointed places, and to curtail his instinctive desires and actions are hard for a young child to learn, but by and large he learns with a manageable amount of frustration when raised by wise, kind, and patient parents. A desire to please, to win approval, and being a part of the social group helps him to learn the necessary social behaviors.

It is in the nature of being human that we tend to perceive selectively. Whether it be a matter of acceptance of, or hostility toward, another person, political party, religious preference, racial bias, or art choice, once we hold an opinion we select from our ongoing experiences those things which reinforce that opinion. Children do the same. A child who has experienced neglect and hostility selects out of his experience those things that reinforce that view, as does the child who has had a more beneficent reception.

The child learns too well, and, like adults, he has difficulty unlearning or correcting his view in the light of later perceptions.

If the child learns early that others cannot be depended upon, if he has been too frequently let down and too keenly disappointed, he may choose never again to invest his feelings too fully in others. The loss of love has been too painful; it is better not to become attached.

Intimate relationships may be difficult for him, loyalty and dependability to friends and family unlikely. Not only is such a person cheated from life's deep feelings and relationships, but he is also likely to become the inadequate parent of the next generation. Without feelings to establish concern, such a person may be more prone to abuse the welfare, feelings, and rights of others.

If there are few consistent others in his life, or if he is shunted from one caretaker to another, it is difficult for him to develop a consistent and accurate image of himself. He may attempt many things inappropriate for himself, or fail to achieve because he has no real notion of who he is or what he can do.

The most unfortunate factor of this situation is that the child must reserve part of his energy for contending with the world. He can never relax; he can never devote all of his energies to being himself, to growing and learning; a portion of those energies must always be reserved for basically a defensive purpose.

Children need an environment which will approve and applaud their positive impulses and actions and which will help them learn how to channel their negative impulses and actions. Children need to grow in a predictable, permanent environment where they are accepted and loved, and where they can learn to care about others. They need an environment in which they are valued for what they are—not because of anything, not in spite of anything, not pending their becoming anything in particular; they are valued unconditionally. Being valued by others, they learn to value themselves. When they value themselves and are free from pressures to defend themselves or to question the reliability of the world, they are free to focus their energies on growing and maturing.

These are things the worker can check out as she works with families.

Bonding and Attachment

The prenatal period is a time of preparation. While the fetus is developing, the soon-to-be parents develop images of what their child will be like. They form expectations and hopes for the child, for themselves as parents, and for their relationship with their child.[2]

Many conditions of the prenatal period affect the kind of attachment that will develop between parent and child. These conditions include such factors as the following:

- Characteristics of the pregnancy itself, such as the timing of the pregnancy;
- Whether or not the pregnancy was planned, desired, tolerated, or resented;
- The mother's condition during the pregnancy, the presence or absence of prenatal complications;
- Maturity of the parents;
- Harmony or disharmony in the marital relationship;
- Financial adequacy of the family;
- Day care availability;
- Experience with previous pregnancies and children, if this is not the first child;
- The kind of parenting that the parents themselves had received.

Development of Bonding in Infancy

Direct bonding between mother and child begins during the very first moments of the child's life. Every mother uses her first contact with her child to explore him, to count fingers and toes, to make sure that all standard parts are present and located in the appropriate places.

The Arousal-Relaxation Cycle[3]

The interactions between parents and child are exchanges between them that involve touch, sound, and visual stimulation.

When an infant experiences displeasure or tension because of either internal or external stimuli, he discharges it. It is clear to everyone when the infant is uncomfortable, for he squirms and cries.

As long as the infant is discharging this tension, his energies are fully engaged, and he cannot participate in, observe, or learn from the outside world. Thus, if an infant or child continuously experiences tension, his ability to perceive what is going on around him is stymied.

The opposite of displeasure in an infant is not happiness or pleasure, but is a state of quiescence, or contentment. The parent's role when the infant is discharging tension is to return the child to a quiescent state.

Most of the interactions between a mother and her newborn child are initiated by the infant. The child fusses and cries; the mother responds. The interaction is pleasurable for both and is likely to continue through a series of activities.

The following diagram[4] depicts a typical, successful interaction between mother and child. The interaction is initiated by the child's need and consequent expression of displeasure and completed by the mother's response.

There are several places where the successful completion of the arousal-relaxation cycle might break down for a mother and child pair.

• Children (and adults) have widely varying pain thresholds. What produces acute pain in one child is unnoticed by another. If a child does not sense pain or discomfort, or if that pain or discomfort is not troublesome, the child will not cry for help, and the caregiver is not alerted to his need.

• The child may cry, but the response is inordinately delayed, or there is no response at all. Neglectful or abusive parents may fail consistently to respond to their child's needs.

• Some parents try earnestly to respond to the child's needs, but, try

The Arousal-Relaxation Cycle

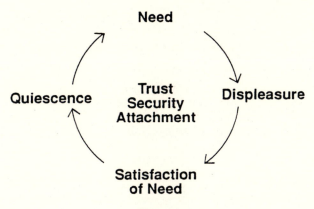

Figure 1.

as they will, they are unable to relieve his discomfort. The colicky baby, the baby with an unusual personality or a special medical condition, or the child who for a host of other reasons is a "fussy baby," is guaranteed to vex the parents as they try, without success, to comfort the child.

• Some parents are overly attentive to their child and meet the needs of the child before he is uncomfortable, or protect him from any stimuli that might disturb him. It may be as harmful to deprive the child of discomfort as it is to deprive him of the feeling of pleasure.

Society is quick to blame parents, particularly the mother, for any disturbance in the child's emotional development. This is an unfair generalization. The possibility of neglect or inappropriate caregiving needs to be explored by the worker, but frequently the parent(s) will be found to be without fault.

The Positive Interaction Cycle[5]

The arousal-relaxation cycle is initiated by the child's needs, and successful completion of this cycle contributes to bonding between mother and child. However, the extent to which the mother initiates interactions with the infant also influences the attachment between them. As the child grows, the degree to which the caregiver initiates interaction with the child may be more important than the caregiver's responses to the child's expressed need. The more social interactions an infant has with someone, the more strongly attached he becomes to that person.

The diagram below illustrates the cycle of positive parent/child interaction that is initiated by the parent.

The Positive Interaction Cycle

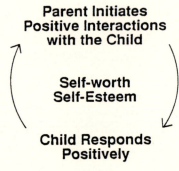

**Parent Initiates
Positive Interactions
with the Child**

**Self-worth
Self-Esteem**

**Child Responds
Positively**

Figure 2.

A child who is well-attached to one person can more easily become attached to others. This is obviously critical for foster care and adoption, for it means that the child who has been attached to a parent can be helped to become attached to a foster parent or adoptive parents.

The primary psychological task for a toddler is to recognize that he and his primary caretaker are two separate individuals. This is eased by the toddler's increasing mobility.

"Peek-a-boo" games and watching his mother disappear into another room and then reappear pay off, and by approximately eighteen months the child has developed enough memory that he can be away from her and realize that she still exists. After the child is three, it becomes easier for him to accept his mother's temporary absence.

However, throughout life attachment behavior increases during times of anxiety and stress. Observing a child when he is tired, frightened, or not feeling well is often a useful way to find out about his attachment to his caretaker. The well-attached child will seek out his primary caretaker at this time and be comforted.

Separation in Infancy

Infants are especially sensitive to developing attachment behaviors during the fourth, fifth, and sixth months of their lives.

In one study,[6] 86 percent of those infants who were moved from a foster home to an adoptive home when they were six months old showed signs of disturbance. Every infant who was moved at the age of seven months or older showed marked disturbance.

After the child is six months old, he is increasingly able to distinguish between family members and strangers, and he has a corresponding anxiety when he is approached by a stranger.

The strength and frequency of this reaction increase as the child nears one year of age. This makes it increasingly difficult for a child to develop an attachment to a new primary caretaker during this period, which has implications for the placing worker and adoptive worker.

According to one researcher[7] the anxious, insecure child may falsely appear more strongly attached to his mother than the secure child who can explore fairly freely in a strange situation, using his mother as a secure base.

The insecure child may not explore even when his mother is present, may become extremely alarmed by the appearance of a stranger and seem helpless and in acute distress when his mother leaves.

The Child's Expanding World

The child functions in ever-widening circles. First he is in the crib; then he graduates to the playpen; then he can roam anywhere in the house, but when he goes into the yard someone has to go with him; then he can play in the yard by himself; next he can go up and down the sidewalk, but he may not cross the street—and so on, until he is old enough and has sufficient judgment to go by himself wherever he wants to go.

His relationships expand in a similar fashion. First there is just mother, then there is father, then siblings, grandparents, aunts and uncles, neighbors, and so on. Each step forward is based upon the cumulative steps from the past.

While his world is expanding in this way, he has increasing responsibilities, which are directed by the adults in his life.

• It starts with toilet training—learning that there are particular circumstances under which the discharge of bodily functions is preferred.

• It goes on to recognizing the property and the rights of others—it is not nice to break his brother's toy; biting his sister is frowned upon, even if he thinks she deserves it.

• Chores are added—cleaning his room, emptying the wastebaskets, carrying out the trash, feeding the dog.

In this interaction between parent and child, the teaching and learning process, the child is introduced to family values, customs, and behavior.

Then comes school, where the teachers have their own ideas about what he should do, and how and when he should do it. Next come clubs, baseball, basketball, the marching band. And gradually the child's horizons expand.

One of the more difficult tasks of parenting is to coordinate parental expectations with the increasing abilities of the child. If parental expectations get too far ahead of the child's abilities, the child may be in danger—from crossing the street, running the lawnmower, driving a car, etc.

On the other hand, if parental expectations lag too far behind the child's abilities, the child is infantilized, and he is forced into either timidity and lack of self esteem or rebellion. Every parent struggles with this balancing act.

THE FAMILY AS A PRIMARY GROUP

Family life is based on a reciprocal relationship between parents and child. The parents do something for the child, and he responds; the child does something for the parent, and they respond.

When he is little, he gurgles and coos, and his parents laugh; when he takes his first step, his parents applaud; when he says his first word—perhaps intelligible only to the parents—they are jubilant, they think this is wonderful, as if he were the first child ever to do such marvelous things—no other child ever talked so clearly or so early. And they feel good about themselves—aren't they the clever ones for having such a brilliant child.

Normal parents respond to the child not just for what he does, but for what he is—he is an extension of themselves, a visible evidence of their love for each other, an indication of their stability and their normalcy in wanting and having a family; he is a promise of their posterity.

The child perceives the delight which his parents have in him, and, in that delight, what he does and, even more, what he is, is validated. He feels good about himself because they feel good about him.

The training he receives from his parents differs in terms of where he is in the family hierarchy. If he is the first child born, he is always the oldest child, no matter how many more come along. If he is the second of three children, he is always the middle child. The last child is forever the "baby" of the family. His perception of himself and other's perception of him is determined in part by the position he holds in the sequence of children.

In the family, the child can experiment with interpersonal relationships, test out ways of coping with and resolving life's concerns and problems, discover the natural consequences of his own behavior, and learn effective ways to deal with his own feelings.

As the child struggles to find a balance between freedom and limitations, the family provides support and encouragement, comfort and healing, approval and recognition, and acceptance and belonging. The child's sense of identity and his feelings of self-worth and self-competence are rooted in his primary group relationships.

The constant in all of these experiences is the family. The child can meet and cope effectively with the relationships and situations he encounters because he has developed and tested his capacities in adequate parent/child relationships and because home is always available.

All of this is to say that the family is the child's first primary group. With the family, you didn't sign an admission application, you did not fulfill any entrance requirements, no skills were needed. You belong to a primary group because that is where you belong.

When, as in placement, the child prematurely loses his first primary group, the family, he must be provided with a replacement primary group, a group in which the learnings given above can be carried on. The placement worker is responsible for ensuring that the placement resource provides such a group.

So far, we have been talking about the traditional thinking of bonding and attachment, and the influence primarily of the mother on the infant and small child.

The bonding and attachment theory has limitations, perhaps the chief being that it is excessively restrictive. For example, in this theory day care is detrimental, since it severs the single most critical relationship in a child's social life and thereby jeopardizes social and emotional development.

The ingredients of healthful early childhood are essentially these:

- Continuity of the environment, both human and nonhuman;
- Reliability, which makes the caregiver's behavior predictable;

  • Graduated adaptation to the changing and expanding needs of the
child, whose growth processes impel him or her toward independence
and adventure;
      • Provision for realizing the child's creative impulse.

These can be achieved in ways other than those described in classical
bonding and attachment. The child's social contacts quickly reach beyond
his mother to include father, siblings, uncles, aunts, grandparents—
and then neighbors, peers, teachers, and others. There is no reason to believe that this social network does not also contribute to the child's
growth.

Following this to its natural conclusion, it is likely that appropriate
day-care can enhance social development by exposing the child to a
variety of experiences with adults and other children. Day care may
become another branch of the child's social network.

Lewis[8] and other researchers have even found that children who were
maltreated at home were able to develop good social relationships if they
were in a good day-care system. Other children, he says, can provide
social experience as good as that provided by mothers.

NEW LEARNING ABOUT INFANCY

New research has shed light on factors which earlier were ignored or
made light of. Let us turn briefly to some examples.

Since 1972, there has been an increased awareness of prenatal influence and experiences of the child in the first days and weeks of life.

It has been found that newborns who heard the sound of the human
heartbeat in the hospital nursery gained more weight and cried less than
those who didn't.

In an experiment at the University of North Carolina, infants suckled
a nipple that activated a tape recorder.[9] One pattern of sucking produced
their mother's voice; another pattern produced another voice. Babies
quickly learned to produce their mother's voice and preferred it.

In another experiment, pregnant women read a children's story aloud
twice a day for six weeks prior to delivery. After birth, their babies
preferred the familiar story.[10]

The same experiment was worked on fetuses, which showed recognition of the familiar story by a change of heartbeat.

The fact is, some learning is taking place prenatally. The implications are yet unclear. Grandma may have been right when she told her pregnant daughter, "Think pure thoughts."

Habituation.[11] Habituation is an indication of basic learning and memory processes that has been detected in newborns. If a stimulus—a sight or sound—is presented to an infant several times in a row, the baby usually will pay less and less attention to it each time, suggesting that he or she remembers having seen or heard it before and is now growing bored with it. If a different stimulus is then presented, the infant will perk up and pay attention to it, suggesting that he or she can discriminate between the two.

Habituation, which becomes increasingly acute over the first ten weeks of life, is commonly assessed as a measure of an infant's maturity and well being and is seen as a good predictor of later intelligence.

Associative Learning.[12] Associative learning has also been detected in infants. In one study, two researchers taught 48- to 96-hour-old infants to discriminate between two different sounds in order to receive a taste of sugar water. After only one half hour of training, these infants learned that turning their heads at the sound of a tone, but not a buzzer, would earn them a reward. During the next half hour, the buzzer-tone combination was reversed, and the babies learned to respond to the buzzer instead of the tone.

Memory.[13] Researchers have found that infants have surprisingly good memories. Two researchers hung a mobile over an infant's crib and attached it by a ribbon to one of the baby's limbs. Six-week-old infants very quickly discovered which arm or leg would move the mobile. Two weeks later, the infants were placed in the same situation, and they remembered which arm or leg to move—even though they weren't attached to the mobile. These early signs of memory are the basis for the kinds of learning from experience that go on throughout life.

Imitation.[14] Imitation is another ability with which babies have surprised us. According to most traditional theories of infant development, the ability to imitate facial gestures occurs at about one year of age. One researcher has moved that development back to the time of birth, and even suggests that babies may be born with the ability to imitate facial gestures.

The researcher and his colleagues originally tested 12- to 21-day-old infants and found that they could imitate certain gestures, such as opening and closing the mouth and sticking out the tongue. Thinking that infants could have learned to imitate such gestures during two or three weeks of close interaction with their mothers, the researchers tested even younger babies. Forty infants younger than three days of age and one only 42 minutes old clearly imitated the gestures.

Facial imitation by infants has implications for social development. The suggestion is that the ability to respond to and imitate a human face means that infants play a very active role in structuring their world right from birth. In particular, it is said, it means that babies are interested in, even fascinated by, the human beings in the world around them.

We do not yet know what all this means, but we do know that these research findings add new dimensions to the meaning of early days of life. The placement worker has concomitantly enhanced responsibility for giving careful attention to the early experiences of the child.

THE CHILD'S MEMORY OF HIS FAMILY

The child does not "remember" his early experiences the way adults remember experiences. The adult can call to mind memories of past events—the first date, getting a driver's license, a certain movie, etc. The child remembers, too, but not in that way. He remembers feelings associated with early events, rather than the details of the events themselves. For example, long after he has forgotten that his mother nursed him, he has feelings he had which were connected with being hugged, fondled, sung to, and played with as mother fed him.

Similarly, in less pleasant experiences, specific details have faded into the subconscious, but feelings associated with the experience remain. The six-year-old who was scared by a dog at age two may retain only enough memory of the incident to be afraid of dogs in general. He doesn't remember specifically why he is afraid, but he is afraid. He has unconscious memories of an earlier event.

The longer a child has lived with his family during these early years, the stronger their influences are upon him. He is more likely to have conscious memories, but also, the more numerous and more solidly established are his unconscious memories.

The child must coordinate new experiences with old experiences and memories. When the child's new experiences are not consistent with his old experiences or memories, in order to make sense of his life the child resorts to fantasy. Fantasies complicate the already complex issue of placement.

Thus, the family the child knows is a composite, made up of many experiences, many facts, and varying amounts of fantasy. The family as he knows it may not be exactly the family as it really is, but as he thinks that it is. That is important. It is the only family he knows, the only family he has. Whether the family is good or bad by community standards is immaterial to him; it is his family, and for him his family is right. If other families (or the standards or values of other families) are different, then they are the ones that are strange.

There is one inescapable fact about the relationship of the family to the child: the family is a permanent part of the child. No amount of effort, skill, or wishes can take the family out of the child.

This is the situation into which the placing worker comes.

NORMAL GROWTH EXPERIENCES: THINGS TO LOOK FOR

Child-rearing principles ensure that some situations are predictable, understandable, or, in some cases, avoidable. The worker may be able to pass some suggestions to caregivers, whether they are biological parents, adoptive parents, or foster parents. For example:

• Approval. The toddler does something—puts two blocks together, scribbles on a piece of paper with a crayon—then looks up, wanting, expecting, and needing approval, for in having what he does approved, he himself is approved. Approval need not be time-consuming: a smile, a nod of the head, a quick clapping of the hands and, "Oh, that's fine!" will suffice. The important thing is that some response from the adult is forthcoming.

• Substitution. Small children like to bang things together. Rock crystal goblets ring nicely, but banging them together tends to turn mothers grey. Simply substituting a pan lid or other unbreakable object for the goblet will reduce the mother's blood pressure and satisfy the child's need to bang. He may wail for ten seconds, but then he will continue his banging contentedly. Needs of both child and parent have been met.

• Curiosity. The normal child is insatiably curious, and he learns through satisfying his curiosity by touching, moving, smelling, and tasting everything in sight. This is fun to watch until he cleans out a dresser drawer, pulls all the toilet paper off the roll, stuffs it in the commode and then flushes, uses the screwdriver on the light switch, and pulls the cat's tail. The patience and understanding which parents show on these occasions help determine whether or not the child will have self confidence. "Baby-proofing" the house will save distress for parents and child.

• Property rights. Toddlers like to mark with pencils, pens, or crayons, and the wall provides a convenient and accessible surface for marking. Parents as a group find this less than amusing. When the child gets to this stage, the parent may keep a supply of scratch paper in a drawer which the child can open—this is "his" drawer; he soon learns that he is free to get the scratch paper whenever he wants it, but scratch paper, not the wall, is for marking. The child can learn what is legitimately accessible to him and what is off limits.

• Whining and tantrums. A parent may despair when the child whines or has a tantrum, and, in desperation, give in. When the child finds that this strategy works, he is sure to repeat it. Instead of having her own tantrum, or despairing and giving in, the parent can devise her own strategy. "You can whine or have a tantrum if you want, but I don't have to listen to it. Go to your room and have your tantrum." If the child is small, he can be carried to his room and the door can be closed. If the child is too large to carry and will not move, the parent can leave the room. When the public relations component of the tantrum is removed, and the child learns that the tantrum or whining will not get what he wants, the behavior will usually diminish.

• Behavior awareness. Adults should be sensitive to age-appropriate behaviors, e.g., if a two-year-old is asked a yes/no question, for the answer will always be "No." Instead of "Do you want to put your jacket on?" the question should be "Do you want to wear your red jacket or your blue jacket?" The latency-age child performs hair-raising acrobatics on his skateboard and bicycle. The teenager experiments with different styles of handwriting, hair styles, dress, speech, emotions, and driving. These are normal behaviors at different ages. Parents do not have to enjoy age-appropriate behaviors, but they are well advised to endure them without major complaint. The phase will pass, and it will pass more quickly and with less strain for both parent and child if it is allowed to wear itself out naturally.

• Consistency. The rules should be the same from day to day. If the child cannot bang unrestrictedly on the piano today, he cannot bang unrestrictedly on the piano tomorrow; if he was not allowed to play with the computer yesterday, he cannot play with it today, etc. In this way he learns the dependability of the world.

• Uniformity of approach by parents. Perhaps the most frequently abused principle of child rearing is coordination of approach of caregivers. Children are skilled at playing one parent against another, and parents must keep alert to the manipulations of the child. If the child wants to leave the supper table, and Dad says, "No," Mother supports this decision, even though, for her part, she would have permitted the child to go. If the child wants to go out and play and Mother says it is too close to mealtime, Dad supports her, even though he would have let the child go. Later, when the child is not present, mother and dad can iron out their differences and develop some mutually agreed-upon rules.

• Respecting the child. A child at play demonstrates real concentration, for children's play is not just play, it is experimentation with life. The child's play has to be coordinated with the daily schedule, of course, but adults must provide some leeway for the child. Instead of saying, "It's bath time right now," the child should be alerted ahead of time. "In fifteen minutes it will be time for your bath." "When the big hand gets to six, it will be time to put your toys away," "When you finish coloring that page, it will be time to wash for supper," etc. Thus, the child is recognized as an individual, and his plans, schedule, rights, and needs are respected.

• Holding to limits. Children of all ages depend upon adults to establish and hold to limits. This is how children define their world and their prerogatives. Holding to limits is essentially an extension of society. Society's law states that one cannot get a driver's license until age 16. Family law says you do not watch TV until homework is finished; a child does not go out to play until his belongings are straightened up and put away; everyone at the table tastes every food that is prepared—or whatever else is appropriate for this particular family. Once the limits have been established, they must be upheld by all adults.

• Consequences. The child should know in advance what the consequences for certain misbehaviors will be, and the consequences should be dependable. The child should have confidence that the penalty will be applied every time there is an offense. He needs to know that someone will help him protect himself from his growing, but largely uncontrolled, strength and abilities.

These are generally observable interactions between parent and child, and through such observations the worker can gain valuable insights into the family dynamics.

As elementary as these principles or procedures sound, they will be news to some of the parents. The worker is well advised to start with the simplest and most obvious before she moves on to the more technical or more esoteric.

SUMMARY

It is apparent that understanding of the importance of the early days of life is still being expanded. The worker must have some understanding of the elements of growth and development for her work with the child and, perhaps especially for her work with parents, as she seeks to avert the need for placement.

The worker seeks as much information she can get as to the nature of family functioning. Such questions as the following may help her as she coordinates the answers with her own knowledge of growth and development:

• What do the parents understand with respect to the needs of the infant and the growing child?

• To what degree do the parents find joy amidst the sometimes frustrating antics of small children?

• To what degree are the parents able to think for themselves, or, conversely, to what degree are the parents enslaved to their own childhood?

• To what degree are relations between parent and child or among family members reciprocal?

• Do the parents only speak to the child, or do they listen to him, too?

• Do parents find pleasure in the child's growing capabilities?

• Do parents respond to the child, or do they require the child to respond to them?

Endnotes

[1]Ross, J. B. and McLaughlin (Eds): A Portable Medieval Reader, NY: 1949, Albert R. Roberts, "Studies of Children Deprived by Human Contact, Interaction and Affection," in Albert R. Roberts (Compiler) *Childhood Deprivation*, Springfield, IL: Charles C Thomas, 1974, p. 21.

[2]Fahlberg, Vera. *Attachment and Separation.* MI Dept of Social Services, 1979, p. 9.

[3]Ibid., pp. 14–15.

[4]Ibid., p. 15. Used with permission.

[5]Ibid., p. 17. Used with permission.

[6]Yarrow, L. J., Research in Dimensions of Early Maternal Care. Merrill-Palmer

Quarterly, 9:1965. Quoted in Fahlberg, Vera. *Attachment and Separation.* MI Dept of Social Services, 1979, p. 12.

[7]Ainsworth, M. D. and Boston, M., Psychodiagnostic Assessments of a Child after Prolonged Separation in Early Childhood. Brit. J. Med Psychol., 25: 1952. Quoted in Fahlberg, Vera. *Attachment and Separation.* MI Dept of Social Services, 1979, p. 13.

[8]Trotter, Robert J. You've Come a Long Way, Baby. *Psychology Today,* 21:1987, p. 45.

[9]Anthony J. DeCasper and William Fifer, quoted in Gina Kolata, "Studying Learning in the Womb." *Science,* 20 July 1984, Vol. 225, No. 4659, p. 302.

[10]Gina Kolata, "Studying Learning in the Womb." *Science,* 20 July 1984, Vol. 225, No. 4659, p. 303.

[11]Trotter, op. cit., p. 38

[12]Ibid.

[13]Ibid., p. 38.

[14]Ibid., pp. 38–39.

Chapter 2

SEPARATION FOR THE CHILD

Enforced separation from his family is the most devastating thing that can happen to a child. Separation is disorienting at best, disastrous at worse, for it may lay the groundwork for lifelong instability. Forcible separation (which is most often the case) removes the child from the security, safety, and "belonging" of his home and family and thrusts him into a strange environment where he does not know, and has no reason to trust, the caregivers. Even though the child was neither safe nor secure at home, he did belong there, and he knows he belongs there. Separation has an immediate effect upon the child and his family, and it has a lasting effect upon the child's later adulthood and upon the family he will establish.

Separation is damaging for several basic reasons:

• Placement occurs when the child still needs to be given to by his family. In placement, nurture which should be provided by his family must be provided by strangers. Alternate caregivers can, indeed, provide affection, physical care, and emotional support, but they cannot replace the "belonging" which is an integral part of family living.

• Placement is an inversion of the natural order of growth and development. In the natural order, separation occurs when the child is old enough and mature enough to survive on his own. In placement, by contrast, separation can occur at any age; more often than not it occurs before the child is ready or able to survive on his own.

• Placement follows a series of negative experiences for child and family. Family disintegration is not a sudden or unpredictable event, it deteriorates gradually until it reaches the point where the parents finally realize that something is wrong or where someone outside the family intervenes.

In many cases, the child who is subject to placement has never received adequate nurture; in more extreme cases, he has been the victim of neglect or abuse. Whatever the circumstances, the child from a deteriorating family is less able even than the child who has had a normal family life to accept alternate caregivers or to function on his own.

25

Factors such as the following add to the trauma of separation:

• An outside force, usually the court, intrudes upon family life. Normatively, a family determines its own life style, makes its own decisions, and constitutes its own authority. To have family life controlled by the intrusion of an outside force is an aberration which, however needed, is resented.

• The child is propelled into an unknown future. No child has experience by which he can envision, gain perspective or insight into life apart from his family.

• Separation from his family may make all future attachments difficult and all future separations painful.

Let us review what happens in the natural sequence of growing up in what we like to think of as a "normal" family.

NORMAL GROWTH

The small child lives in an adult's world, physically, emotionally, and intellectually. Adults make the rules, adults enforce the rules, and adults impose the penalties when the rules have been broken. Every child is aware of this.

Adults are physically three times the size of small children. If we lived in a comparable world, we would live in a world populated by 18-footers. If we lived in such a world, most of us would attempt to get one of those giants on our side just in self defense. This is precisely what the child does. When the child tells his playmate, "My daddy can lick your daddy!" he is less interested in the physical prowess of his father than in his own safety. The child is telling himself that "Nothing can hurt me, because my daddy will protect me and take care of me." Out of his perceived need for protection, that is, his awareness of the difference in strength, power, and authority between adults and children, the child believes—he must believe—in the omnipotence and omniscience of his parents. His family is his protection until he is old enough and capable enough to protect himself.

Home is a refuge. When the world becomes too threatening, the child can go inside, slam the door, and stay inside until he has recouped his strength and courage and is ready to return to the battle. As one little fellow said, "Home is where, when you go there, they have to take you in."

The child is identified by his family. He is the "Jones kid," she is the "carpenter's daughter," or he is "the kid who lives in the big yellow house on the corner." Others perceive him as such, and he perceives himself as such.

As the child grows older, he grows in his ability to survive on his own, and parental involvement decreases correspondingly.

At birth the child is totally dependent upon others; nothing is more helpless than the newborn human. From birth to age 18, however, the line of dependency should decline steadily until age 18, the age of legal adulthood, when the child should be emotionally and intellectually prepared for independent living. The triangle of age/dependency shown below depicts the desired pattern of growth and development.

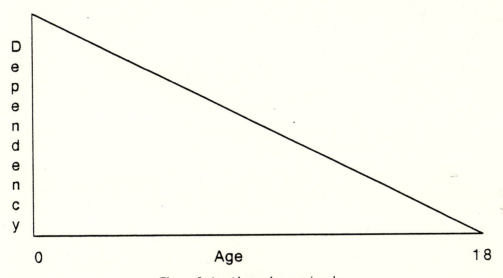

Figure 3. Age/dependency triangle.

Obviously, progress toward independence is not as unremitting as the diagram suggests. At various ages, perhaps most dramatically in adolescence, the line waffles up and down as independence appears alternately desirable and fearsome to the child. Allowing for temporary resurgences of dependence, however, movement toward independence should be relatively constant.

The child who has grown up in an adequate family has been provided with the conditions necessary for maturation, and he has gradually assumed more and more responsibilities, he has been given more and more privileges and leeway to do what he wishes, and his growing independence is a matter of satisfaction to his family and to him.

For the child in an intact family, failing to achieve independence by the target date of 18 is not calamitous, for most families remain interested, supportive, and involved with their child even after he legally becomes an adult, leaves home, and marries.

The separated child, on the other hand, may have no family support from the time of separation or before. If this child misses the target age of 18 in developing the capacity for independent living, better that he miss it on the near side rather than the far side, so that he is assured of the ability to handle legal adulthood when he gets there. When he turns 18, he can sign contracts, vote, marry, enlist in the armed forces without permission, and he is entitled to all of the other privileges and responsibilities of adulthood. If residual immaturity gets this child into trouble after he turns 18, he may have no one who is interested, supportive, or involved to whom to turn for help.

NORMAL SEPARATION

Every child has some experience in separation. Children learn to play out of sight of Mom and Dad, they go to school, they go to visit Grandma, they roam the woods or city streets and alleys, dad and mother go to work each day, etc. All of these are normal experiences of separation, and they are previews—practice runs, if you will—of the separation which is completed in adulthood.

Under normal circumstances, as when the child lives with his own family, preparation for social and emotional independence and self support is a gradual process. The child is, in effect, weaned from dependence while still being given to by his parents. Growing up means growing away from family, home, and the familiar associations which have provided the child with sufficient emotional satisfaction and self confidence to liberate him for new experiences with new people.

Normal separations have identifiable qualities which minimize the pain of separation and turn separation into a positive experience. Those qualities include the following:

- The child knows the reason for separation and its probable duration.
- The child has the assurance of reunion with his family when the purpose of the separation has been fulfilled.
- The child has confidence that his family will not change during the separation.

• The child knows that his family's love will continue during separation.

• The child has confidence that he will be welcomed home when separation is over.

Some natural separations, of course, are not followed by reunion. The family dog is hit by a car, someone in the family or in the neighborhood dies. Death is final. The child in his own family still has an advantage, for parents and other family members provide support and explanations.

Separations are natural occurrences in life as it changes and expands, and they prepare the child for final separation from his family. Separation is a healthy and desirable experience when the child is ready for it.

BACKGROUND OF PLACED CHILDREN

Separation is quite different for the placed child. Placed children, too, were shaped by their early experiences, but their family experiences may have been substantially less salutary than those of the children described above. Children who are vulnerable to placement come from families with varying types and degrees of dysfunction.

These children may have grown up in families where

• Children were not wanted;

• There was no dependability and little predictability in parenting;

• Parents had little understanding either of the nature of childhood or of parental responsibilities;

• The parents were preoccupied with their own problems and had little time or energy for children's problems or needs;

• Parents may have been overwhelmed by the rate of change in society and were trying to cope with today's world using tools of a generation ago—poor education, perhaps to the point of functional illiteracy; few skills;

• Parents may have no insight into the world as it really is; they may have little adaptive capacity to a rapidly-changing society.

These children may have grown up in a harsh world in which their needs were met erratically; were met in a surly, begrudging fashion; or were not met at all. The cuddling and playing with the infant which is a part of normal mothering may have been chaotic, unpredictable, or non-existent; the expanding abilities of the growing child were unrecognized or unappreciated. It may be that no one ever developed a dependable relationship with them. With their needs unmet or poorly met, they concluded that the world is a hostile, frustrating place.

Manifestly, a child with these early experiences has a poor foundation for maturation.

Typically, these children tend to be:

- Careless;
- Emotionally immature and unstable;
- Inept in interpersonal relationships;
- Lacking in any goal in life;
- Victims of life, rather than choosers in life;
- Not interested in school; and
- Unwilling or unable to attempt to solve problems if they can run away.

The shock of placement on top of inadequate early experiences may result in the child's emotional growth's being halted. His journey toward maturity may be arrested at whatever stage of development he had achieved when he was placed. This is depicted in Figure 4 below. Child A was placed at age 7, Child B was placed at age 10; Child C was placed at age 13. These children arrived at the chronological age of 18 with emotional ages of 7, 10, and 13 respectively. At 18 they were as immature and dependent as was appropriate for the age at which they were placed.

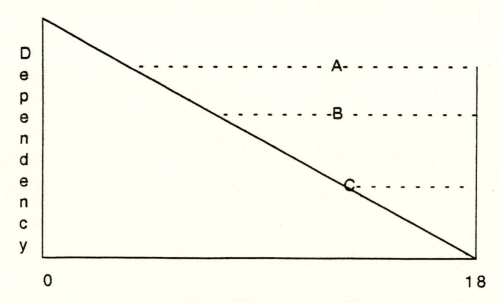

Figure 4. Age/dependency triangle—arrested emotional development.

This emotional arrest, which results in a difference between chronological age and functional age, is the more insidious for being invisible.

At age 18 the child looks like an adult, and everyone around him—employer, instructors, colleagues, friends—expects him to behave in a manner commensurate with his age and appearance. The results are predictable—flunking in school, bad work record, many job changes, unsatisfactory relations with peers, broken friendships.

There is a cumulative effect upon the child: immature behavior breeds unacceptable actions; unacceptable actions produce unsatisfactory life experiences; unsatisfactory life experiences reduce self esteem; reduced self esteem promotes immature behavior. And the cycle starts all over again.

Placement is not alone at fault in delaying development, but the stress of separation and placement on top of inadequate nurture or a dysfunctional family may doom the child to prolonged immaturity.

The social worker often enters the case first when placement has been requested, ordered, or is likely. If the worker ascertains whether or not the child has had access to, or has been denied, adequate nurture and a reasonable opportunity for maturation, she may identify one factor of the chronological age/functional age differential.

The social worker may help the child to move through the placement process in a manner which preserves the process of the child's development, and thus may help him to avoid arrested emotional development.

FEELINGS TOWARD FAMILY

When placement is necessary, the child inevitably has strong feelings about everyone involved. Because of the primacy of his family in his life, his feelings may first be focused on his family.

The child knows intuitively that he is not ready for independence; he knows that his family is supposed to take care of him, so it is not to be wondered at that the child reacts negatively to the family who "gives him away," "throws him out," or allows him to be taken away by the social worker or by the court. This is contrary to what he—and to what all of society—expects from families. Confronting placement, the child forgets family neglect or controversy, school difficulties, behavioral or other problems, and he spends his energy resenting what is happening to him.

The worker must be aware of several feelings toward families which are common for the placed child:

• He feels abandoned by his family. All of our culture says that parents support their child until he is able to go on his own. For him, that support has suddenly been rescinded.

• His life pattern has suddenly been reversed. He had expected to have increasing decision-making authority for his own life. Now, however, he is again being told what he must do—something is being been "done to" him, rather than "with" him, which pushes him back down the ladder of development.

• He feels betrayed. Someone from outside the home has come in and ripped him out of his family, *and the family did nothing about it.* In the child's mind, moreover, the family actually may have aided and abetted the placement worker's activities.

• His powerlessness is emphasized. The child knows he is powerless, and he depends upon his family to wield any power necessary to protect him. With placement, it is obvious that his family either has failed or has entered a conspiracy to get rid of him. Even the thought of a conspiracy is more tolerable than the thought of family impotence.

As long as power exists, the possibility of redirecting it remains, but if the family is also powerless, the child has no hope.

• He learns distrust. In his feeling of having been abandoned by those he trusted, he begins to distrust his family. If he cannot trust his own family, whom can he trust? It is only a short step from distrusting his family to distrusting all adults.

• He harbors a sense of favoritism. His brother and sister stayed home; obviously his parents preferred them to him. Children have a rigid sense of fairness, and to be selected from among siblings for placement violates his code of fairness.

• He is protective of family, despite the foregoing. To the small child in our society, parents are right. Even with his anger at his parents, the separated child idealizes his family; he fantasizes about life with them, especially when he is separated from them for long periods without an opportunity to experience family living again. His memory of the bad tends to disappear.

Sherry, twelve years of age, had been in an institution for six years. She described in detail to the social worker the ranch-style home where her mother lived. Sherry took the worker verbally through the house, describing the furnishings, the swimming pool, the horses, and the cars. Altogether she described an upper-class country estate.

The fact of the matter was her mother lived in one room in the poorest section of a small midwestern city. Before Sherry was four years of age, her mother had twice hitchhiked with Sherry from

Illinois to California and back and once from Illinois to Texas and back. Sherry had blocked out those experiences and, having no facts to go on, idealized her mother's situation.

Was Sherry lying? Of course not. Having no facts and having suppressed bad memories, she, like all children who do not have facts, had only her fantasies to sustain her.

After the child has been placed, he continues to believe the best about his family. Mother promises to come to visit, and he believes her. It doesn't matter how often she has promised this and then didn't arrive—on the appointed day he paces the floor waiting for her.

The child is still longing for the parents to give to him, and hence he cannot be free of the ties he has to them.

The child does not give up hope. Despite the events which have transpired, the child continues to hope that placement can be averted or, having taken place, can be terminated. Love and hate are equally deep emotions and are closely intertwined. His love for his family will provide him with hope; when that hope is dashed, his love can be turned instantly to hate.

The abiding questions for the placed child, of course, are, will they ever accept him back, and is he worthy of being accepted back?

FEELINGS TOWARD SELF

The worker also needs to be aware that, just as he has strong feelings about his family in face of placement, the child has strong feelings about himself.

- Unwanted. His first reaction may be that he is unwanted; therefore, he has been deported, banished to Siberia, and he will never be able to go home again.
- Anger. A basic response of many children in the initial stage of placement is anger. He protests against what is happening to him; he grieves for what he has lost, and the process of grief always includes some anger.

The child does not know at whom to direct his anger, so whoever comes into his line of fire becomes the target: foster parent, child care worker, school teacher or principal, and especially the placing worker.

Anger creates guilt. It is not acceptable to be angry at one's parents or other authority figures. Students routinely get in trouble for showing anger to a parent, teacher, or principal. Being angry, therefore, he also feels guilty.

• Guilt. A more direct guilt arises from his belief that somehow he managed to break up his family. Since his own parents cannot be at fault—remember, he has to believe in their omnipotence and omniscience—he has to be the guilty one. And this is confusing, for he doesn't know how he did it. He wasn't behaving any worse than the kid next door, and that kid is still living in his family. Carrying a load of self-appointed but erroneous guilt is one of the most common characteristics of newly placed children.

• Power. If he broke up his family, somehow he has exercised power that he didn't know he had. He doesn't know what it is or where it came from; he doesn't know how or when he used it; he doesn't know when the power may come again, or what effect it may have the next time. He doesn't know who will help him to identify and control this mysterious power which has been so devastating. This is scary. He does know that it is inappropriate for children to have power, and it is especially inappropriate for children to exercise power over adults.

• Punishment. Bad boys deserve to be punished, and anyone who broke up his family certainly deserves to be punished. The first step in that punishment, as he sees it, is placement. If the first step of punishment is losing your family, he has to wonder what the next step will be.

• Worthlessness. In his eyes, his parents have thrown him out or permitted him to be thrown out. The only thing you throw out is garbage; therefore, he is the human equivalent of garbage, abandoned, rejected, and worthless. Even though he has tried to deny these feelings, these suppressed thoughts come through loud and clear:

—Nobody loves me; nobody wants me.
—There must be nothing in me worth keeping, or this wouldn't be happening to me.
—I have nothing to offer.
—I am not worthy of being loved.

• Shame. Following immediately upon a feeling of worthlessness is a sense of shame. Guilt can be differentiated from shame: guilt arises from a feeling of wrongdoing; shame arises from a feeling of inferiority.[1] The shame, then, is for what he is, not for what he has done.

• Lack of self esteem. Lack of self esteem probably is the most common problem of placed children. Adults frequently unwittingly play a role in the child's loss of self esteem by a careless choice of words. "You're no good." "You're stupid." "You'll never amount to anything." This is a prophecy, and the child is likely to take it seriously and set about making it come true. Adults must be careful to differentiate what the child is from what he has done.

• Depression. It is not to be wondered at that these feelings lead to the possibility of depression. Feeling abandoned by those who should support him, feeling unloved and, even worse, unworthy of being loved is enough to cause depression in anyone. Children do not have the perspective or experience to reason their way through these feelings alone. If they are to escape depression, the placing worker is the most likely source of help.

These are some of the characteristics that children may demonstrate in separation. Not every child will demonstrate each one, but these are things the worker can look for.

The social worker must get behind the intellectual awareness of these possibilities and tune in to what the child is feeling—to "get inside his skin," so to speak, to see the world exactly as he sees it and to feel the situation as he feels it. The child may not be able to identify or list his feelings, and some feelings which he can name are forbidden topics in his family. Almost no child will tell the worker in words what he is feeling; the worker must extrapolate feelings from the child's actions, from his lack of actions, from what he says and from what he does not say.

WHAT THE CHILD LOSES

The worker is on somewhat clearer ground when it comes to what the child is losing through placement. The worker must perceive the loss through the eyes of the child. For the child, the loss is not academic, it is intensely personal. The social worker cannot remove his pain, but she can convey to him the fact that she understands and that she may be able to share his pain.

What the child loses and misses most in placement is in part age-stage related. For the young child, it is the mother primarily, but also the father, and the more dependent he is the more is he damaged by the loss.[2]

For the school-age child, in addition to his parents and siblings, his peers are of great importance, for after he starts to school he is involved increasingly with the associations with his friends and his activities outside his home. For the adolescent, there is his special buddy who shares with him the turbulence of adolescence and the alternating anticipation and anxiety of approaching adulthood.

More specifically, the child loses such things as the following:

- His family as a unit, its ways, its customs, its shared memories, the family system of which he has been a part;
- His sense of identity, his feeling of belonging to something stable;

• Customary ways of finding comfort, of turning to some familiar person, place, or object for reassurance;

• Relationships within the family, each of which has had its place in his life, whether primarily positive or negative. Having a sibling to envy, tease, emulate, or play with.

• Familiarity of his home, his bed, his dog, and his possessions;

• His position on the school team, his place in the classroom—he may be the best student or the worst student or somewhere in between, but he knows where he fits into the classroom hierarchy;

• The secret places where he goes with his best friend, the places available for cheap amusement; today, perhaps the safest and cheapest place to get drugs and where to use them without getting caught;

• The ordinary routines of family life. Even with abusive families, life may have a predictability, e.g., if Dad routinely comes home from work drunk, one learns to get under a table, make oneself scarce in the house, or leave;

• His neighborhood, which may be deteriorated, the friends few and even undesirable, the educational opportunities inferior—but these are adult perceptions, the child himself does not feel this way. To him they are known and familiar, they are his world. All of the small mysteries and rituals of a child and his feelings about these places and activities are a part of his life in a specific environment; they are his ways of gaining comfort and gratification, his ways of solving some of his problems of living.[3]

Thus, the child has ample reason to grieve in separation. The worker must somehow relate to these profound losses in the child's life and help the child make sense of that which to him is insensible.

REACTIONS TO PLACEMENT

The reactions of the child to the whole placement process do not end, of course, when he arrives at his destination. His reactions continue, and the placing worker has the responsibility for ensuring that his continuing reactions are dealt with in a positive manner.

The adaptive tasks that confront the child in the placement experience are contained in three major elements of change and in his ability to deal with his feelings about them:[4]

• Loss of the family and extended environment (persons and places), described above;

• Introduction of the placing agency and its personnel (strange persons and places) to assume responsibility for planning, securing direct care, and providing other services normally provided by family members;

• Introduction to a new family or group facility and extended environment.

The child may deal with the pain of placement in a number of ways, such as defiance, regression, withdrawal, depression, or by some combination of these.

In spite of all preplacement preparation, the child may face the real pain of separation only after it actually has occurred. Often he maintains (and believes) that the "shock" of separation has taught him his "lesson" and that, therefore, now, a week or so after his arrival, he should return home. All other problems which plagued him before, which in fact caused the separation, are blocked out by this overwhelming experience.

Conversely, he may deny separation pain, for he feels he has been rescued now from the tensions and conflicts of his previous life.

Sometimes he thinks that the mere fact of placement has solved his problem. He refuses to involve himself in further treatment. It is as though he said, "I have done my share by consenting to be placed; now leave me alone."[5]

In some children there is an ambivalence about placement, welcoming it as rescue and still feeling crushed by it. Anger and gratitude, suspicion and trust, despair and hope may be very much intermingled during the first weeks of a child's stay.

In some way, the worker must sort out these conflicting emotions help the child deal with them.

AFTER PLACEMENT

When the worst has happened, and placement really has taken place, the child may have one or more of various standard reactions.

• If he is bad, as obviously he is, since he broke up his family, he can expect more punishment. If losing his family is the first step of that punishment, what might the next step be? Bread and water? Solitary confinement? Execution?

• Who will administer the next step in punishment? Obviously, it will be the people with whom he now lives, foster parents or institutional staff. He knows he must treat them warily.

• If he provokes mild punishment for something he did, the new caregivers may get distracted from remembering how bad he really is and what serious punishment he deserves. Also, in that case he will know what the punishment is for. This may account for much initial acting out.

• Beware of the new caregiver, whose ways are unknown. The child expects the same treatment, the same reactions, from the caregiver as his parents gave him. When the new caregivers react differently, he may be confused.

• In placement, the child faces changed rules, e.g.:

—Speech. Language customary at home may not be acceptable. This is true not only of the foster home or institution, but of the community at large.

A teen-age girl who lived in an institution spent an hour in after-school detention. The van was a few minutes late, and when she was released from detention and found that the van was not waiting for her, in exasperation she exclaimed, to no one in particular, "Where the hell is the van; don't they know that detention is over at four o'clock?" The school secretary overheard her and pronounced, "I don't need to listen to that kind of language," and put the girl on detention for three more days.

—Actions. Actions which were normal at home may not be acceptable here.

A boy lived in a group home in which the bedrooms were on second floor and the bathroom was on first floor. Being accustomed to solving problems in the most direct way, when he had to go to the bathroom in the middle of the night, instead of walking downstairs to the bathroom, he urinated out the upstairs window. As punishment, he was required to drink a glass of his own urine.

• How long will this new caregiver keep him? Will she throw him out like his parents did? And how is he to know what will provoke her into throwing him out, since he never figured out what he did to get thrown out of home in the first place?

• There is the threat of closeness in the new parent. Child care workers have been known to sneak away in the middle of the night; a staff member resigns; another gets fired. Even seeing staff members take time off or go on vacations may be a threat that they will disappear. If he is just going to lose her like he lost his parents, why bother to get close?

• He must fulfill the prophecies that have been made saying that he is inadequate.

Willie, a handsome, husky fourteen-year-old, had problems with school. He said, "I can't learn; I'm dumb." Willie knew that he was dumb because his teachers and his parents had told him that he was.

Teachers and parents are powerful; he dare not contradict them. Predictably, he had problems with learning.

When he came into institutional care, hard work by three highly skilled and caring teachers helped him overcome his early indoctrination. Eventually came the day when Willie was found reading a book on the noon hour—not because reading had been assigned, but because he had discovered that books contain interesting things, and reading is exciting. When that point had been reached, his learning problems were essentially over. He was not dumb.

- Getting close to the foster parent or child care worker may imply disloyalty to his parents. He may think he cannot have a meaningful relationship both with his parents and with the new caregiver—it has to be one or the other.
- There is a threat of separation from new caregiver. If he has begun a relationship, he may become highly sensitive to any threat of separation. The child care worker takes a day off, goes on vacation; she simply is not home when the child expected her to be there. In some cases, it is not enough that the child care worker be at home when the child returns from school—she must be in a particular room.[6]
- Drive the caregivers away. The child may attempt to alienate the caregivers, usually through provocative behavior. This may be a deliberate, although unconscious, ploy to determine to what extent the caregivers are serious when they say that they care.

If the foster parents or child care workers misunderstand this dynamic, they may unwittingly play into his attempts to provoke rejection, which is simply testing. If they reject him, his expectations and fears are reinforced. The worker must help caregivers to understand this testing behavior for what it is and support them as they struggle to withstand the child's onslaught.

On the other hand, the insatiable need of the child for affection and attention may overwhelm the caregivers and finally drive them away.

Janie, a sixteen-year-old, entered an institution 400 miles from home, but within 25 miles of her two sisters. The sisters were initially delighted to have Janie nearby, and they attempted to establish a relationship with her. Janie had been deprived of emotional support for so long, however, that she became increasingly shrill in her demands for her sisters' time, gifts, and attention. Finally they had to withdraw to keep from being smothered. Janie promptly became pregnant.

Girls have this distinct advantage over boys: they can always create someone to love them. When girls feel particularly unloved, the predictable result is an "unexpected" pregnancy.

> • Life may be confusing. When another child leaves the cottage, the reasons for the discharge are not explained, and all remaining children wonder whether or not they will be next and for what reasons they may be discharged.
> • Honeymoon period. Frequently a child will appear to make an immediate adjustment to his new living arrangements. He is polite, obedient, respectful; he quickly learns the rules and follows them; he interacts appropriately with adults and other residents; he falls all over himself being helpful to staff, and in general he is an asset to the residence.

The inexperienced or unwary foster parent, child care worker, or social worker may take this complaisant behavior at face value and rejoice that the child's transition has been painless.

Experienced workers know better; they know that the child is just biding his time. Everything is strange; he may essentially be in shock from the separation, he may be too frightened of the new caregivers or residents and/or of the new surroundings to act naturally. He has to get acquainted and develop a degree of comfort before he can risk being himself; he has to assess the limits and the consequences for exceeding the limits. Until he has some confidence in his own safety and chances for survival, he dare not reveal himself to others.

As long as he remains in this defensive posture, his energies are not available to any program designed to bring about attitudinal or behavioral change.

The honeymoon period may end with a bang or a whimper, but no one is in doubt when it is over. Everyone breathes a sigh of relief when the child is comfortable enough to be himself and his new behavior is within reasonable bounds. The "model child" which existed during the honeymoon period has departed, probably never to return. The important fact is, however, that his feelings are again accessible, and real work can begin.

> • Lack of information. After placement—even months or years after placement—many children are still confused as to why they have been placed. Children in alternate care who have been asked why they are there have given a variety of reasons, often totally at variance with the facts. Sadly, in some cases even the social worker may not know why the child is in alternate care.

One new institutional executive discovered that one teenager had been in residence for more than four years. The boy was an excellent student, he had no apparent behavioral problems, and the record was unclear as to the reason for his continued placement. When the executive contacted the placing caseworker, she confessed that she did not know, either, why the boy had never been returned home.

• Erroneous information. If the child did not understand clearly why he was being separated from his family, he may harbor wildly erroneous ideas as to why he was placed.

The child may blame specific incidents for his initial separation: he was angry at a sibling or parent; he may have had thoughts about his parents or siblings which he knew would be unacceptable, but didn't know they knew; he may have said things which elicited a vigorous response from his parents.

Natural growing-up processes, especially sexual desires, may have elicited comments of displeasure from his parents, which led the child to believe that this was the reason for separation. When the child realizes that these feelings have not disappeared with placement, he may fear that the worker will throw him out if she learns about them.

It should be noted that the delinquent child has one real advantage over the dependent/neglected/abused child. The child who has been adjudged delinquent knows that there was a specific offense; that he appeared in court and the judge decreed placement. In other words, his trouble started with a known event and a specific date; the issue is clearcut. With this specificity, the delinquent child may accept placement more readily, and he may be easier to handle than non delinquents. The dynamics of the delinquency—the fact that his delinquency may have been an unconscious protest against family dysfunction and its effects—may forever elude the child, but still he may be better off than the child who has no reliable information as to the reason for his separation.

How the child gets through the pre-placement and placement procedures influences his adjustment in the immediate post-placement stage.

Irrespective of the adequacy of advance preparation, typically the placement experience involves some regression. The areas of regression depend to some extent on the age and developmental stage of the child. The young child who has just learned to speak or has recently achieved bowel or bladder control is the most likely to regress temporarily in these areas. Regression in some areas, such as fear of the dark, fear of being alone, disturbances in eating and sleeping, shortened attention span, agitation, and destructiveness, may occur at any age.[7]

To the degree that the child is able to understand what is happening and senses continuing support, these regressions will be temporary. If he does not understand what is going on, if he is left with unanswered questions, or if the pain of separation is unrelieved, his emotional development may be arrested.

A simple example: children learn the word "no" as one of their first words. This word appears around age 18 months, and the child is intrigued with this powerful little word, which prevents him from doing so many things he wants to do. For a time, he uses the word to answer every question. "Do you want to go to bed?" "No!" "Do you want to get up?" "No!" "Do you want a piece of candy?" "No!" Adults take the vehement "No!" of a two-year-old in stride—"He's just going through phase," which is exactly right. If, however, the child gets stuck at that point of his development, he may go through life as a "nay-sayer," reacting instinctively to any new situation, question, or possibility with a resounding "No!" Negative behavior in a two-year-old tends to be charming; the same behavior in a fifteen-year-old or a thirty-year-old is less appealing.

Children may get stuck at any other point of their development with comparable effects.

It is not difficult to construct the future scenario for the child who has been subjected to the stresses and strains which we have been discussing. When artificial or contrived conditions, such as placement with its attendant dynamics, impinge upon the child, his personality may be changed.

Bereft of the security of home and family, convinced of his own worthlessness and guilt, and facing alone a future which he cannot even imagine, he has little alternative to using people around him to serve his needs. If no one else will meet his needs, he has to do something about them himself.

Perhaps the most common characteristic of the placed child who has had inadequate help with separation is the development of a shallow, manipulative personality.

Typically, this child cannot form emotional ties—he does not have experience with emotional ties, and he cannot imagine that anyone would want to be his friend. He appears selfish, greedy, and ungrateful; his behavior alienates others, who understandably resist being rebuffed or used, and draw away from the child. Thus, the negative circle is complete, but sadly, for it is completed for reasons the child misunderstands. He thinks he is rejected for what he is, whereas, in reality, he is rejected for what he has done—he has been manipulative and hostile.

On the other hand, children may function well for some time—even years—in placement, but when some new stress enters their life, their adjustment breaks down. Frequently, this is when they enter puberty and begin normal sexual acting out. How often have foster placements that worked well for years fallen apart when the child reached age 13, and foster parents were unable to cope with the stresses of adolescence.

The more mature the child and the more he understands and participates in the placement process, the less severe his reactions after he is placed. That is, if he is free to ask questions, if he gets answers to his questions, if he is permitted to give open and honest expression to his feelings; if he is helped to move step by step through the need for placement, shares in the selection of the placement resource, knows the probable duration of placement and the conditions which must exist before placement can be terminated, and if he knows the responsibilities of everyone concerned in the placement, he has a fighting chance of surviving without emotional damage. His thoughts and feelings must be recognized and validated throughout the process, for he is the one to whom placement is happening.

The child who does not have a realistic sense of his own future produces plans that are as fanciful as they are unrealistic. He plans to leave school and get a job which will enable him to buy a house and a car; she will marry a rich man; he plans the details of spending the ten million dollar sweepstakes; etc. These plans are so real to the children, and their personalities can be so strong, that the worker has to be on guard that she doesn't get caught up in them. More than one social worker has caught herself thinking, "Dear God, he doesn't even know what a checking account is—what will he do with ten million dollars?!"

Underneath these unrealistic dreams, of course, are realistic questions:

- When can I go home?
- What do I have to do to get to go home?
- If home won't have me, what will I do?

The effects of separation reach beyond the pain of the initial separation. In any subsequent separation, all of his feelings about the original separation may be reactivated—the anger, the feelings of helplessness and guilt, sense of abandonment, desolation, and worthlessness.

Thus, when the child's family visits him in the foster home or institution; when parents bring him back from a home visit and then prepare to depart, when he prepares to leave home to return to placement, when a friend is discharged, when a staff member resigns, when a pet dies—or whenever any type of separation occurs, he may react violently. His violence is not a response to the immediate situation, it is a reaction to the pain of the original separation and to the cumulative pain of all subsequent separations.

The worker must understand this dynamic, for, if separation is left untreated, this disproportionate reaction to separation may last a lifetime.

Surrogate caregivers also must understand, lest they provide salubrious physical surroundings and material gifts and then wonder why their efforts are not appreciated. The child's need is emotional, not physical.

SUMMARY

The social worker's first task is to understand what is happening to the child, what the child feels, and why he feels and acts as he does. The social worker has the responsibility and the opportunity to help the child move through the experience of placement in a manner which will minimize disruption of emotional growth, which will preserve, restore, or develop self esteem for the child, and which will leave minimal residual damage to the child and to his family.

The social worker's task will include helping the child to incorporate the agency, specifically, the worker, into his network of relationships, for ultimately, it is in the agency that he must gain a sense of trust and continuity before he can feel confident about his future care. This means that the child must accept the transfer of many parental responsibilities from his parents to the agency, since for the duration of placement the agency, rather than his parents, will have primary responsibility for deciding where he is to live and what kind of life he is to have.

Then the worker's task is to help the child live with the pain of separation and to avoid having arrested emotional development. Initially, the child's task is to master, to some extent, the anxiety that the experience arouses. This mastery will emerge from the relationship developed with the worker; the child cannot do it alone.

The worker helps the placed child to perceive his situation and his family's situation realistically, recognize and accept any anger he feels toward his parents and toward himself, and she helps him verbalize his pain and guilt.

The worker confronts the child with tasks that can be accomplished in small steps and then only to the degree that his relationship with her will support him in his uncertainties.

The worker will help the child gain some understanding about how his conflicts affect his adjustment in placement. She will help the foster parents understand the basis for the child's behavior so they can respond to the child's behavior in an objective and helpful manner.

Foster parents can be helpful to the child, and they can accept much deviant behavior if they are aware of its underlying causes. Referral material to an institution will contain this information, but too often foster parents are denied this essential tool, either through inadvertence or through lack of trust.

The worker must deal with separation while it is fresh. Some children, of course, have been placed previously, perhaps repeatedly, and it is not to be expected that their reaction to placement will be the same as in an initial placement. Old separation feelings may be re-activated, but they will be less willing to talk about it. Thus, separation must be dealt with thoroughly the first time.

Endnotes

[1]Kline, Draza and Overstreet, Helen-Mary, *Foster Care of Children.* New York: Columbia University Press, 1972, p. 172.

[2]Ibid., pp. 72–73.

[3]Ibid., pp. 72–73.

[4]Ibid., p. 70.

[5]Mayer, Morris F., and Blum, Arthur. *Healing Through Living.* Springfield, IL: Charles C Thomas, 1971, p. 18. Used with permission.

[6]Littner, Ner, *Problems of Separation and Placement — Diagnosis, Prevention and Treatment.* Second Winter Seminar for Social Workers, Chapel Hill, NC: 1971, p. 9.

[7]Kline and Overstreet, op. cit., p. 77.

Chapter 3

PARENT SEPARATION

PARENTHOOD

Parents are also affected by separation, a fact sometimes overlooked, especially in these days when caseloads are heavy and many cases are emergencies. The worker, who usually enters the case on the child's behalf, may find family circumstances to be so harsh or the child's condition so importunate that she disparages or ignores the parents.

Irrespective of the cause of separation, parents and their feelings must be dealt with. Parents are part of the problem; therefore, they must have a part in the solution. Despite the problem, most parents are not monsters; they are the product of their own upbringing, of the times and circumstances in which they live, and of their own adaptability.

The worker must extrapolate from the existing conditions the formative factors of the family situation. Awareness of causative conditions does not condone neglect or abuse, nor does it permit parents to justify their actions by virtue of events or circumstances of the past, irrespective of how deplorable those may have been. Awareness of causative conditions will, however, help the worker to understand what is going on, and it may suggest to her some ideas as to how to proceed.

It may be fair to say that while family reunification remains a possibility, the child will gain mastery over his life in proportion to the extent that his parents gain mastery over theirs. This is where the worker comes into her own, for the social worker is admirably equipped to nurture individual and family functioning.

We can best start with the family where the family starts.

DEVELOPMENT OF THE FAMILY

In the traditional pattern, parents are individuals first, then they become a couple, and finally they become parents. Each of these roles has a process of development. If even one parent is not fully mature as an individual before marrying, the need to mature as an individual over-laps with the need to participate in the give-and-take of marriage. Similarly, the adjustment to marriage may not be well established before it becomes necessary to make adjustments to provide care for a child.

A cumulative effect, either positive or negative, obtains in moving through the roles of individual, parent, and spouse, i.e., the more mature the individual, the better the prospects for a successful marriage; the more successful the marriage, the greater the likelihood that the couple will become adequate parents.

Conversely, the less mature the individual, the less likely it is that the marriage will be successful; the less successful the marriage, the less likely it is that the couple will be adequate parents.

If even one parent, much less both, is caught up in unmet needs either as an individual or as a spouse, energy will be expended on meeting these needs, and little energy may left for parenting.

Becoming Parents

Adults become parents for diverse reasons, including the following:

• Some have children as a tangible evidence and the culmination of their love for each other. They plan to have children, and they organize their lives and finances toward that end.

• Some couples have children because that is what one does when one gets married. This is in part a residual effect of an agrarian society wherein children were economic assets.

• Some couples have children because of pressure of society, peers, or parents. Peers bring pressure; parents are notorious for wanting to become grandparents and for urging their children to bring this situation about.

• Some couples have a child to cement a faltering marriage.

• Still other couples have children simply because they do not know how to avoid having them.

Even the couple which wants a child may be more enamored of the status of parenthood than with the task of parenting. They have a mental image of proudly pushing the baby buggy down the street or taking their well-dressed—and, of course, well-behaved—child to show him off to relatives. Dreams and reality are not necessarily synonymous.

The Parent and the Child's Needs

Irrespective of the motivation for parenthood, unless at least one member of the couple has had experience with infants, the new parents are due for a rude awakening when the baby arrives. At least one parent must be prepared for diaper changes, feeding the baby, the crying in the night, the frighteningly sudden temperatures to which babies are subject, the exploration and denuding of dresser drawers, and all of the other needs, activities, and incessant demands of the growing, normally curious child.

This is the part of parenthood that is overlooked by, or unknown to, couples who have had no experience with children, and who do not appreciate the enormity of the socialization process of the infant.

In his first two years, the child has an astonishing learning task. The way he learns best is to investigate, feel, smell, and taste. He must learn to use and control his body, he must observe and adjust to a new environment, he must learn to talk, and he must learn to relate to others.

In practice, this process is both entertaining and frustrating. When the baby can crawl, he opens the stove drawer and finds that pan lids make a bang which is more satisfying to him than to his mother. Other learnings can be equally nerve-wracking.

Moreover, when the parent is in a hurry and least able to interact with the child, the child senses the inattention, and his needs escalate. In turn, the parent's impatience—even desperation—increases in response to the increasingly strident demands of the child. The parent begins to think that in this two-year-old body is a scheming, conniving adult mind which is malevolently calculating how most effectively to plague the parent.

Parental involvement in the child's learning is essential, even though it has a price for the parents. Of course it is easier to vacuum the carpet without having the child tag along with his hand on the vacuum cleaner; of course it is simpler to do the dishes without having the child stand on a chair "helping"; of course it is more efficient to put toys away and straighten up the room without his assistance, but this is how he learns. He imitates, he attempts and fails, then he attempts again and again until he achieves his goal. Every type of learning proceeds along this same path, and all learning takes time and requires the support and encouragement of adults.

The parent who is impatient, is perpetually in a hurry, is preoccupied, or who fails to appreciate the really prodigious task of the child to learn, develop, and grow, may react to the child in a manner that discourages him, puts him down, or in other ways conveys to him that the world is a daunting place to be. To say in words or actions, "Get out of my way," is to belittle his efforts and to make him feel inadequate and unworthy.

The demands and parental involvement with the special needs child are substantially greater: the autistic child, the Down's syndrome child, the cerebral palsied child, the child with spina bifida, etc., require incomparably more parental time and energy.

Parents can fight this if they wish—and many do, because they do not realize that adult schedules, priorities, and pressures have no meaning to the child. It is a fight, however, which they cannot win.

The Parent's Needs

Apart from the child's needs, the parent may be worried, preoccupied, or driven by his own internal unrest or disturbance. He may be fighting a losing battle with the world—poor education, unemployment, outdated job skills, inflation, mounting expenses with each additional child. This parent typically has no internal resources, no flexibility; he perceives himself as being caught in a corner from which there is no escape. A frequent refuge from this demoralizing situation is alcohol or drugs.

For people like this, who have never developed any inner strength or controls, life is a continuous harassment. They cannot cope with anything; every element of their life is a source of frustration, anger, anguish, and, finally, hopelessness.

For the parent who is burdened by his own concerns, the child's learning can be an intrusion, e.g., beginning attempts at speech are an annoyance because they require translation. The harried parent is in no condition to appreciate the child's progress from "muh" to "muk" to "milk"; if this parent ever heard of Dr. Seuss, he doesn't have time, patience, or inclination to read about the cat in the hat. Thus, the child's needs fall victim to the parent's problems.

Because of the parent's own needs, he may expect the child to provide the gratification which his own circumstances have denied him. This is doomed to failure, of course. Children are to be given to, not taken from; they are to be nurtured—they are not expected to be the nurturers.

Whatever the nature of the parents' development as individuals, as spouses, or as parents, however, they and the child make some adjustment to each other. That adjustment may be like or unlike the adjustments made in other families; the adjustment may be considered to be healthy or unhealthy by the community. Given the background and nature of these parents and this child, however, the adjustment is natural and normal for them. Any disturbance of the adjustment the parents and child have made to each other has an effect upon the parent as well as upon the child.

The threat of separation may force the parent to think about parts of his life which he has suppressed. He suppressed them because it was too painful to think about them, and when he did think about them he could find no solution for them. Both for having those elements in his life and for not being able to solve them, he may feel guilty.

The worker is well advised to ascertain which of these factors—or others—lies behind the circumstances which suggest separation. Sometimes workers complicate a situation by seeking esoteric explanations for what is basically an understandable and logical situation.

The worker probably will have a problem in establishing a relationship with this parent. The parent simply may not know how to interact with other people, he may be consumed with his own problems, and he cannot believe that others might be seriously be concerned about him.

Parents are not deliberately or intentionally neurotic, and rarely are they intentionally or by calculation negligent, argumentative, excessively passive or hostile to their children. When they are neglectful or abusive, those characteristics may reflect primarily their own frustrations, their lack of understanding, or their impatience with childhood growth patterns.

We need to take time to examine and compare abuse and neglect.

ABUSE VS. NEGLECT

Abusive acts are acts of commission which result in harm to children; neglectful acts are acts of omission which have negative effects upon children.[1]

Abusing parents may or may not neglect their children, depending probably upon their social and economic class, but neglecting parents typically do not abuse their children.

Neglecting and abusing parents are generally put in the same category, but, although they have some characteristics in common, they are different in behavior and different in their potential for the future.

Neglectful Families

Neglectful families tend to be poor, with all of the negatives associated with poverty, e.g., poor housing, poor nutrition, high infant mortality, alcoholism, drug addiction, etc. The chronically poor are second-class citizens: if they have medical care, they must use public clinics; if they are to eat, they must have food stamps or welfare; if they can get a job it is unskilled labor at minimum wage, because of lack of education or training.

Perhaps the most damaging aspect of chronic poverty is that the human psyche can withstand only a finite number of defeats before the psyche itself is defeated. Eventually, apathy sets in, and when action is demanded the apathetic cannot respond; it is easier to deny, ignore, or run away from a problem. Apathy may be so pervasive that the consequences of problem-evasion are irrelevant.

The crux of the problem is that the poor live on a different plane and in a different culture from those who establish community laws and mores and who decide when those laws and mores have been violated, and there is no natural channel of communication between these two groups. Neglectful families may be members in good standing in their own culture—family, neighborhood, or community, but they have no relationship to or contact with the ruling class. Neglectful parents are not opposed to the ruling class—they simply do not give it thought. They drift along, caught up in forces which they neither understand nor oppose.[2]

Neglectful families typically have no support system outside their own narrow associations. The poor are not joiners: they do not belong to the Rotary Club, they cannot afford the YMCA, and they may have no church affiliation. They do not seek out to those organizations, and those organizations do not seek them out.

The behaviors which are common to their culture may be at variance with the culture of the larger community, e.g., when incest is uncovered in a family, two questions typically are asked by that family: first, "so what?" second, "doesn't everyone?"

Neglectful families will reach out for tangible help—welfare or medical assistance—in time of crisis, but the thought of seeking intangible help such as counseling, training in parenting skills, guidance in shopping, etc., would never occur to them. If they are to be helped in these ways, someone must reach out to them, and our society provides few reasons to offer help in the absence of an observable crisis.

Abusive Families

In almost every case, abusive parents were themselves abused as children. This should not be surprising, for a child learns how to parent by observing his parents. What abusive parents learned as children is that when a child vexes the parent, the parent hits the child. If these parents, as children, were never parented in a real sense, how could they learn to be adequate parents.

The result of this deficiency is perhaps more serious to the person as an individual than as a future parent. Denied the example of a "normal" parent, the child has no opportunity to learn about close relationships. The child may be headed for a life of essential loneliness, not knowing how to care for others, feeling that he is not cared for by others, and, ultimately most tragically, believing that he is not worth caring about. This deficit cannot fail to have an effect upon all relationships, first with his spouse, then with his children, and finally in his business and social dealings. In all of his life he may be struggling with his own identity and worth as an individual, as a spouse, and as a parent.

Abusive families cut right across the economic spectrum.

In one study, 90% of the abusive parents indicated no spontaneous expression of regret: on the contrary, they seemed to see no need for such a reaction. When they were criticized, they blamed other people, often the children, accusing them of the behavior that was in fact their own. More than one parent said angrily that there was nothing else he could do when the children were so "bad," but there were no specifics about what the children had done. There was just a general indictment of "badness." More than any other group, the severely abusive families blamed others. Often the children, in desperation, blamed themselves.[3]

Two Kinds of Abuse

Situational Abuse

Two kinds of abuse exist. The first might be termed "situational abuse." This is the unpremeditated, unplanned, unintended, unexpected abuse which is the result of an overreaction of an adult to a specific situation. Every parent has been in a position where this type of abuse was possible; for example:

At three o'clock in the morning the baby has been crying for five hours. Mother and father are desperate. They changed the baby and fed him, and they know that he is full, clean, and dry; but he kept on crying. They picked the baby up; he kept on crying. They put the baby down; he kept on crying. They put more covers on him; he kept on crying. They took covers off of him; he kept on crying. They have taken turns walking the floor with him, rocking him, singing to him, ignoring him, and entertaining him; he kept on crying.

Now, after five hours, the parents are frantic. First, they are upset for the baby's sake. A five-hour crying jag cannot be good anyone, and they feel bad for him. And they feel guilty. For some reason, they cannot understand what his behavior is saying. Surely, they think, if they were adequate parents they would be able to figure out what he is trying to tell them.

Secondly, they are concerned for themselves—the alarm is going to ring in three hours to send them to work, and they know that the boss is very fond of having his employees at least half awake, even in those early afternoon hours which may drag under the best of circumstances. How can they possibly get up, go to work, and be productive if they don't get some sleep tonight?

Every parent has gone through this. By 3:00 a.m. it is "wild idea" time, when every parent has cast around for some way—just any way, no matter how outlandish—of quieting the child. In exploring all possibilities, most parents have thought—however fleetingly, and without the least intention of doing so, "Hold a pillow over his face, maybe that will do it." or "Hit his head on the wall, then maybe he will be quiet." These are not serious options—this is desperation speaking; they are simply ideas used to vent frustration.

Most parents have sufficient self control in that moment not to do anything bizarre or violent. Most parents have enough knowledge of infant growth and development to know that crying is one of the things babies do best, and occasionally they cry for long periods of time and for no discernible reason. The parent just has to tough it out, and sooner or later the baby will exhaust himself and fall asleep.

Some parents, however, lack self control; they do not have any understanding of periodic crying jags or any other infant behavior; they run off the far end of their patience, and they do take impulsive action, and the child is hurt. This is child abuse, but it is a type of abuse to which every parent can relate, and which every parent can understand, at least to some degree.

Situational abuse includes circumstances in which the child knows he can expect punishment.

If Dad comes home drunk every night at five o'clock and starts throwing furniture, from the child's point of view, dynamically this is not so serious, for it is predictable behavior, and at least the older child can defend himself: he can crawl under a table, escape into another room, or leave the house.

In situational abuse, deplorable as the outcome may be, a cause-and-effect relationship exists, so the child's life retains some rational basis.

Classical Abuse

The second type of abuse may be termed "classical abuse." This is abuse which is reported by a neighbor, a physician, the police, the emergency room attendant, or the coroner.

Classical abuse is not punishment for something the child has done. Classical abuse is punishment as an end in itself, without rational reason or purpose—not punishment to fit the crime, but punishment in the absence of a crime.[4]

Perhaps the most devastating emotional part of classical abuse for the child is that the abuse is unpredictable; the abuse does not follow any pattern, it comes without warning, and consequently there is no defense. What is acceptable one day brings violence the next day and is again acceptable the third day. No cause-and-effect relationship exists; there is only effect.

The father made his five-year-old daughter walk in circles in front of him and every time she passed him he hit her, was behaving illogically. Her plaintive, "Daddy, I'll be good; I'll be good, Daddy" had no effect. There was no precipitating act on the child's part; therefore, she could not anticipate and avoid the situation, and she was too small to escape it.

The child who was kept locked in a closet for eight years, the child who was hung by his feet in the closet, the child who had multiple cigarette burns on his little body, the child who was force-fed quarts of water could not have done anything to merit such treatment.

Everyone who reads the newspaper, as well as the social worker, can provide additional illustrations of the point. Classical abuse is not the fault of the child, it is not a reaction to what the child has done. Clearly, classical abuse is indicative that something is amiss with the adult.

The practical result of classical child abuse, aside from physical damage, is that the child goes through his little life always looking over his shoulder to see who is going to hit him next. Even if the child survives, and many do, these lessons are durable, as are all lessons learned in childhood, and more than likely these lessons will last a lifetime. In adulthood, the child, now grown up, habitually expects other people to abuse or misuse him—and, of course, they oblige.

Unfortunately, abusive families may be highly successful in the business world, accustomed to ordering people around; they may have strong, even overpowering personalities; they may be articulate and persuasive. Families like these require the most experienced caseworkers available, people who are clear in their purpose and comfortable with authority.

Similarities of Neglectful and Abusive Families

In one respect, neglectful families and abusive families are alike: they do not seek help with their family problems. It is not clear that they even perceive the family behavior as a problem; for many of them the problem is community pressure and interference.[5] They have to be discovered by someone or some agency in the community, and intervention in their affairs is the result of concern from the outside, not of parental volition.

By and large neglectful parents seek outside help only for economic need or in some drastic family crisis, and then they want only the help they have requested. Preponderantly under-educated, they have no reference point to suggest that counseling—talking—can help solve their problems. Understandably, they resist what appears to them to be a futile and time-consuming activity.

Prevention of neglect involves extensive education, from literacy and job training to parenting and relationship skills; it involves developing support groups—and many more things which the social worker can list.

Abusive parents, less often destitute, have less reason to seek economic or other tangible help, and they are more likely to scorn any help offered.

In one study, as a group, abusing parents seemed to see other people as victims, resources, or enemies. They made contacts rather than friends; they trusted no one. They did not often visit other people, and they invited few into their houses. They rarely joined groups or organizations, and most of them did not participate in religious groups. Their motives were what they conceived to be their own best interests. As they frightened others, so they themselves responded chiefly to fear. They tended to evaluate any social worker, or anyone else, for that matter, in terms of how much power over them that person has.[6]

Prevention of child abuse requires that schools, hospitals, doctors, courts, churches, and social agencies work cooperatively in a system of identifying and treating families whose children are at risk of abuse.

The schools see more children regularly at an earlier age than any other community entity, and thus must be an integral part of this cooperative effort. The school cannot be expected to treat such children and their families; schools already have more than they can do. School personnel can be trained, however, to recognize and report to the appropriate agency children who appear to be in the need of help. The human service delivery system must then be coordinated and equipped to make prompt and effective response to provide help for the child and the family.

Work with Neglectful and Abusive Families

The family is a unit, and it must be treated as such. The family may be neurotic, psychotic, or bizarre in some other way, but the child and family belong together, and the worker must accept and work with both the parents and the child if anything positive is to be accomplished.

The worker must accept the parents not only for their sake, but for the sake of the child, who will be quick to discern the worker's condescension or disapproval of the parents. When, in the child's presence, the worker accepts the parents despite their shortcomings, the child is free to feel that he, too, is accepted despite his shortcomings.

The child cannot feel accepted by the worker who does not also accept his family. Because of neglect or abuse, the child may feel personally rejected and inferior, which means that he has no status or recognition in his own family.[7]

It may help the worker to remember that accepting the parent does not mean accepting what the parent has done or failed to do.

The parent is not only a parent, he or she is a son or daughter, frequently a spouse, perhaps an employee. Additionally, he or she is an individual with hopes, dreams, biases, habits, prejudices, fears, frustrations, needs, tendencies, habitual actions and reactions, talents, and potential. This is what the parent is, and this can be accepted.

The parent has neglected or abused the child. This is what the parent has done, and this is not accepted. Not only in her work, but also in her thinking, the worker must separate what the parent is from what the parent has done or failed to do.

Work with neglectful parents may start with underlying problems: limited education, no job skills, not enough money, difficult living conditions, insufficient health care, etc. As the underlying problems are relieved, neglect may diminish.

With abusive parents, the approach is the other way around: the first concern is to protect the child. Once the child is safe, the worker can focus on the underlying problems.

THE PARENTS IN SEPARATION

Normal separation is a mark of success and achievement; it is the result of a natural sequence: the child grew and matured, and when he finished high school or college he moved out on his own. The child is ready to go, and the parents are ready to have him leave. There is sadness, because parents and child will miss each other, but there is an accompanying sense of fulfillment; there is a naturalness about this new stage in life to which both child and parents adapt.

Separation in placement, by definition, is not a normal separation. Placement is an artificial separation, usually imposed upon the family by an outside force, contrived to replace an injurious environment with a more salubrious one. Parents relinquish their authority not to the child, as in normal separation, but to an agency.

To place on parents full responsibility for the problems which led to placement may be erroneous. Contributing factors certainly can be identified, but in many cases the full explanation is beyond current understanding. No one has explained fully how it is that in one family one son becomes an archbishop while his brother heads the Mafia. Some children simply have a rougher time in growing up than others, especially in adolescence.

The family system and its dynamics are too complex for any one person to be the sole cause of problems within the family.

Parents' Feelings About Themselves in Separation

Because of the circumstances which have been described, many parents who face separation will think first about themselves. We can list some of the feelings they may have to which the worker will wish to be sensitive and responsive.

• Placement casts aspersion on these parents as persons and as adults, and parents know this. From childhood, every child dreams of "When I grow up, no one will be able to tell me what to do; I will decide what I am going to do and when I am going to do it."

Now, with placement, whether imposed by the court or by circumstances which have made parents request placement, these parents have been shoved back toward childhood. They are grown up, but someone is still telling them what to do. What they thought about, dreamed about, and depended upon didn't turn out the way they expected and intended.

• The child's need of placement reveals the parents' inadequacy as parents and as persons. The qualities of their life which they had concealed from others—and perhaps from themselves—are now paraded in public. The worker is likely to find guilt, shame, and feelings of failure, accompanied by the common defense mechanisms of denial, displacement, and projection. These feelings and these defenses may well be overlaid by anger that their secret has been revealed.[8]

• Parents know they will be stigmatized in the community. They will always be identified as "that family whose child was taken away from them," or "that family that gave their child away."

A social worker appeared in court, at the judge's request, while a family case was heard. The decision was made to place the two children, and the social worker took the children from the courtroom to put them in her Volkswagen. The father trailed her down from the courtroom, and as the children entered the car, their father pounded on top of the car, swearing, "If you take those children, I'll kill you, I'll kill you, I'll kill you!" The judge, leaning out of an upstairs courtroom window, called, "Now, John, I wouldn't do that if I were you," and the social worker and children drove off.

On the following Saturday, the father visited his children at the institution. Given his behavior outside the courthouse, there was some anxiety as to what to expect. When the father appeared at the institution, however, he was the perfect gentleman, cordial, well-behaved, and appreciative that the institution could provide for his children in a way that he could not.

The explanation of the father's histrionics outside the courthouse seemed to be that the courthouse lawn was the gathering place for all of the idlers and unemployed of the county. The father might be unable to provide adequately for his children, but he still had his pride, and he had to demonstrate to his friends that he was a proper father, for he did not give his children up without a struggle.

• Humanly, the parents attempt to escape incrimination by blaming someone else—just anyone else—for perpetrating their pain. The less adequate the parents are as individuals, spouses, or parents, of course, the more acrimonious will be their attack.

• Relinquishing a child besmirches the parent/child relationship. Many parents consider that placement means that they have been of no value to their child. The pain and bitterness of the need for placement has obliterated the good times, the warm, tender moments, the shared experiences, the good things they have done for their child. Additionally, parents often feel they no longer have a useful function; their parental rights are being entirely severed.[9]

• When the parents realize that placement is, in fact, to take place, characteristically, after initial resistance, they simply cave in. Understanding the process of placement and the dynamics leading up to it is too complicated, developing a cure is too threatening and too energy-consuming. To understand the child and their problems with him is to understand themselves, which is painful.[10]

It is simplest to turn full responsibility for the child over to the agency. The decision to run away seems less intolerable than facing thoughts about losing him or of wrestling their way to understanding the total situation and doing something about it. This is apathy again.

The result of this feeling is that parents feel that the placement resource will do all of the work, and this further confirms their helplessness, their inadequacy, and their feelings of being unwanted. If, after placement, the foster family or the placement facility tends to shut the family out, their feelings of uselessness are exacerbated.

To avoid pain, the parents may agree quickly, impulsively to place the child. This is a time for the social worker to be especially alert and available. The worker can make a profound difference in family/child relationships by persisting and insisting that the parents remain involved and that they retain and exercise all of the rights and decision-making authority possible.

Parents' Feelings About the Child in Separation

Just on the surface, the parent will have the feelings which are normally associated with separation. If a relatively normal parent/child relationship exists, the parent feels the loss that every parent feels when the child leaves.

Humanly, the thought of separation brings a feeling of isolation and loneliness. Very simply, they grieve over their loss. In one study of the feelings of parents on the day of placement, sadness was the major feeling reported, as shown in the table below. Also high in frequency among the feelings expressed were worry and nervousness.

Parental Feelings Reported as Experienced on the Day of Placement[11]

Feeling	Percent of Mothers N = 297	Percent of Fathers N = 137
Sad	87	90
Worried	74	68
Nervous	68	56
Empty	60	42
Angry	50	45
Bitter	43	43
Thankful	42	57
Relieved	40	42
Guilty	39	30
Ashamed	36	39
Numb	19	14
Paralyzed	16	11

Even when the parent holds strongly negative feelings about the child, the parent may be distressed about no longer being in daily touch with the child.

On a deeper level, the worker knows that the parent's feelings will be conflicted with respect to the child. Uncertain of his own adequacy, the parent may have put undue reliance on the child's success, which, in the parent's mind, authenticates the parent's existence. Now that the child is to be placed, the success of the child is diminished, and the reputation of the parent is proportionately tarnished.

Separation may affect the parent's emotional stability, resulting in regression by the parent. The more the parent regresses, of course, the less accessible he is to participate meaningfully in a problem-solving activity with the worker. Part of the worker's task may be to help the parent re-establish emotional equilibrium in the absence of the child.

In placement, then, the parent's feelings about the child cannot be severed from his feelings about himself. The child and what the child represents are so intertwined with the parent's own identity that the two are indivisible. When the parent separates from the child, he is separating from a part of himself, a part of himself which he may partly love and partly hate. His guilt, which may be the most evident feeling, is based on what he has failed to do for his child, or for what he has done and is doing to his child. Underlying all of these feelings is his sense of inadequacy.[12]

Additionally, the parents may have other normal parental concerns about the child, including, but not limited to, the following:

- Will the child be safe and well?
- Who will console the child when he cries? Who will take up for him when there is controversy?
- Will the surrogate parents really love the child?
- What kind of discipline will be used in the new setting?
- Will the child learn to love the alternate caregivers and cease to love his own parents?
- What if the child is glad to leave home—will he ever want to return?
- After losing touch with the rhythm of his family life will the child and the family ever become in "synch" with each other again?
- What if neither the child nor his relationship with them improves; will he respect their authority when he returns home?
- Even if the child is given the opportunity to grow, to get well, he may fail, and perhaps it would be better not to risk this failure after a series of so many failures—why gamble and risk finding out that there is no hope whatsoever?[13]

Thus, in separation the feelings of the parent vis-a-vis the child are a mixture of concern for the child and self image for the parent. The worker cannot overlook the honest sadness of the parent at losing the child, but she will not be deceived that this is the only—or even the basic—issue at stake.

PARENTS' FEELINGS ABOUT PLACEMENT

At the Time of Placement

Parents' feelings about placement depend to some degree, of course, upon their adequacy as individuals, spouses, and parents. Parents who are adequate as individuals and who enjoy their role as parents, will react to the placement of their child as they would to any loss: they regret the necessity of placement and they grieve over the loss of their child, but they participate in planning with respect to the placement in order to expedite reunion. Even in separation, they are not diminished as individuals; their personal integrity and strength continue.

If the parents are reasonably adequate, they may be able not only to handle their own feelings, but also to help the child with his. This is more likely when the placement is voluntary than when it is mandated by the court.

Several positive factors obtain in the case of a voluntary placement: the parent who has the insight and initiative to seek placement is likely to have thought about and worked through available options, and consequently he can handle more credibly the objections of the child. This parent is usually more sagacious and emotionally more intact than the one for whom placement is mandated.

Parents who are less adequate are more likely to be personally devastated by placement, and participating in plans which will result in the child's return is more difficult. These parents tend to take an all-or-nothing approach to placement: they had struggled with the problem, they had wrestled with their concerns, but still they lost the battle; therefore, all is lost.

The parent for whom placement is mandated is in the position of everyone who has an unwanted decision forced upon him, i.e., his instinctive reaction is to strike out against whoever is doing something to him, rather than confronting the situation itself. Taking this defensive posture is antithetical to entering a helping or cooperative relationship.

This parent may have wildly unrealistic expectations of placement. He may expect the worker to "fix" the child and then bring him back. With the child's problems taken care of, he will be "ready" to return, after which life can return to normal, except that now the child will be well-behaved. Manifestly, these parents are defending themselves against their pain by not acknowledging their share in the faulty family dynamics which led to placement.

What Placement Means

Parents know that in placement they must enter a new relationship with their child; they must relinquish a portion of their independence by sharing authority and responsibility with the court and a social agency. Henceforth, parental decisions vis-a-vis the child are valid only with the concurrence of those agencies.

On a personal note, other persons will take over some of the parental role which the parents have enjoyed—caring for everyday needs of the child, observing growth and development, giving and receiving affection, having daily interaction with the child. Even in the worst cases, there must have been some pleasurable days or moments between parent and child, and those days or moments are now to be lost.

It is unavoidable that some of the child will be lost to the family and some of the family will be lost to the child. Family and child will each have experiences which are not—cannot be—shared by the other, and in the absence of shared experiences, to some degree they will be strangers to each other when they meet again.

Concern for Site and Caregivers

The parent has questions about the new caregivers.

- Will the new caregivers treat the child well?
- Will the new caregivers share with the parents what is going on with the child?
- What will the new caregivers think and feel about a parent whose child is placed?
- Will the parents be able to visit the child, and, if so, how will they be treated by the new caregivers?
- The parents are also afraid that they who are "bad" parents will be replaced by "good" parents in the eyes of those who have authority. Unfortunately, this fear is sometimes reinforced by the foster family or by the residential staff.[14]
- What if, under the tutelage of alternate caregivers, the child has outgrown the parents after a period in placement?

The child is going to live with strangers in a strange place, and the parent may fear the impact of an unknown residence, school, and neighborhood. The parent has questions about these:

- Will the child be safe?
- What are the other children like who are already in residence?
- If the child is picked on, will someone stick up for him and, if necessary, protect him?
- Will the new school be more appealing to the child than his old school?

• Will the child be permitted to participate in school sports? Will he be required to participate in school sports?
• Who will wash his clothes?
• Will the child be confined, even locked up, or will he have freedom to move around the neighborhood?

In some cases, the parents may fear that the placement resource will not be sufficiently restrictive to control the child. The parents may envision prison bars and a repressive regimen which the child cannot conceivably outwit or overpower. Some parents may have threatened the child with just such a dire fate if he did not behave himself, which is to say if the child did not do what the parents wanted him to do.

Parental Behavior

The parent's behaviors are variable. Parents may be cooperative; often, their behavior will be negative. Behavior may take the form of antagonism to the worker in all of its infinite variations, e.g., refusing to respond to written communications, not returning telephone calls, failing to be home when the worker has said she would come, slamming the door in the worker's face, etc. When the worker does catch up with the parent, he may deny his responsibility in the problems of the child and the need for placement. He may verbally abuse the worker; he may threaten physical violence to the worker or to the judge, although usually this is bluster.

When the child is to be placed, new behaviors emerge, such as the following:

• The parent may refuse to accompany the child on the pre-placement visit or on placement day.
• The parent may not follow instructions to notify the school that the child is leaving.
• The child's clothes may not be ready to go; the clothes that are ready do not conform to the list of required clothing.
• The parent may have "forgotten" to take the child for a medical examination.

After the child has been placed, still more behaviors emerge, such as the following:

• The parent may not follow visiting policies, either in a foster home or group setting. He appears at odd hours without appointment, often just at mealtime.
• The parent may be critical of the living arrangements for his

child, stating unequivocally that they are inferior to what the child had at home.

• The parent may be discourteous to foster parents and to child care workers.

• The parent may supply his child with contraband items, e.g., cigarettes, liquor, drugs; he may supply other children in residence with the same items.

• The parent may spend lavishly on his child's wardrobe and personal possessions — TV, bicycle, stuffed animals, etc.

• The parent may seek to ingratiate himself with the new caregivers and with other residents by bringing them gifts.

• The parent may seek to countermand the instructions of the new caregivers; he may tell the child that he does not have to follow the rules.

• The parent may damage property of the foster parents or group facility — always accidentally, of course.

• The parent may promise repeatedly to visit the child, but then does not show up. When he bothers to explain at all, his explanations are patently false, e.g., he had car trouble; the neighbor would not transport him; he unexpectedly had to go to work on his day off; he wasn't feeling well, etc.

• The parent may give false promises to the child with respect to the child's return home.

The list could go on indefinitely. The worker will recognize that these behaviors are indicative of the parent's pain; he is seeking to re-establish some control over his life, and, since he cannot control in order, he will control in disorder.

The alternative to these behaviors is for the parent to withdraw and disappear. This is a real tragedy both for parent and child. Let us look at two examples.

Three teen-age siblings were in long-term care in one institution, for they were told that their mother had been dead for ten years. The three were popular with other children and with staff, they were doing well in school, they were excellent, conscientious workers. In sum, they appeared to be well adjusted. One can get over death and go on.

However, one Saturday morning their mother walked up the front walk and inquired about her children.

In retrospect, no one knows exactly what happened. It does not matter, however, that no one deliberately lied, that an accidental oversight occurred somewhere, that earnest efforts may have been made to find the mother. The fact is that for ten years the children were led to believe that their mother was dead when in reality she was alive and well, and that is all that mattered.

Another institution had a 17-year-old girl who had been in placement for 15 years. Workers consistently declared that no family was available.

An assistant executive director took the record, followed up on various clues and finally found the father's telephone number and address in a distant state. He promptly called the father, who said that he had tried repeatedly to get his daughter back, but that no one would ever help him, so he finally gave up.

At that point, it was discovered that the girl knew where her father was, she had his telephone number, and periodically she would dial his number, but when the telephone was picked up at the other end, she would hang up, unable to face the possibility of rejection.

The girl was reunited with her father, subsequently attended college and became a CPA. She is the first to say that if she had not found her father, she would never have finished school.

This case contains several issues: First, some workers simply quit too soon. The father was abandoned by the system, so he and his daughter lost fifteen years with each other.

Secondly, in fifteen years of alternate-care living, no one managed to get close enough to this girl to realize that she had kept track of her father. What a lonely life for a little girl, in all of her growing-up years to have no one to whom she could confide her fears, her hopes and dreams.

Within the family, too, parental behavior may follow certain patterns. Retaining a sense of family unity when one member is absent is difficult. The parent makes changes which exclude the placed child: family vacations are taken, the family moves to a different house without informing the placed child; clothes, toys, and bicycle are given away, the child's room is assigned to a sibling, and other evidence of the child's existence are eliminated. For all practical purposes, the child disappears from family life and planning. Family activities and interaction cannot be held in abeyance until the absent member returns, but the empty chair is always there.

In one sense, this is logical and necessary, for life does go on. In a deeper sense, however, this can be disastrous, for it tends to weaken the tie and make reunion more difficult. This underscores again the need for ongoing work with the family.

When the parent does begin to get involved in the process, he may seek specific, simplistic solutions which will obviate the need for placement or bring its speedy termination: a move to better housing, finding a job, joining Alcoholics Anonymous, reuniting with a spouse, etc. The fact that physical considerations are generally least important is beyond him. The worker helps him to focus on what is essential, upon the fact that the important work goes on not outside an individual, but inside.

Negative behaviors are annoying for the worker, but they do contain one positive: the parent is still fighting. As long as the parent has energy to fight, the possibility exists that that energy can be redirected into more positive channels.

Reunion

Generally, the idea of separation initiates the wish for the child's return.

In most cases, the parent says he wants the child back. He may really want the child back, or he may feel that as a parent he is supposed to want his child back, in which case his stated desire to have the child back may reflect his impulsivity or guilt, and may be in the service of denying his role in the child's painful past.

Combined with wanting reunion is the fear of it.

Parents fear that the child will return "too soon" and that they will not be able to cope with him. Questions come to their minds, such as:

• Will they be any better able to handle the child when he comes home than when he left?
• Will he have grown so far apart from them that there is no point of meeting?

This is where the worker's contribution is essential. She reassures the parent that not only is all not lost, but that the parent's continued involvement with the child is crucial to his well-being—and to theirs.

The parent may find it difficult to accept the worker's authoritative expectation that he participate in an extended process of involvement, in order to ensure that the child's needs for a stable, caring environment can be met.

The worker must be alert to a subtle but important possibility, the possibility that the parents may harbor a secret hope that the placement will fail, for if it succeeds and the child succeeds, this will mean they have solved things in the past in the wrong way. These are forbidden thoughts that arouse guilt and the fear that if discerned, further disapprobation will be brought on themselves and they will be rejected as worthless. On the other hand, if placement should fail, it will mean that their own failure is less, for the child is beyond anyone's power to help.[15]

The parent and the child each face the paradox of wanting the other to remain unchanged, yet demanding change, since the current situation is intolerable.

Each may feel that when reunion comes, a change will have occurred, bringing a resolution of all difficulties. Perhaps mixed in with the idea of change is the mythic notion that reunion in and of itself may be curative.[16]

The only reassurance that most parents have, and that they in turn can give the child, is their confidence in the ability of the agency (i.e., the worker) and in alternate living arrangements to help their child. If they lack this confidence, it is much more difficult to handle the separation trauma with them or to use their assistance in helping the child with it.

SUMMARY

The feelings and reactions of parents are a crucial factor in the placement process. Not all parents can participate meaningfully either in attempts to avoid placement or in the process of placing the child.

The worker will be careful, however, to be sensitive to the feelings of parents in spite of their surface behaviors, which very likely are negative in direct proportion to the acuteness of their pain.

Placement is not a punishment, and separation is more than a matter of suspended animation with a subsequent continuation of old routines; it is a matter of healing and growth. Absence, if it is sustained by the relationship with the social worker, has a healing power.

Placement, properly used, is an opportunity for this healing. When supported by the skills and relationship of the social worker, separation from the child and from a stressful situation affords parents an opportunity to recover health and strength, to identify anew—or perhaps for the first time—their own strengths and to use them, to reassess their relationship with each other and their relationships with others; to find a new competence in life. With the worker's help, they can identify the needs or problems which have been concealed by their absorption in their struggles with their own problems or with the problems of their child.[17]

When the worker enters the scene to assure the parents that all is not lost; that placement is not the end, but the beginning, and in this beginning not only is their presence and participation desired, it is critical, parents can be reassured.

Parents can also be unnerved by this assurance. Their rights as parents have been abrogated by the removal of their child, but now they learn that separation did not absolve them of responsibility; they are expected to work. Their work is to understand their child and, in the process, to understand themselves. And this is expected of parents who have customarily run away from problems or turned their problems over to someone else.

The worker need not hesitate to bring up serious issues for fear that she might push the parent into withdrawal or disintegration. People are astonishingly resilient and durable, and, given steadfast support from a worker—and that is a crucial condition—strengths can be uncovered which even the parent, much less the worker, did not suspect existed. Many parents will find it refreshing to have someone deal openly and honestly with them and to support them as they deal openly and honestly— perhaps for the first time—with themselves.

The major work with parents precedes the child's admission to group care and is focused on prevention of or preparation for placement. Once the child is in placement, there are eight different areas that are to be discussed.

- Reassuring the parents that the child is in good hands;
- Reassuring the parents of their own continuing role in the life of their child;
- Defining the functions, rights, and duties of the parents during placement;
- Supporting the child's placement and treatment;
- Helping parents to change their own attitude toward the child;
- Helping the parents with problems that are not directly related to the child;
- Helping parents to resume full-time parenthood;
- Aftercare. The work with the child and his family after his discharge to his home is as important as the work before and during his placement.[18]

Work related to the successful use of aggressive outreach has been ably summarized as follows:

- The approach must be purposeful, related to a definite problem in the situation. It may be delinquency or truancy or other evidence of child neglect;

• The approach should be open-minded; ready to hear and really understand the family's point of view;

• It should be made with genuine confidence in the ultimate potential of each human being and respect for human dignity;

• It should be persistent. We must go often enough, stay long enough, go, despite rebuffs, discourtesy, frank hostility, and nonchalant denial of need or wish to use our service.[19]

Endnotes

[1]Giovannoni, "Parental Mistreatment: Perpetrators and Victims." *Journal of Marriage and the Family,* November 1971, p. 649.

[2]Young, Leontine. *Wednesday's Children.* New York: McGraw-Hill, 1964, p. 85.

[3]Ibid., p. 68.

[4]Ibid., p. 45.

[5]Ibid., pp. 36–37.

[6]Ibid., pp. 134–135.

[7]Glickman, Esther, *Child Placement Through Clinically Oriented Casework.* New York: Columbia University Press, 1957, p. 332.

[8]Mandelbaum, Arthur, "Parent-Child Separation: Its Significance to Parents." *Social Work,* October 1962, pp. 29–30.

[9]Ibid., pp. 29–30.

[10]Ibid., p. 28.

[11]Jenkins, Shirley, and Norman, Elaine, *Filial Deprivation and Foster Care.* New York: Columbia University Press, 1972, pp. 106–107. Used with permission.

[12]Freud, Clarice, "Meaning of Separation to Parents and Children as Seen in Child Placement." *Public Welfare,* 13, No. 1 (January 1955). p. 15.

[13]Mandelbaum, op. cit., pp. 29–30.

[14]Ibid., op. cit., pp. 30–31.

[15]Ibid., p. 29.

[16]Moss, Sidney Z., *Separation and Reunion: Interwoven Themes in Child Placement.* 12th Winter Seminar for Social Workers, Chapel Hill, 1981, pp. 8–9.

[17]Mandelbaum, op. cit., p. 33.

[18]Mayer, Morris, Richman, Leon, and Balcerzak, Edwin. *Group Care of Children: Crossroads and Transitions.* New York: CWLA, 1977, pp. 115–116. Used with permission.

[19]Bryce, Marvin and Lloyd, June (Eds.). *Treating Families in the Home.* Springfield, IL: Charles C Thomas, 1981, p. 16. Used with permission.

Chapter 4

INTAKE STUDY

The specifics of an intake study will be spelled out in the administrative manual of most agencies. The new worker will not be at a loss for what to include in the study, for although the sequence and organization of the study will vary from agency to agency, the content will generally be the same. The framework within which the study is conducted may be less obvious.

In making an intake study, the worker must be careful to work *with* the parents, not do something *to* the parents. The intake process is the process of assessment, only one result of which may be placement. Many other kinds of results are possible.

The intake process does not aim at a decision for alternate care, irrespective of the nature of the referral. Rather, intake focuses on a beginning understanding of the total problem. The intake process involves the parents and maintains their rights for making any decision within their capability.

Once the parents understand this, they will not feel pressured; their anxiety and their resistance will be relieved by the realization that their child will not be placed until he is understood, until they are understood, and without their sharing in whatever decisions are made.

It is all too easy for the worker to make decisions for the family and to direct the whole process in order to put speedy closure to the situation. This is quick, and the overworked social worker will be tempted to do just that. This is short-term gain at the expense of long-term loss, however, for parents cannot be held responsible for decisions they did not make. When plans made by the worker fail, parents have an easy out.

Only by guiding, encouraging, and supporting the parents in thinking through their whole situation, identifying the problem and options, and finally choosing and following through upon an option, can a permanent resolution be developed. They cannot do this alone; they must have the support of the worker. The worker's task is to help the parents to identify the problems, not to assign blame. Both parents and child should be helped to understand that the problems exist within a system that is capable of change. It is only from such a process that the appropriateness of the use of alternate care can evolve.

One challenge of the worker is not to allow parents to abdicate their decision-making function. When parents are helped to make a decision and then are held accountable for it, their self esteem is increased, and they tend to find strength which even they did not realize they had to cope with the present situation. As they begin to utilize their own strength in this situation, they are better able to handle other situations in their life. The family must be permitted and required to "own" their own problem.

While the family may be receptive to the worker's help eventually, if not at first, the family is also threatened by the knowledge that the worker is not only the catalyst for change, but the power that determines when, and if, enough change has occurred. This revives the parent's feeling of powerlessness.

If, after the total situation is understood and alternatives exhausted, placement appears to be the best plan, the worker must have clearly in mind the purpose and function of alternate care. Placement is a tool of treatment—a tool whose use is arrived at diagnostically and whose handling requires the utmost thought and care. Placement is properly used only in conjunction with other tools.

If the worker perceives alternate care as either a "quick fix" for a troubled family situation, or, conversely, as a resource to be used only when all else has failed, she will convey this perception to the family. They will sense that, once again, they are being manipulated by powers beyond their control, which pushes them into a one-down feeling. Parents of children who are at risk of placement are all too prone to consider themselves victims; they need no help from the worker on that score.

THE INTAKE PROCESS

The focus at intake is on identifying the basic problem and then upon change in family relationships.

In facing change, the family is caught on the horns of a dilemma, for change includes both promise and threat. If change materializes, the family will be more stable than before, and this promise, considered in the abstract, is desirable.

The threat is that change itself is scary. Change takes effort, and change is painful. Additionally, one cannot change alone, for as one person changes, all relationships in the family network also change. If one changes and other family members do not, the change is self-defeating, and the one who changed is worse off than ever, for the old relationships are gone, and new relationships cannot be established unilaterally. Family members could wind up as strangers to each other. Thus, neither child nor parent want too much change to occur.

On the other hand, if too little change occurs, the problematic situation will reassert itself, and this is unacceptable. The catalyst for change is the worker.

One of the worker's goals, then, is to "empower" the parents, most of whom have a long history of powerlessness. If their powerlessness is permitted or encouraged, the parents' sense of failure is increased if the child is placed. The results then are predictable: visits to the child diminish, parents are less available to the worker, and the child finds himself unable to re-enter his own family, which may have restructured itself and found satisfaction without him.

Ideally, the family and the child will feel that they are partners with the worker in identifying problems, setting goals, and in evaluating their progress and the prospects for eventual reunion.

In the process of assessment, several questions are consistently examined:

• What is the basic problem in functioning and in relationships within the family?
• What circumstances would have to change in order for the family to function adequately and for the child to continue to live at home?
• Are parents and the child willing and able, with the support of the worker, to make those changes?
• If not, do the parents have strength to permit the child to live apart from them?
• Can the parents see alternate care as just one factor in a process of change which will result in growth and maturation for the child and for his family?
• What community resources exist which can help the family? Community resources are closer, and, consequently, more accessible to the family than the worker. The family can have more frequent contacts with community resources than with the worker, and community resources are less threatening to the family than the worker. As an incidental matter, community resources save time for the worker.

If these questions are not carefully deliberated, at the first sign of stress the healing process will falter, which constitutes additional trauma for the parents, the child, and, if placement ensues, for the foster parents or the staff of the residential center.

The term "working alliance" has been used to designate the relationship between the caseworker and parent-client, within which the cooperative role of the parent can be nurtured and implemented.[1]

With some parents, the achievement of a working alliance may come with relative ease. With other parents, achieving a working alliance may be the initial task of the worker and may call for the use of various reaching-out techniques and activities.

Cooperation might appear to be an unduly limited objective in relation to long-term plans. Actually, however, nothing can be achieved either with the parents' problems or with the child's problems until a climate of cooperation is achieved. The parents' capacity to cooperate and to act on their own behalf is an index to progress or lack of it.

The impediments to the parents' cooperation with the worker should not be underestimated. Attitudinal change precedes behavioral change. Cooperation very likely first will entail such changes for the parents as the following:

- Overcoming fear of and hostility toward authority;
- Beginning to see that their constructive thoughts and actions, however meager, are recognized and accepted by the worker;
- Learning that they retain some responsibility and decision-making authority with respect to their child;
- Learning to make decisions based upon a considered evaluation of facts;
- Beginning to gain or regain a sense of power—or call it maturity—in their own lives.

The development of trust with adults, as with children, is a slow process, and comes only with the opportunity to test and experience the attitudes and reliability of the worker and agency. To the degree that the parent is distrustful, afraid, and hostile in his relationships with adults, his ability to enter into a working alliance is limited. This will be especially true with respect to the worker or with any other adult who represents authority.

As has been noted, the parents' common anxieties and fears in this relationship may include the following:

- Fear of losing the child;
- Feeling of failure as a parent and as an adult;
- Fear of disapproval by friends, family, and neighbors;

- Expectation of rejection and blame by the person who represents authority;
- Fear of personal disintegration.

Emotionally fragile to begin with as individuals, spouses, and/or as parents, this threat may be enough to make them disintegrate or to feel that they will fall apart. The worker's support at this point is crucial to reassure parents and child that there is a future and that she will help them find that future.

The child has an even greater need of reassurance. Parents easily and unwittingly pass their fears on to the child, who may erroneously conclude that he is responsible for his parents' fears and disintegration. He needs permission to be a child who wants, needs, and deserves to receive care from powerful but safe adults; he does not need to feel that he is responsible for his parents' failings.

Active parental involvement provides concrete evidence to the child that worker and family are working together, openly gaining support from each other.

Not only parents are involved. In making decisions regarding intake of disturbed children, the support of relatives, friends, and the home community are of great importance. Family dysfunction and a child's problems are more amenable to treatment if support is available apart from the worker.

Parents' Expectations During Intake

Nowhere is the basic social work dictum of "Start where the client is" more pertinent than in working with parents of a child in need. It is necessary to explore what the parents expect and wish the agency to do in regard to the problem.

Bringing out the parents' ideas as to how they think the agency functions, what it can do for them and the child, where their rights and the agency's authority intersect, and any other ideas they have about the agency will establish a base line for both worker and parents.

As a practical matter, the worker should explore the parents' ideas and feelings before explaining the agency's service, procedures, and authority. If the nature of agency services differs from the parents' hopes and expectations, they may be too embarrassed or disappointed to be honest with the worker about their ideas. Unless corrected, their expectations will continue to operate, and they will taint and undermine future efforts of parents and worker.[2]

After hearing the parents' expectations, the worker will describe the agency's services and, in the process, she will make it clear that help will be a joint agency/family activity: the agency will help the family, not take over for them.

The needs of the child cannot be divorced from the needs of the parents, and frequently the worker will find that she must first address the parents' needs. Parents with problems typically are not accustomed to thinking problems through to arrive at an action plan; they are more likely simply to act or react. From the worker they may want physical, tangible, observable action or services. This may involve specific assistance in housing, unemployment, medical care, financial help, etc. The need for help in these basic areas of living may initially take priority over other problems, and it may be a necessary part of starting where they are.

Obtaining tangible services for the parents meets their needs; it also gives them an opportunity to test the worker to see whether or not her concern is real. Once parents have experienced positive action by the worker, i.e., when tangible problems have been relieved, they may be more inclined to trust the worker in planning for their child. Later, after they have accepted help on behalf of their child, they may seek help with the intangibles of their lives.

Even though a working alliance has been established, the worker will be careful not to make excessive demands upon the parents, whose emotional strength is fragile. Many are still at the bottom of the employment heap, at the bottom of the emotional heap, at the bottom of every other heap, and they may still be struggling with their own sense of adulthood. Dealing with intangibles is still foreign to them; consequently, more energy is required.

Piled on top of those things are the pain and anxieties created by the present situation. When these factors have been diluted by the giving of gratification, there will be a somewhat diminished drain on their energies and they will have more energy available for better functioning.

Such parents are not to be expected to think and plan with regard to their children's welfare first, or to become involved in a casework approach which includes struggling with their own guilt, anger and its meaning, pain, and confusions in order to become freer to take care of their children. It may be sufficient initially to get their cooperation in acting on their own behalf.

It is so easy for people who are accustomed to having their problems taken away from them simply to dump the whole situation in the agency's lap and withdraw. The worker has to prevent this if she can, and she can't prevent it by doing the parents' work for them.

If a decision is made that placement is needed, the parents will enter an agreement with the agency—usually called the agency/family plan of care—which will record the specific responsibilities of agency, parents, and child. Most plans of care will set forth conditions which, if met, will result in the reunification of family and child. In some cases, the plan will provide for long-term alternate care of the child and will establish the conditions for appropriate involvement of the family with the child. The parents and the agency must demonstrate to each other that they have fulfilled their respective share of the agreement.

With placement, the parents enter a new role with their child. The parents will share decision-making with the agency, even though in cases of involuntary placement the agency has authority over the parents. In any placement, the parents are in the position of having to earn the right to resume full child care and decision-making responsibility. The worker will help the parents identify the means by which this can be accomplished.

The question the parents may have, but be unable to ask, is whether or not they will ever again be parents to their child. They may just assume that when this chapter of the child's life is over, they and the child will pick up where they left off. For them, placement is just an unexpected, uninvited, unwanted interval in the life of the family, and when the court has done its thing, or when the social worker gets tired of messing with the kid, the child will come back and they will resume life as they know it. The worker will constantly counter this assumption.

Occasionally a parent will abandon, or appear to have abandoned, the child. In rare instances, this may reflect a lack of interest in the child. Far more frequently, abandonment is a mixture of guilt, pain, personal inadequacy, and disbelief that they can change sufficiently so as to provide adequately for the child.

During intake, the worker will do everything she can to keep the family involved—or, at the very least, in contact. If the parent is scared off, and his whereabouts is unknown, the worker really has a problem. Anyone who has worked with a child in residential care who doesn't know where his family is will testify that this is not a fun situation.

As indicated, when the parents have a working alliance with the worker, the parents may be ready for more intensive work on the intangibles in their own lives. This may occur while plans are being made for the child, or it may emerge after the child's problems have been solved or action plans are complete. The parents' needs may include such things as the following:

> • Easing guilt and shame, which will free them to function more adequately;
> • Increasing impulse control;
> • Reinforcing desirable patterns of behavior;
> • Beginning to gain new insights into the family's problems;
> • Beginning to see the problems from the child's perspective.
> • Identifying self-defeating patterns of behavior in interpersonal relationships and in role functioning;
> • Changing their feelings and behavior in relationships with other adults;
> • Changing their feelings and behavior toward each other and toward their child;

Thus, the worker's responsibilities vis-a-vis the family extend far beyond the question of whether or not to place the child.

SIBLINGS

Siblings may be the forgotten figures in the placement equation. In families where there is more than one child, but placement is being considered for only one, the worker must be sensitive to the placed child's feelings about siblings' remaining at home, and to their feelings toward the child who is being placed.

The child who is being considered for placement may understandably be resentful of a sibling who will remain at home. Care must be taken that the real reason for placement is clear to the child.

The child who will stay at home may feel guilt in being worthy to remain, just as, in some circumstances, he may feel a secret satisfaction and relief, too. There may also be feelings of sorrow for the one going into placement. Additionally, the one who remains lives under the threat that in the future, placement could be considered for him, too; after all, he is living with parents who do place children. These feelings must be recognized by the worker and, when appropriate, explored and dealt with.

VOLUNTARY PLACEMENT

There is a difference, of course, in intake in voluntary and involuntary placements.

In a voluntary placement, the intake process is most helpful in helping the parents decide whether or not placement of the child is the best course or the only one left after considering available alternatives.

Neither the referral nor the parent's request for placement should be taken at face value; rather, a careful evaluation should be made with the parent as to whether or not placement is needed, either for psychological or for social reasons.

Understanding the usual patterns in the parental relationships and in parent-child relationships, with allowances for individual differences within these categories, will serve to establish the goal of placement. It is the cumulative understanding of the parents, of the child, and of their relationship, which determines whether or not placement is indicated and, if so, the length and goal of placement. That is, will placement be only temporary, indefinite for a long time, or definitely permanent; specifically what is to be accomplished through placement?

INVOLUNTARY PLACEMENT

In working with parents who are involuntary clients, ordinarily the agency must take the initiative for the initial contact. Most parents can be located at the time of the court referral, even though this may require visiting the parents in a hospital or a jail, or searching for them through relatives, neighbors, employers, previous addresses, or through other means.

In the involuntary situation, where placement has been ordered by the court, the worker still conducts an intake study to establish a relationship with the family and help them deal with the court order. If court records are available, these will expedite the study process. The court and the placing agency normally operate from different perspectives, however, and their studies may have disparate emphases. The court may be primarily concerned with whether or not a law has been broken or the immediate protection of the child; the placing agency is concerned with overall prospects of family rehabilitation. In some cases, the more comprehensive study of the worker may provide evidence which will permit the court to allow alternative measures.

If the court has ordered placement and the decision has to stand, the worker still needs to know what she is working with, for usually the court will not follow the family except to receive periodic reports; ongoing work or contact with the family will be the worker's responsibility. Even with a court-ordered placement, goals have to be set, and the worker cannot set goals if she doesn't know what the individual family members are and what the family system is.

In a court-ordered placement, the worker may have less time for the intake study than in a voluntary placement, and much less time than is desired or necessary. This is reality, and the worker has to do the best she can in the time available.

SUMMARY

Many workers give up on parents of children who are at risk of placement, believing that the parents are not interested in being helped in their relationship with their children. It is true, of course, that some parents are not interested, and others are so beset by problems that they cannot be interested.

Many parents, however, may seem uninterested because they simply do not have enough energy to use in considering and planning for their children both before and after placement; hence, they do not respond to the worker's efforts with them in that direction. They have been down so long that they have given up hope of ever having a better life.

These parents may respond to approaches made to involve them for their own sake. This is because they are so in need of gratification themselves and so lacking in personal resources for obtaining it. They have to be given to in order to replenish their own psychic energy first before they can muster any to apply to the problems involving their children.

The parent's paramount psychological tasks in reaction to the child's possible placement, are to find a new maturity within himself and a new equilibrium in his relationship with other family members and with the child.[3]

The kind of help the parent-clients can use is differentially determined on the basis of a variety of factors. These factors include:

- The parent's view of the purpose of his contacts with the agency;
- The problem areas he presents for discussion which provide the

opportunity for mutual identification of the areas of work to be undertaken at any given time;

• The degree of dysfunction in major life roles (parenting, marriage, work, etc.);

• The nature of the defenses against underlying dependency which determine the degree to which he can use constructively the realistic dependence inherent in accepting help and the level at which help can be offered.[4]

Theoretically, it can be assumed that the parent's fear of the helping relationship is at least equalled by the extent of his underlying need.

When placement has been decided upon, the parent's involvement in and acceptance of the placement plan may mean the difference between success and failure of treatment. It includes his adapting his visiting, gift-giving, correspondence, and so forth, to the plan of care. It means that ultimately the child's return to his home depends on joint planning and effort.

Several questions will be answered by the intake study:

• What are the basic problems in this family?

• What alternative solutions to the problems are available?

• What strengths do the parents have to involve themselves in the process of strengthening the family and providing adequate care for the child?

• Should the child be placed in view of what such a move will mean to him and in the light of the unpredictability of alternate care?

• If placement of the child is indicated, is the parent ready to move in that direction?

• If placement of the child is indicated, what are the goals of placement for the child and for the family?

• If placement of the child is indicated, what placement resources are available, and how can they meet the needs of this child and family?

• What strengths does the child have which will enable him to survive placement?

• What measures can be used to assess the family's readiness to receive the child again?

• If placement is indicated, will this be temporary or permanent? If the separation is to be permanent, should termination of parental rights be commenced at the time of separation?

The intake study and the reasons given for separation will follow the child throughout his placement(s). Subsequent workers, foster parents, and/or institutional personnel must have a clear statement of the reasons for placement; they must have a clear assessment of the nature of the child's family and support system in order that all planning for child and family will be based upon reality.

Nowhere is the professionalism of the worker put to a more crucial test than in the intake process.

Endnotes

[1]Kline, Draza, and Overstreet Helen-Mary. *Foster Care of Children.* New York: Columbia University Press, 1972, p. 162.
[2]Glickman, Esther. *Child Placement Through Clinically Oriented Casework.* New York: Columbia University Press, 1957, pp. 8–9.
[3]Kline and Overstreet, op. cit., p. 177.
[4]Ibid., pp. 183–184.

Chapter 5

DECISION TO PLACE

Making the decision to place a child is where all of the skill and the professionalism of the worker come into focus. The worker must put aside personal biases, culture, and values in order to concentrate objectively upon the specific child and family with whom she is working. This is more easily said than done.

Workers with any experience at all have been exposed to sub-standard homes, some of them extremely sub-standard. Most workers are middle class, and their initial reaction to a child's living conditions may be one of revulsion. The human reaction of the social worker of "I wouldn't want my child to grow up there" is irrelevant—that is not the question. No child should have to leave home because of lack of food, shelter, or cleanliness.

A child may be ill-fed, and ill-sheltered, he may be dirty and suffering from disease, he may be ill-treated, but unless his parents have totally rejected him, he is secure in the knowledge that there is someone to whom he is of value and who will try, even though inadequately, to provide for him until such time as he can survive on his own.[1] This security must be preserved while existing problems are relieved. Placement is only one option available to the worker by which this can be accomplished.

The question is whether or not this child can have a reasonable chance for safety, development, and maturation in this place and with these people and whether or not he is valued by his primary caretakers.

PREVIOUS EXPERIENCE IN PLACEMENT

The history of placement practice leaves much to be desired.

In one study, in cases where the child had been in foster home care prior to the placement in question, the parent was asked whether or not she had seen a social worker during the interim.

85

• About one-half of the parents of children who had been placed more than once replied in the negative. Very likely if there had been more adequate follow-up on discharged cases, at least some of the subsequent placements might be avoided.

• Almost 30% of the parents felt that, in retrospect, placing their child in foster homes was not necessary.

• Another 23.3% of the parents reported that they thought placement could have been avoided if they had been able to receive quicker or more intensive family counseling.

• Another 16.7% thought that having a homemaker would have been all that was necessary.[2]

In another study, more than 70% of the fathers and mothers of the children either had no relationship with the agencies responsible for the care of their children, or their relationship was erratic or untrusting.

In many instances, the agencies' resources were such that their staff's time was entirely consumed with the day-to-day job of caring for the children. They had no time for the kind of continuous work with the parents of the children which could effect the rehabilitation of the home.

Frequently agencies failed to appreciate the dynamics of intrafamily relationships as a whole and worked only with the child.[3]

In still another study, according to the parents there was almost no initial consideration of options to the necessity of the child's going into alternate care.

• Homemakers were discussed in about 3% of the cases;
• Day care was only talked about in less than 2%, and
• Other child care arrangements were talked about in 2.5% of the cases.

This was in spite of the fact that 28.8% of the parents felt that accessibility to day care alone would have been enough to make a substantial difference in the decision.

The parents were asked about their perception of whether or not they were given a realistic picture of foster home care by the social worker prior to the placement.

• 20% stated that they were not;
• Of greater concern, however, is the fact that 42.5% of the parents reported that it was not talked about at all.

When the parents were asked about whether or not their child agreed with the necessity of a foster home placement,

• Almost half the children were said to be too young to understand the issues;

• However, 27.9% of the children were against the plan, and an equal proportion were either in favor from the beginning or eventually adjusted to the idea.

• 19% of the children did not really understand what was happening, and

• About 20% of the children were "pressured" into entering care.

• Sadly, 25.3% of the parents did not know how the child felt.

• Most important, 60% of the parents stated that they felt as if they were excluded from participating in the process with their children when it came to dealing with their reactions.[4]

These data tend to show that the workers were intent on placement; they show a callous disregard of the effects of separation on child and family and of the alternatives which might have eliminated the need for placement. Excessive caseloads notwithstanding, such practices can no longer be tolerated.

DECIDING TO PLACE

In considering the placement of a child, social workers typically make one of two mistakes:

• They place too easily and too soon;
• They do not place soon enough.

Workers place children too easily and too soon because placement is a quick solution to—actually, an evasion of—complex problems. Working with problems is time-consuming and enervating; it is far simpler to place a child and then get on to other cases on the caseload.

On the other hand, the worker may delay placing a child because she hopes that the situation will improve, even though realistically she knows that it will not. Delay simply exacerbates the situation; damage to the child and to the family deepens.

Once a social worker's assessment has led her to the belief that placement is indicated, she should use it with conviction and move promptly to begin the placement process.

The worker must have some conceptual base against which to measure a specific situation. The following two questions are a starting point:

• What constitutes minimally adequate care for children, the level below which the home is so destructive that children can only be seriously and permanently damaged in character, personality, and behavior?

   • Secondly, in what homes can change toward greater family integration take place within the time limits set by the inexorable rate of children's physical and psychological growth?[5]

The worker does not have unlimited years at her disposal. Children grow quickly, and when making the decision as to whether or not to place, the worker must take into account the amount of time she has available in relation to the child's growth and development.

In the individual case, the worker must answer other basic questions:

   • Can this child be protected in his home? Can someone come into the home; can the family be directed to some help in the community; can support of some kind be introduced so that the child will not have to be separated from his family, but still be protected?

   • If the child cannot be protected in his own home, is an alternative available for the child which clearly is superior to his home situation? In what specific ways is the placement resource superior to his own home?

   • If the child is placed, are services available to child and family which will preserve their relationship and increase the likelihood of their reunion? Whose responsibility is it to activate those services?

   • What steps should be taken at the time of placement to ensure continuity in the life of the child? Who is responsible for taking those steps?

   • If the parent/child relationship is such that it cannot, or should not, be maintained, is a *permanent* alternative available for the child?

   • When placement has been considered, are the reasons for the decision to place or not to place clearly documented in the child's record?

How does the social worker decide when it is time to break up a family group?

Traditionally, separation has been used when there has been physical or sexual abuse or physical or emotional neglect.

Physical abuse usually is relatively easy to identify. More often than not, the worker will have evidence from neighbors, physicians, the hospital emergency room staff, or others to support her case.

Physical neglect is more obscure. The worker must be careful that apparent neglect does not constitute more an offense to her middle-class standards than danger to the child. Children can grow up happy and content amidst squalor, provided they have love and emotional support.

Lack of food, adequate school clothes, poor housing, or some other comparable deficiency should not be a reason for separation.

Housing or dietary standards which are hazardous for the child are equally hazardous for other members of the family and must be remedied. Unless the worker can place the entire family, in such cases a plan other than placement of the child is likely to be more appropriate.

The controlling question with respect to physical neglect is not the amount of dirt, but the amount of love and support. This is not to say that physical neglect is never a factor in the decision. It is to say that many conditions of neglect can be relieved without breaking up the family.

Emotional neglect is extremely hard to define; some experts argue that it should not be a basis for intervention. Children probably should not be removed in cases of emotional neglect unless emotional damage is defined very carefully and unless adequate facilities or services are available to help the child. If the worker does not have something substantially better to offer the child than he has at home, she should leave him where he is. There is little merit in replacing parental neglect with state neglect.

The answer to whether or not to place should not lie in the exact kind or degree of neglect or rejection, but rather in the future chances of parents and child to succeed in living together.

The basic question is, "Is this child safe, or can he be protected in his own home?

Basically, state intervention should be limited to instances where a child has suffered serious physical harm, serious and narrowly defined emotional damage, or sexual abuse, or where there is a strong probability that the child imminently will suffer such harm.

When the worker can predict quite clearly that a harmful situation will continue, or almost certainly reach that slightly worse point at which the parents "break," abandon, or are brought to court for their failures, she can be fairly sure that she is facing a placement situation.

We cannot say too often that the worker has to allow for her own biases and prejudices. She is not looking for an ideal family situation; she is not looking for a replication of her own family life or of the family life of her dreams. She is looking for a place where a child can have at least minimal assurance of having physical and emotional needs met; where he is free from the pressures or trauma of a dysfunctional family in which he has been victimized, and where the damage of placement is less severe to the child, to the parent, and to the child/parent relationship than the damage of leaving the child in the home.

The child who faces placement because his parents have requested it is not nearly so damaged as if this plan is imposed upon him and his parents by an outside force. The parent, however disturbed, who has enough insight and strength to ask for help has, by that very act, demonstrated that chances of family rehabilitation exist.

THINGS TO GUARD AGAINST

The worker is well advised to guard herself against several issues.

• Historically, placement has been used "in the best interests of the child." No matter how well intentioned and how high-sounding it might be, there are certain deficiencies in this phrase.

One obvious objection to the "best interests of the child" test is that by its very terms it ignores the interests of the parents. By excluding consideration of parental interests, this test reflects a now outmoded philosophy.

As we have seen, the parents have an involvement over and above their interest in and concern for their child. Aside from the satisfaction and pleasures which may be derived from their relationship with their child, the parents' adequacy as individuals, spouses, and parents are all on the block and may well be destroyed when the child is placed.

The best interests of the child cannot be divorced, therefore, from the best interests of the family.

• In deciding who should care for a particular child, the court is comparing an existing family with a largely unknown alternative, the foster care system. The foster care system is well known in theory, but its practical deficiencies are unknown to the general public—and to the court.

One 4-year-old New York boy was placed in 37 different homes in two months. Another boy was put in 17 homes in 25 days. Twenty-five percent of the children in foster care in another city were abused.[6]

• Applying the "best interests of the child" test assumes that the judge will compare the probable consequences for the child of remaining in the home with the probable consequences of removal.

The court does not have—and cannot be expected to have—expertise in the dynamics of placement. Some judges, it is true, have acquired broad understanding of family dynamics and the principles of placement. Those judges, to their credit, have taken the initiative to educate themselves in these matters. Such insight cannot be assumed, however, nor do judges who do not possess such insights deserve criticism. The court's responsibility is to interpret and to apply the law.

Judges are still predominantly male, white, and middle class, and they may have biases about the very issues which are involved in placement decisions: illegitimacy, sexual permissiveness, life styles, drug use, child-rearing practices, etc. Furthermore, their biases may well reflect the biases of the community, which may bring pressure to take a child away from his family for what social workers would consider to be frivolous or capricious reasons—surface behavior, physical cleanliness, etc.

Probation officers and social workers who investigate the facts and report to the judge also have biases. Even if they have a graduate degree—which most do not—childrearing is still an art rather than a science, and graduate schools in the human services are primarily staffed by middle-class teachers, with little direct experience of slum life or minority group culture.[7] Fortunately, this is changing, but many practicing social workers received their education in an earlier era.

Thus, the worker must be prepared to work with the court and to interpret to the court the reasons for or against placement and the ramifications of that decision.

It is no longer considered sufficient that a child be afforded a placement situation in which his basic needs are being cared for in terms of shelter, food, and clothing, and a benign environment in which positive emotional growth can be enhanced.

The placement resource must have a mechanism which will take positive action on behalf of the child and which will permit positive action on the part of the child. The placement resource must be able to measure and document progress.

The child must have specific goals toward which to work, goals which he has had a share in developing. He must have a sense of progression in his work to achieve those goals.

Unless a placement resource is available which possesses these qualities, the child might be better off remaining at home.

• A criterion which is an integral part of assessing the adequacy of an agency's performance is whether a child can be assured continuity of relationships and permanency in his living arrangements.

It is not enough that the child might be placed in a setting that offers him care. If he cannot regard the people he is living with as his family on a permanent basis for as long as he needs them, his situation reflects something less than an adequate resolution of his life situation. This obtains whether the child is placed in foster family care or an institution.

One teenager had lived in an institution for six months. He said, "When I came here, they said I would never have to move again. In four months I was moved four times."

A move from one living unit to another within an institution is nearly as complicated dynamically as a move from home to the institution.

• Parents have widely differing abilities to contend with behaviors of their children. The worker must take these differences into account. "Different" means only "unlike"; it does not mean better or worse. The parent may well be dealing admirably with a situation which is so difficult that the worker has a problem recognizing the adequacy of care. For example:

A single mother provided 24-hour-a-day care for a severely retarded, but physically agile nine-year-old. The apartment, three rooms over a commercial establishment, reeked of urine, for the girl was incontinent; all flat surfaces were bare, because the girl would climb across dressers, counter tops, the buffet, and all tables. Wherever the mother went, the girl had to go—to the store, to the basement to wash clothes, to the clothesline to hang up the clothes, etc. The girl could never be out of the mother's sight.

The impressive thing about this situation was that the mother did not complain. Her practical, no-nonsense approach to a confining life style was refreshing. When the worker spotted on the kitchen table a new bottle of medicine, obviously a tranquilizer, she commented on it. The mother replied, "Yes, they gave it to me for Brenda, but it didn't do her any good, so I took it myself, and I feel a lot better!"

A foster mother accepted into care a husky 17-year-old boy who had spent four of his early teen years cleaning up after incontinent men on an adult ward of a mental hospital. David was an exceedingly difficult charge; moody, his behavior was highly unpredictable.

When David chopped the garden hose into one-foot lengths, the foster mother shrugged it off. When he came into the foster mother's bedroom one morning and threw the covers off of her, she said that he didn't mean anything by this, he had awakened early, he was hungry, and this was his way of getting her to move. Most foster parents—and most parents—would have been terrified to have a burly, teen-age male suddenly pull the covers off of a sleeping female.

Other parents and foster parents deal adequately with children with comparable, although totally different, problems. The point is that the difficulty or complexity of the problem does not, in and of itself, indicate placement or re-placement. One must take into account the parents' ability to cope.

> • All children's disorders are negative interactions between inner and outer forces. The family members' reaction to a child's problems, apart from their role in creating it, is often as important a criterion for accepting a child into alternate care as the problem itself.[8]

The worker must be aware of the possibility of negative follow-up by the family. For example:

> • Parents of an acting-out child may be so relieved, yet so guilt-ridden, when the child is placed that they scheme with the child to circumvent the authority of the placement setting;
> • Parents may unconsciously encourage the child to act out their own delinquent fantasies when he is in someone else's care;
> • Some parents seek to gain their child's favor in placement by providing him and his friends with lavish gifts, parties, or drugs;
> • Some parents may be so angry with their child that they consider any controls placed upon the child by the caregivers to be insufficient;
> • Some parents may unconsciously set the child up for delinquent behavior, as when the car keys are "accidentally" left in the car when the child is home for a visit.

Needless to say, these reactions are counter productive. The worker may or may not be able to identify such potential behaviors in advance, but she must be alert to their possible development and keep such possibilities in mind when making a decision to place.

PRESSURES ON THE FAMILY TO CONTINUE FOSTER CARE

One of the factors in making a decision to place is the realization that placement is easier to initiate than to terminate.

In most cases, having the child at home increases the financial pressure of the biological parent: no one can rear children without spending money. Even if financial stress did not contribute to the child's placement, it may prevent his return. The family budget, developed with the child out of the home, may appear to be simply inadequate for the family to accept the child back home.

While the foster parent and the institution are reimbursed for some or all of the expenses related to care of the child, the natural parent receives no funds for support of the child unless he is on welfare. Thus, finances provide a disincentive for restoration of the biological family.

This pressure extends to the extended family which provides care for a child. Because of drugs and alcohol problems, increasing numbers of grandparents are providing care for grandchildren, either informally or through legal guardianship or adoption. In retirement, when their own income is reduced and at a time when they should be free to pursue their own interests, they are faced again with child-rearing expenses and a drain upon reduced physical and emotional energy. Placement can be the easier course for them, and in the absence of financial help, they may encourage continued placement of their grandchild.

UNWORKABLE FAMILIES

It is true, of course, that some families are unworkable. Their dysfunction is so profound, or their involvement in the alcohol or drug scene is so deep seated, or for various other reasons they simply will not or cannot respond to the most sensitive help from the worker.

In such cases, placement is surely indicated. Having made this decision, the worker then will assess carefully the degree to which continued contact with the family is necessary for the child's continued growth, with or without termination of parental rights. Variations on the placement theme are infinite, and the worker will use her best professional judgment to put closure on the case. No worker can responsibly say either that she will always opt for return of the child to the family or, conversely, that she will always opt for termination of parental rights. As one sensitive executive stated, "All questions in child care have the same answer: 'It all depends.' "

DOCUMENTATION WITH RESPECT TO REMOVAL OF A CHILD

All aspects of the placement decision must be documented, for several reasons:

- Documenting the reasons for a decision forces the worker to think through her actions with greater precision than simply thinking them through;
- In case of litigation, the evidence presented was established at the time the action was taken, rather than after the fact; hence it is more nearly accurate and complete;
- Future workers with child or family will have an adequate background upon which to base their work, thus providing continuity of services for family and child.

The contents of the report upon which the decision to place a child is based have been ably listed as follows:

- If removal is recommended, a full description of the reasons why the child cannot be protected adequately in the home, including a description of any previous efforts to work with the parents and the child in the home; the in-home treatment programs, e.g., homemakers, which have been considered and rejected, and the parents' attitude toward placement of the child;
- A statement of the specific harm(s) to the child, as defined by statute, that intervention is designed to alleviate;
- A description of the specific programs, for both the parents and the child, that are needed in order to prevent further harm to the child; the reasons why such programs are likely to be useful; the availability of any proposed services, and the agency's overall plan for ensuring that the services will be delivered;
- A statement of the measures, e.g., specific changes in parental behavior, that will be used to determine that placement is no longer necessary;
- A statement of the likely harms the child will suffer as a result of removal. This section should include an exploration of the nature of the parent/child attachment and the meaning of separation and loss to both the parents and the child;
- A description of the steps that will be taken to minimize the harm to the child that may result if separation occurs.[9]

CORRECTING ABUSES RESULTING FROM
AN ANTI FAMILY BIAS IN PLACEMENT

Steps necessary to correct abuses which result from the long-standing anti-family bias in placement have been ably summarized as follows:

• No child should be removed from his home unless services designed to prevent unnecessary out-of-home care have been provided to the family, or offered and refused. The only exception should be in emergency situations, where the child is in danger of substantial physical or emotional harm.

• If the child is placed "voluntarily," i.e., without court involvement, there should be a written agreement spelling out the obligations and rights of both the parents and the agency. The parents should be informed both verbally and in writing of their right, upon request, to the return of a voluntarily placed child within a reasonable period unless the state files a dependency, neglect, or abuse petition.

• If the placement is involuntary, i.e., as a result of a court proceeding, the parents and child should have the right to counsel.

• If a child must be placed, priority should be given to the formal placement of the child with willing relatives with reimbursement at the foster care rate. If such placement is not possible, the child should be placed in the least restrictive setting appropriate to his needs, within reasonable proximity to family and home community.

• While the child is in placement, the public agency with responsibility for the child should have a statutory obligation to maintain and encourage, whenever possible, parent/child contact and provide specific restorative services designed to reunify the family. Parents should have a statutory right to receive progress reports.

• There must be independent (of the agency or person providing services) reviews of children out of their homes at least every six months to determine progress toward reunification.

• No later than 18 months after entry into care, there should be a dispositional review conducted by a court or specially designated board, independent of service providers and appealable to the courts. The purpose of this review should be to determine whether the child should be returned home, continued for a specified period in foster care until reunification, freed for adoption, or, in special circumstances, placed in permanent foster care. All interested parties should be notified of this review and have the right to participate. A mechanism should be mandated to ensure that recommended dispositions are carried out.

• Statutory provisions regarding termination of parental rights and adoption subsidy should be reviewed and strengthened as necessary. All children should have separately appointed counsel in termination proceedings.

• Parents, foster parents, and children should have access to grievance mechanisms to register complaints about the care or treatment they are receiving.

• Community advocacy groups should closely monitor, evaluate, and seek to correct inadequate policies and practices toward children at risk of placement or in placement and their families. Budgets should be reviewed to ensure adequate funds for preventive, restorative, and adoptive services, as well as for review procedures.[10]

SUMMARY

The history of placement of children is replete with examples of a bias against the child's family. This bias is no longer acceptable. It is true, of course, that some children must be placed for their protection or to ensure their chances of maturation. Today this does not mean riding rough-shod over the parents' rights or wishes. Parents must be afforded an opportunity to participate within their capability in decisions which involve their child, and they must be offered assistance in increasing their capabilities. The worker is the one to offer this support.

The worker should perceive placement as an opportunity for parents and child to come to an understanding of themselves and one another that will make it possible for them to come back together and again to function as a family—or to separate amicably, with understanding, and with emotional needs of both parent and child met insofar as possible.

Whether casework planning should be directed toward permanent removal of a child from the family or toward greater integration of the family members is not a decision that should rest with personal biases, preconceived assumptions, or idealized aims, however lofty, that have small chance of realization.

The basic questions to be answered in the placement decision are:

• Is this child safe and given a *reasonable* chance for growth and maturation in his own home?

• What services are available by which the child can be protected and provided with a reasonable chance for growth and maturation in his own home?

• If the child cannot be protected in his own home, is a placement resource available which clearly provides the services the child needs?

• Who is working with the family, and to what ends is that work directed?

• What arrangements are being made in this case for permanent resolution of the problem—reunion of the family, termination of parental rights, or some other responsible plan?

Endnotes

[1]Katz, Sanford: *When Parents Fail: The Law's Response to Family Breakdown.* Boston: Beacon Press, 1971, p. 62.

[2]Gruber, Alan R. *Children in Foster Care.* New York: Human Sciences Press, 1978, pp. 140–141. Used with permission.

[3]Maas, Henry and Engler, Richard E., Jr.: *Children in Need of Parents.* New York: Columbia University Press, 1959, pp. 390–391.

[4]Gruber, op. cit., pp. 141–142.

[5]Young, Leontine. *Wednesday's Children.* New York: McGraw-Hill, 1964, pp. 120–121.

[6]*NASW News,* Vol. 33, Number 7, July 1988.

[7]Mandell, Betty: *Where Are the Children?* Lexington, MA: Lexington Books, 1973, pp. 56–57.

[8]Mayer, Morris, Richman, Leon, and Balcerzak, Edwin: *Group Care of Children, Crossroads and Transitions.* New York, Child Welfare League of America, 1977, pp. 89–91.

[9]Wald, Michael S.: State Interventions on Behalf of "Neglected" Children: Standards for Removal of Children from Their Homes, Monitoring the Status of Children in Foster Care, and Termination of Parental Rights. *Stanford Law Review,* April 1976, Vol. 28: Page 623. Used with permission.

[10]Knitzer, Jane, Allen, Mary Lee, and McGowan, Brenda: *Children Without Homes.* Washington, D.C.: Children's Defense Fund, 1978, pp. 34–35. Used with permission.

PART TWO
PLACEMENT AS A PROCESS

Chapter 6

PREPARATION FOR PLACEMENT

When the decision has been made to place the child, the child and the family must be prepared for this traumatic event.

Adequate preparation for placement accomplishes several things:

- The pain of separation is diminished for parents and child;
- Continuity of life is preserved for the child and the family;
- The integrity and self determination of individuals is preserved insofar as possible;
- Family and child receive help with their individual problems and with problems in their relationship;
- Disappearance of the family may be prevented;
- The likelihood of success of the placement is enhanced;
- Reunion of the family and child is more likely.

At the very least, the child's preparation for placement should include:

- The opportunity to develop a sufficient relationship with the caseworker to enable him to accompany the caseworker without overwhelming anxiety;
- Increasing understanding of the circumstances which led to placement;
- Clarification of incorrect perceptions about placement and the placement resource;
- Opportunity to react to every aspect of the situation;
- Direct help with his fear and anxiety;
- Support from his parents to whatever extent they are able to participate constructively;
- Awareness of his own responsibility and his parents' responsibility in achieving reunion.
- Opportunity to become acquainted with the oncoming parent surrogates and other family or group members and the new physical environment before placement;
- Assurance of continuing support from the placing agency, especially, the worker.

PREPARATION WITH THE CHILD

The Infant

Infants have perhaps been least well served in the placement process. Because infants cannot talk, the assumption seems to be that they cannot feel or react and that they are oblivious to their surroundings. As was seen in Chapter One, such is not the case. Because the infant cannot react like an older child, the bridge from one placement to another must be constructed with care even with infants.

Ideally, if the worker is to move the infant, get-acquainted visits by the worker should be daily for probably a week before placement. During those visits, the worker needs to handle the child to accustom the child to being handled by someone other than his usual caregiver.

The social worker should take the child on two or three pre-placement visits to familiarize him with what will be his new surroundings and encourage the new caregiver to handle him during the pre-placement visits.

Alternatively, the permanent foster parents or adoptive parents may visit the child in his temporary foster home. This will save the worker time.

The visits should not be hurried; the first foster parents should encourage the new caregivers to feed, clothe, bathe, and cuddle the child. Thus, in a gentle and gradual way, the infant's transfer from one home to another is eased, his world is continuous, and his security remains intact.

One well-intentioned error that is frequently made in placing infants is to provide an entirely new set of clothes and blankets on placement day, forgetting that the infant's world is largely sensory. On placement day, the worker should ensure that the infant is dressed in familiar clothes and wrapped in a familiar blanket. When moving into a new placement, the infant at the very least should have the advantage of familiar textures, odors, and voices around him.

Today's caseloads and the increasing numbers of babies who are born with substance addiction or other problems may cause the worker to exclaim that she does not have time to prepare for placement of an infant. Precisely because of the unusual intensity of need of these little ones, however, they must be given every possible advantage. Time inappropriately saved in any placement process will more than be made up for in later work with child and the new caregivers.

The worker is quite free to improvise procedures which will save time. Improvisations are acceptable provided they adhere to professional principles.

Preparing the Older Child

Meeting the Child

In any placement situation, whether voluntary or involuntary, the placement worker's making his first contact with the child by coming to his home for the purpose of eventually removing him will most likely leave the impression with the child that the worker is an invading enemy. This creates a barrier which will impede the worker's further attempts to help the child both in the process of separation and in later adjustment.[1]

A simple technique to remedy this impression is to have the first interview with the child in the worker's office. If the parent brings the child to the office for the first visit, the likelihood that the worker will be perceived as the initiator of the action will be reduced. If office visits are not feasible, arrangements can be made to meet in a neutral setting—a city hall, a restaurant, etc. Often a church will loan an office or room for such a meeting.

There should be little difference in using this technique whether the placement is voluntary or involuntary. When the parents request placement, asking them to come to the office is a natural response to their request.

When the court has ordered the placement, the parents will not be surprised by a request to come to the office, and very likely they will keep the third or fourth appointment set for them.

In some cases, of course, it is not possible to avoid meeting the child early on. The worker may have investigated a neglect or abuse charge; she may have been present when the judge ordered placement, she may first meet the child in a detention center, etc. If this is the case, she proceeds with her task and deals with the child's hostility toward her as it arises.

Giving Up the Old

Quite naturally, the child has fears about giving up the old, for obvious reasons:

• The old is the known. Even though he has been badly treated in his family, in one way or another he has learned to live with it and survive. He has no perspective on what he is missing.

• The new is the unknown. He can only assume that the unknown will be worse than the known, and he has to face the unknown without the support of his family.

• Every child knows that adults are in charge of the world and of his world, and great unhappiness can result for the child who criticizes adults, including—and perhaps especially—his family. If the child admits that his family is in some way defective, he is left defenseless. Every child knows intuitively that he is not ready to function on his own, and thus he knows his basic dependence, although few teenagers will admit this openly.

The worker's task is to help the child perceive that life continues after separation, that he is not being asked to go into the unknown alone. She will go with him and provide the support which normally would come from the family.

Developing a Relationship

The first function in preparing the child for placement is to build a relationship with the child. The mechanics of building a relationship with the child vary with the age of the child, but the principles are the same: the worker gets acquainted with the child and, equally important, lets him get acquainted with her. He will quiz the worker, test her, and in other ways make his own determination as to whether or not she is to be trusted.

At least two significant factors make the relationship-building phase an exciting and challenging time for the social worker:

• The social worker may be the first adult the child has ever known who has been honest and open and unafraid of feelings;

• Frequently the child will indicate by behavior, rather than by words, what he is feeling, and the social worker must translate the message into words, first of all for herself, so that she knows what is being communicated, and second for the child, so that he knows that she knows what is going on.

For many children, adults are all alike and uniformly negative.

Adults are much more inclined to talk to children than to listen to them or converse with them, and their speech is frequently directive in nature. "Do this," "Do that." "Don't do this."

Adults want explanations from children, especially when things have gone wrong. Adults love the word "why." "Why did you break that window?" "Why did you use drugs?" Always "Why?" Most of the time the children do not know why, and, even if they did, they would not tell the adult. If pushed, children will lie just to get adults off their backs.

Adults are very likely to discount or, even worse, to forbid feelings. From time immemorial, adults have said to children, "You shouldn't feel that way," just as if children—or adults—were able to change the way they feel. Feelings come without being invited; therefore, any feeling is legitimate.

We cannot control how we feel, but we can control how we function in light of those feelings. Most of all, we can learn to confront our feelings, whatever they are, and eventually, by dealing with them and understanding them, we may be able to change them or to change the conditions under which they developed.

Adults often fail to differentiate between what a child is and what he does. The child hears, "You're stupid," instead of "You did a stupid thing." When the parent fails to make this differentiation, the child feels—and is—rejected.

For the teenager, the situation may be even more tense, for he is struggling with encroaching maturity, he is sorting out what he believes and what he is, and his opinions are likely to be at variance with adults' opinions. Many parents get into needless hassles with their teenage offspring by pouncing ruthlessly upon adolescent reasoning.

The social worker is a different kind of adult—or should be. In the first place, the social worker has time. The social worker is, or should seem to be, in no hurry. If a social worker communicates her pressures and busyness to a youngster at the point of establishing a relationship, he will feel rejected again by knowing that even with her he has a low priority.

At the beginning of the interview, the worker may say, "I have an hour to spend with you," but she doesn't resort to the parental, "Come on, I haven't got all day!" For the small child, she may say, "We have an hour to spend together. See—that means until the big hand gets all the way around to here." Setting time limits is acceptable; rushing a child to speak so that one can get on to other business is counterproductive.[2]

More than that, the social worker talks with the child and actually listens to him. If the child doesn't feel like talking, the worker doesn't insist that he say something; silences do not disturb her. Enduring silences without anxiety or discomfort is learned behavior for most adults, but it is an inherent part of the social worker's task.

Most important of all, she is not distressed by his comments. Instead of "Oh my, hating is not nice; you shouldn't hate," he hears, "He really made you angry, didn't he?"

Now, perhaps for the first time, the child has an adult who does not demand that he do away with ugly thoughts and feelings; rather, she encourages him to bring these thoughts out and look at them. She does not approve, condone, or deny them; she simply acknowledges that they exist and demonstrates that it is all right to talk about them. Moreover, she understands what he is thinking, even without asking "why?"

Even if words slip out against the social worker, she is not distressed. Rather, she helps him put his feelings into words: "You are really angry with me today, aren't you. You feel that I'm the one who is making you leave home."

Gradually, the child learns that the social worker is someone he can trust. She is honest and open. If she makes a promise she keeps it; even when he talks or feels bad or mean, her feelings about him do not change. As trust develops, he begins to have something he can hang onto as he moves into this frightening experience of placement.

Proceeding Incrementally

Given a relationship with the child, handling with him the need for placement proceeds in steps which are determined by the age and degree of understanding of the child, by the nature of the placement resource, and, to a degree, by the time available for the whole process.

The caseworker confronts the child with tasks that can be mastered in small steps. She will give the child as much information as he can accept in his present state of adjustment. The worker helps relate the facts to each other so that he gets the whole picture as fast as he can absorb and understand it. His relationship with the worker will sustain him as he begins to understand and adapt to the changing conditions of his life.

The worker will identify with the child's wishes and attitudes, which will range from extreme reluctance to leave home to relief at leaving a disturbed family. She will accept his feelings, empathize with him, and regret with him the circumstances which made separation necessary.

Rarely will the worker have time to let her relationship with the child develop to the point that she can discuss with him his deepest feelings. More likely, placement is imminent, and she will have to leave the deeper feelings for exploration in the placement setting, either by foster parent or institutional staff. At the moment, she will deal primarily with his feelings that pertain to the placement itself. She will give him brief, factual information about the reason for his placement, give him time to react, and then deal with those reactions.

Because time usually will not permit the worker to do complete work with the child, she can lay the groundwork for future work by suggesting that he has feelings which they have not discussed. This gives him tacit permission to have such feelings, but allows him to hold onto his defenses until he is ready to give them up. The way is thus opened for later work by placement personnel or by a future worker.

Frequently a child brings out his resentment at the worker in the accusation that if it were not for the worker, placement would not happen. This is dealt with relatively easily. The court or parents can make a placement without the agency; however, since placement is to be made, it is preferable that it be carried out by one who is familiar with the procedures. If this worker were not here, some other worker would be assigned.

The placing worker must make it clear to the child whether she will continue with him after placement or that another worker will be assigned. When the child has been placed, a worker will serve as a resource to the foster family or to the institution in working with the child's deeper feelings.

Description of Placement

The beginning of the description to the child of what placement entails should occur soon after he is told he is to be placed so that the child can gain intellectual mastery of it. The worker may describe placement and the placement resource in broad strokes, filling in details in response to the child's questions. If the worker has pictures of the foster home or institution, these can help the child to think specifically about what lies ahead. If the child asks questions which the worker cannot answer, it is fair to say that she does not know, but she—or they—can get the answer. She should jot the question down so that it is not forgotten.

The worker may need to correct distortions about placement which the child received from his parents. Parents may unintentionally or intentionally mislead a child, giving either a rosy description of placement — "you will have your own room, your own bicycle and horse; you can go swimming whenever you like ... " or, conversely, they may make dire predictions of the horrors awaiting the child. This can happen with foster parents, also.

When one worker transported a girl from a foster home to an excellent institution, the closer they came to the institution, the quieter and more subdued the girl became. Although the worker had a reasonably good relationship with the girl, it was not until they drove onto the institutional grounds that the problem was revealed: the foster mother, exasperated with the girl's behavior, had given a macabre account of the cell and the diet, restricted mostly to bread and water, which awaited her as retribution for her behavior.

Ideally, the larger part of the description of life in placement should be given only after the child has settled some of the feelings he is struggling with in relation to the fact of placement. Until he has mastered to some degree the fact that he is going to be placed, very likely he will be too preoccupied to hear details or descriptions of the placement resource.

Sometimes it is prudent not to tell the child about some of the positives of the new placement. One social worker was placing a boy who was interested in ham radios with a foster family in which the father was also interested in ham radios and had one. She deliberately omitted this from the description, because, as she said, "Sometimes kids like to find these things out for themselves."[3]

The Importance of Early Intervention

The child's feelings about placement and about his parents are most accessible early in his placement. To ignore his feelings is to miss the best opportunity to prevent the longterm effects of denial, repression and fantasy. Years later a psychiatrist may make a good living in bringing out what was easily available at the time of placement.

With today's caseloads, the worker cannot personally deal at length with the child's feelings. She can, however, help the child transfer his trust in her to the foster family or to institutional staff who can comfort the child and help him make peace with the facts of his life. The important concern is not who helps him, but the assurance that he be helped and that there be continuity in the helping process.

Counseling of a parent and of the foster parent should, if feasible, precede or be given simultaneously with counseling to the child to ensure that the child gets the same story from all sources. Children do go from one source to another seeking clarification.

The conforming, achieving child may progress well until the usual conflicts of the maturation process set in—either in the years between three and six or, when it is more obvious, in the adolescent years, at which times the child has greater challenges to meet. At these crisis periods of life, the defenses for his trauma, which previously were successful, are broken down by the weight of the stress indigenous to them, the pressures from increased sexual and social needs. There follows the release of accumulated underlying disturbances which can seriously disrupt social functioning.[4]

Abrupt changes should be avoided for children of all ages. Appropriate preparation applies to any placement or replacement of a child, whether he is going from his own home to a foster home or institution, being transferred from one foster home to another, being transferred from one cottage to another within the institution, or returning home from placement.

> One institution director called the placing worker to come within thirty minutes to get a boy she had placed in their facility. She lived more than fifty miles from the institution, but she got there as quickly as she could. When she arrived, she found that no one in the institution had even told the boy that he was being expelled. When she told him, he burst into tears.

When Can I Come Home?

Sooner or later every child will ask the question for which both parents and worker must be prepared: "When can I come home?"

The intake study assessed the character structure of parents and child, the nature of the relationship among family members, and the need for placement. The intake study may give clues as to whether or not changes in the parents' life situation are likely to occur: a hospitalized parent may return home, a new job may be found, addiction treated, etc. Further, the study may provide clues as to the parents' future capacity to parent, their willingness to participate in a guided growth experience in order to be able to parent, and the authenticity of their stated desire to have the child return.

The intake study, augmented by the experience of the placement resource, either foster family or institution, will give indications of the child's treatability for emotional disturbance, if that is necessary, or his increasing maturity, self reliance, and understanding and acceptance of the family circumstances, if that is what is appropriate.

When the placement clearly is a temporary one, both that fact and the reasons supporting it were shared with the child at the time of placement, and they can now be reviewed.

If, on the other hand, the placement appears to be an indefinite one, so must be the reply, but without ever entirely closing the door to hope. Fanning vague hope and stifling all hope are equally damaging: the former keeps the child in a state of suspense and makes him unable to settle down to benefit from alternate care; the latter closes the future for him and leaves him entirely alone, a state for which he knows he is not ready.

An example of the sort of statement a worker might make when the duration of placement is indefinite is, "I hope you can go home after awhile, but I really don't know. It depends on what happens to your mother (or father). It will be easier for you while waiting to see what is going to happen if you will settle down here and enjoy yourself."

Another answer that might be given, when appropriate, is, "When you are less upset and have fewer worries, you will then enjoy living at home." Whichever answer is given, it will require repeated reworking throughout the alternate care experience.[5]

The assumption, of course, is that a worker will be in regular contact with the child and will bring him current information on his family. Especially when the placement is indefinite, the child constantly needs to have someone he can trust implicitly.

Dealing with the Past

Inevitably, placement means dealing with the past.

Children who come from what we are pleased to call "normal" families grow up with the assurance of unconditional love: they are valued for what they are, not in spite of what they are or pending their becoming something in which the parents can have pride and take pleasure.

Most children who are going into placement have had little experience with unconditional love. Whatever acceptance they knew was predicated on behavior that met with parental approval. This may continue long after the child is placed—or beyond.

> Tony, age 17, went home from the institution for a long weekend. When he returned, he was asked how the visit went. "It was okay except when I cut the grass. My dad and I always get in a fight when I cut the grass."

The child who is going into placement resists revealing his feelings about the past in which his family figures prominently, because he is afraid he will thereby lose all chance to stay with or to return to the family, a hope he clings to openly, unconsciously, or in fantasy. Even though he is assured that his confidences will not be revealed to his family, he is still controlled by their past omnipotence. He is still the child; they are still the adults.

Further, he senses, and correctly, too, that if he shares in the work of freeing himself from some part of his past, he will lose his tie to it, and he feels that he needs it badly in the absence of any new ties as strong as these.[6]

The worker cannot ignore the child's past, nor can she permit him to suppress it. She can refer to the past and allow his growing relationship with her to assure him that talking about the past and feeling about the past are safe subjects to discuss with the worker. If her work with him is limited to the intake study and placement process, she will attempt to transfer his growing trust in her to a new worker or to the new caregivers, who will have more time with him to deal with the past.

Again, the crucial concern is not who helps the child but that he be helped. The worker has the responsibility for ensuring that someone is available and that there is continuity from one helper to another.

Telling the Child

When possible, the parents should be the ones who tell the child about placement and interpret its meaning. The worker then becomes the agent who assists in carrying out a plan made by the parents. This keeps the responsibility where it belongs, with the parents.

The parents may have told the child in none-too-helpful terms that he will be placed. Perhaps the child, hearing it many times, has become used to it as a disciplinary threat, and thus believes it will not actually happen.

Manifestly, the capacity of the parents to tell the child will grow out of their increasing relationship with the worker. The parents will need to be advised either how to tell the child initially or how to correct inaccurate information already given.

The parents may, however, in their own fear and guilt, block off the task of telling the child about placement, and to counteract this possibility they need to be supported all along the way.

The worker still has to ascertain whether the child has been told and what he was told. This should begin early. It may be found that the child has, after all, not been told anything, or has been given a distorted explanation, so that it then becomes necessary for the worker to help the parents, when all are present, to tell the child or to correct misinformation.

If the parents are not available or are wholly unable to tell the child about the placement, the task devolves upon the worker. When possible, the worker should tell the child in the presence of the parents. Even if the parents say nothing, their presence gives tacit approval of what the worker is saying.

Siblings

Siblings have been mentioned as often the forgotten ingredient in a placement situation. They are part of the family, too, and if they are to remain at home while one child is placed, their feelings and fears must be acknowledged and addressed.

If these feelings are not handled, the remaining sibling is likely to spend his time and energies on avoiding placement, and thus be impeded from doing his schoolwork or engaging in normal growing-up activities.

PREPARATION FOR PLACEMENT WITH THE PARENT

The first task of the social worker in working with parents is to understand and get her own feelings toward the natural parents under control, which may include feelings such as the following:

- Anger, that parents could treat a child the way this child has been treated;
- Morality, if the natural parent smokes, drinks, or uses drugs and she doesn't;
- Piety, if she is a churchgoer, but the parent is not;

• Perplexity, when the child openly prefers his own parents to her or the foster parents;

• Hurt, that her efforts are not accepted and trusted by the child and his parents;

• Anguish, at what the parents continue to do to their child and at seeing his reactions;

• Pride, that she is not like the child's parents;

• Frustration, that the parents are unwilling or unable to perceive that which is so clear to her;

• Judgmentalism, that what the parents are doing is wrong;

• Impatience, that the family is slow to understand and/or to respond to her, for other cases are awaiting her attention, and time is short.

Relationship Building

The development of a relationship with the parents starts out as in all generic casework, which means an offer of service with respect for the individual's right to selfdetermination.

From the very first step, the guiding principle is to obtain the active participation of the parents insofar as the parent's circumstances and resistances will permit. The worker seeks to empower the parents, i.e., to encourage, guide, and support them as they take action on their own behalf, rather than taking action for them. In this way, their fear of what is going to happen and the feeling of impotence and the feeling of being "done to" is reduced.

The specific needs of the parents must be understood and met at the point where they are now. This alone may be a unique experience for the parents, who may never have been understood; who may never have had anyone who was interested in understanding. In assessing the status of the parents, the worker walks the thin line of knowing how to be giving and at which points, and also of what not to be accepting. She cannot accept everything the parents say, but she explores in a way that separates fact from fiction without incurring their wrath, distrust, or resignation.

Where are the parents in their life experiences and in their thinking? Here the worker may find what appear to be bizarre things: the family is falling apart, a child has been neglected or abused, placement is imminent, the worker is there to help sort out what is going on, and the mother is talking about new kitchen curtains.

The worker's first thought is, my God, woman, wake up and smell the coffee. But if kitchen curtains are what she is talking about, interested in, or worried about, that's where her energy is, and that's where to start. She may actually be concerned about kitchen curtains; more likely, she is talking about kitchen curtains to avoid the issue at hand. Whichever the case, the worker starts with kitchen curtains to put that subject to rest one way or another, and so free the mother to talk about other things. Although the worker starts with kitchen curtains, she does not spend the next six interviews talking about kitchen curtains.

In many ways, work with the parents is essentially the same as work with the child, for the same factors which were at work in developing a relationship with the child are at work in developing a relationship with the family.

   • The social worker may be the first adult—especially the first adult who is in a position of authority—who has been honest, open, and unafraid of feelings.
   • The family, like the child, will indicate by its behavior, rather than by words, what they are feeling and thinking, and the social worker has the responsibility for translating their message into words, first for herself, and second for the family.
   • The social worker may be the first person in the experience of the family who came in not to criticize or to judge, but to help.
   • Finally, this may be the first time the family has had someone come in to help who didn't come with preconceived ideas of how they were to solve their problems, what they were to do and how they were to do it.

It must be remembered that before arriving at the point of placement, most families have had recurrent contacts with social workers and with other representatives of the community power structure. They know the Department of Social Services; some parents and children know the social services manual better than the new worker and can give their social history in sequence with proper paragraph headings. They have been through the Department of Mental Health, the local health clinic, and the Youth Service Commission; they may have had repeated interviews with school personnel, the probation department, the police department, and the sheriff's office.

In each of these places the parents have sat in waiting rooms with hard chairs and outdated magazines—and they don't even like to read in the first place. They were fenced out of the area where action takes place and where decisions are made; they watched social workers move freely back and forth through the little gate, talking with each other, sometimes in idle chat about personal or frivolous matters; they have seen that the social workers are on friendly terms with the decision-makers, e.g., judges and lawyers.

All of this is background for the worker who intends to help the family. Understandably, it may take some time for parents to invest themselves in a relationship with this new worker.

The worker and the parents come together as individuals whose first task is to get acquainted and to develop the beginnings of trust. With placement a real possibility, parents need some dispassionate person to whom to express their feelings, someone who will not judge them or look down upon them for acting or feeling as they do, someone who will help them understand the total situation; someone who will see the total process through to a conclusion with them.

The worker elicits the feelings of the parents; she helps them to ventilate those feelings. She does not stop with helping parents to ventilate, however; she goes on to help them to think through what the feelings mean, where the feelings come from, what the parents can do in light of their feelings, and what they can do in the situation to regain control.

Whether the placement is voluntary or involuntary, parents are encouraged and supported in taking whatever action is possible for them. Part of pain reduction is helping the parents to identify whatever power and authority they can exert, for to remove all power and authority from them is to infantilize them. The worker does not do anything for them which they can do for themselves.

Pain reduction involves determining reality, ascertaining the outside limits of the situation, clarifying issues, identifying problems, handling feelings, seeking alternative courses of action, and assigning responsibility. The worker supports the parents as they work through these tasks.

Detail Clarification

Placement is familiar to the worker; it is unfamiliar to the parents. Hence, the worker must proceed with care so that she does not move faster than the parents can understand.

Simple, honest explanations of the unknown along the way, given with reassurances, serve to cut down the suspense and help both the family and the child gradually to absorb some of the trauma.[7]

The parents are counseled by the worker in a manner designed to clarify the details of their situation and those of the unknown placement situation for their consideration and to elicit their reactions to them. Issues such as the following will be included in the clarification process:

• Clarify the facts of the situation with them. As has been said, intake is a process of examining the total situation. The worker finds some working agreement with the parents about what the total situation is. Actually, this is a matter of defining the problem.

• Consider the alternatives: what will happen if the child remains home; what will happen if the child leaves?

• What do the parents understand about the nature of out-of-home placement? What is placement all about?

What is to be accomplished through placement?
What rights will the parents retain?
What decisions will they have to make?
What decisions will they have to share or yield to someone else?

• What is to take place while the child is in placement?

What is expected of the child in placement?
What is expected of the family while the child is away?

Support is given to enable them to view these difficult areas. Such discussions aim to help the parents see the child more realistically and to see what placement will mean to the child and to them.

The worker keeps the responsibility where it belongs—with the family— but helps them satisfy themselves that the process has been completed. They have been helped to think and feel their way through the situation until they are as satisfied as it is possible for them to be, under the circumstances. They understand; the worker understands; and each knows the other understands. There has been closure on the situation.

The result of adequate preparation is that the parents are better able to tolerate placement, and thus the likelihood of their interfering with the placement is reduced.

Help Parents Solve Their Problems

In most instances, the parent who remains in the picture and is kept involved in the placement needs help with his personal problems or with problems in the family relationships.

Even if the parent does not address family problems apart from the placement itself, the effect of a supportive relationship with the worker and active involvement with a placed child will usually result in an improved parent/child relationship, whether the family is restored relatively soon or long-time placement results. When the parent has worried alone, agonized, and tormented himself about his child or about himself, and perhaps has despaired of ever getting things straightened out, suddenly to have an empathetic ear available may release a flood of feeling.

In more instances than not, when the parent sees progress being made with the child, he will solicit help for his own problems. This becomes an extension of placement, inasmuch as reduction of family or parental problems has a direct implication upon the length of placement.

The worker starts where they are. What is the biggest, most pressing problem for them? It may not be at all what the worker sees it to be, but it is real to them. For example:

• Clothes for the children. Clothes don't have to come from Saks 5th Avenue—is a thrift shop available? Where is it? Does the mother have transportation to it?

• Jobs. What employment agencies are available? Are vocational training programs available in the community? Where does the family start, to take advantage of these programs?

• Parenting skills. Are there parenting classes around? Are there parent groups in the community? Can the worker start a parent group to discuss common problems? One common phenomenon of parent groups is that after the first several meetings, parents begin to call each other apart from the group to share recipes, news about shopping bargains, job opportunities, etc. The effect is that they are taking responsibility for their own support.

• Support Group. Help the family to find or develop a support group. Churches are one place to begin; some churches will take a family under their wing, but the church members may need help in using their energies wisely. The family does not need to have sixteen different people coming in to help them. The worker should get personally acquainted with the group leaders to guide the group in their efforts.

• Household details. The first task of one social worker was to teach a mother to light her gas kitchen stove. The mother was retarded, and there was some concern that she might blow the house up. There was no alternative, however, if the family was not to eat uncooked food.

• Glasses for the children. If the Department can't furnish glasses, the Lions Club has done excellent sight-saving work.

• Shopping. The worker may have to help the mother with shopping. The worker may have to teach the mother something about planning a balanced diet and weaning the family from junk foods. The mother may not know that generic foods may be just as good as brand-name foods at a fraction of the cost; coupons from newspaper and magazine advertisements can save money, as can comparative shopping. Making a grocery list in advance may reduce impulse buying.

• Entertainment and learning experiences for the children. Is a Boys' or Girls' Club available? Do any local service clubs sponsor YMCA memberships or camp scholarships?

This list is, of course, incomplete. It is intended only to illustrate different ways in which the worker can respond sensitively to the needs of the parents. The worker will be guided by her growing knowledge of the family and by her familiarity with the community.

Involuntary Placement

When the court has ordered placement, the principle of self determination can nevertheless still be followed within the limits of that authority. The authoritative force is represented to the parents as a reality, painful as it is, over which the worker has no control.

The parents are not entirely powerless in an involuntary placement. Decisions the parents can make include, but are not limited to, the following:

• If the parents need counselling, will they contract with a private counsellor, use the resources of the Department of Mental Health, or find some other source of help?

• If physical living conditions are a problem, how will they go about finding a new apartment or house?

• If drugs or alcohol are a problem, what will the parents do about that? AA and other sources of help are available; which will they use? Will they enroll themselves, or do they need help from the worker in finding a resource and enrolling in it?

• If parenting skills are an issue, which parent group will they join; will they sign up for — and attend — parenting classes? Where are these classes located?

• When the child is placed, what payment can the parents make toward the child's care; will the parents make that payment directly to the placement resource or to the court?

• Will they accompany the child on the pre-placement visit and on placement day?

• How often can the parents arrange to visit the child; do they have sufficient funds for gas or bus fare?

Empowering the family to make these decisions involves them in the whole process. Resistance to participation is an indicator of the pain they are feeling.

Court-ordered placements are enhanced if the worker and court personnel have a working relationship. If the court trusts the worker, she may be able to make some impact upon court decisions and especially upon the timing of a placement mandated by the court, which may make a substantive difference in the success of work with the family.

The worker does not back away from the authority of the court. She works with the feelings of the family which result from a court-ordered placement, but she does not minimize the fact that placement will take place whether the parents like it or not, and, if necessary, irrespective of their feelings. She uses the authority of the court constructively to nudge the parents in the direction in which they need to go.

Voluntary Placement

Where parents voluntarily request placement, even though placement is not appropriate, respect at the start for the parents' need to wish it will help them eventually to seek another solution.

Every institution executive and most social workers periodically receive a frantic call from a parent who wants to place his child yet that day. More often than not, this telephone call was made in a moment of frustration, desperation, or weariness, and the request really is invalid.

The parent's urgency to place the child may bring pressure on the worker for an immediate placement, even when circumstances actually would permit time for planning.

These parents seek to escape the guilt and anxiety they feel over the situation by getting rid of the child. It would be a mistake for the worker to yield to the pressure of the parents' momentary need and to make the placement, for the very urgency of the need to be free of the burden of the child's care, even when reality pressures are present, will bring greater guilt once the placement is accomplished. These guilt feelings can then either cause the parents to interfere and hence upset the placement or create in the parents the need to suppress the pain or avoid it by disappearing.

If the request proves to be a valid one and there really is a need for placement, absent severe physical abuse, there is time for planning.

Whereas in many cases the worker is encouraging the parents to act, here the worker encourages the parents to slow down, and in most such cases placement can be avoided. The issue, of course, is not the request for placement, but the feelings of the parents. As in most cases of working with people, feelings need to be worked with before facts. If the feelings are brought under control, the facts will take care of themselves.

Family Work

Adequate work with families is enormously time-consuming.

In an informal survey of social workers of various state departments of social services, the question was asked, "Do you work with families of children in placement?" Without exception, the response was a resounding, "Of course we work with families!" When asked how often they visited the families, invariably the response was in terms of the requirements of the social service manual: some states required two family visits per year; other states required four.

Four visits a year are hardly sufficient to effect change in a dysfunctional family; trust cannot be earned in quarterly visits.

If the worker is not prepared to stay the course with the family, far better that she not pretend to help the family. If a worker intervenes in a family to place the child, indicates that she wants to help the family, and then disappears for a three-month period or appears at erratic intervals, the family can only conclude that she was just like all of the other workers they knew. Better not to hold out hope at all than to raise their hopes and then fail to follow through, for nothing is more demeaning to the family than to have even the worker reject them.

If a trusting relationship is to be developed and the family is to be helped to change, the worker will appear as frequently as necessary to do the job. This may mean from one to five or more visits a week in the initial period. Needless to say, the caseloads of most social workers, particularly in public agencies, preclude visits of such frequency. There are many ways of providing help, however.

Ideally, the initial worker will provide ongoing work with the family. Alternatively, when she has performed her basic function of getting the child placed, she can get the family to the kind of help it needs.

If the child is placed in an institution which is equipped to serve both the child and the family, work with the family may be transferred to the institution social worker. Written reports from the institution will discharge the department's legal obligation to the family and child.

If the institution cannot provide the service, a local family service association or other private counselling agency may be available.

Transferring the family to another agency is not quite as simple as giving the family the name, address, and telephone number of the new agency, however, for if left of their own, the family will never get there. The worker must take time to make arrangements with the alternative resource, introduce the family to the new worker, and provide support as this transfer is made. She will still make her quarterly visits, but she will coordinate her work with the work of the counselling agency.

The more the problems and the harder the parents are to get along with, the more they need help.

SUMMARY

The task of preparing the child and the parents for placement, then, is essentially the same:

- Accept them as individuals.
- Start where they are.
- Deal with the facts, but their feelings are even more important, because the feelings will determine how the facts are understood and used. The court can handle the facts; the social worker is concerned with what is going inside the person.
- Preserve their right of self determination to the maximum extent possible.
- Review the circumstances of their life and the reality of placement, including the conditions necessary for the return of their child.
- Encourage them to act on their own behalf, support them when they try, and help them to pick themselves up when they try and fail.
- Clarify the situation.
- Give them time to react.
- Help them with their fear, anxiety, guilt, and whatever other feelings they may have.
- Correct misinterpretations.
- Provide information and support.
- Use authority appropriately.

Endnotes

[1]Glickman, Esther: *Child Placement Through Clinically Oriented Casework.* New York: Columbia Press, 1957, p. 119.

[2]Charnley, Jean: *The Art of Child Placement.* Minneapolis: University of Minnesota Press, 1955, p. 48.

[3]Ibid., p. 127.

[4]Glickman, op. cit., pp. 328–329.

[5]Ibid., pp. 127–128.

[6]Ibid., pp. 254–255.

[7]Ibid., pp. 115–116.

Chapter 7

THE PRE-PLACEMENT VISIT

A pre-placement visit is an integral part of every placement. The placing worker is responsible for ensuring that a pre-placement visit is made and that the pre-placement visit is planned so that it fulfills its purpose.

For the worker, the pre-placement visit may be an inconvenience, and unquestionably it takes time, but in the long run it will save time in the present placement, and very possibly it will prevent a re-placement.

Ultimately, the child is the one who will determine whether or not the placement is successful; therefore, at the outset, the child must be introduced to the placement resource at a rate and in a manner which will enable him to experience, assess, experiment with, test, and finally accept it. A child is not a UPS package which can be shipped impersonally here or there. Taking a child to a new situation and simply leaving him there, or, even worse, sending him alone by bus or plane to a new living situation, is unthinkable.

For the child, the pre-placement visit introduces the child to his new environment before he is irrevocably thrust into it; it gives him an opportunity to react to the situation, to express his feelings, and it legitimizes those feelings; it reduces his anxiety, and, in so doing, makes possible some positive feelings toward the placement. Just as important, a pre-placement visit strengthens the child's ego by making him a participator in the placement process.

For the parents, the pre-placement visit does all of these things. Additionally, the pre-placement visit inherently acknowledges their role and rights as parents, it reduces their fear that they are losing their child, and it sustains the hope, intention, and plan of reunion.

OVERVIEW OF THE PRE-PLACEMENT VISIT

The purpose of the pre-placement visit is to ease the change from one living situation to another, to enable a child and his family to sample a new situation and to adjust incrementally to altered life circumstances.

The principle of the pre-placement visit is to enable the child and family to see and experience the placement resource, then return to their own home and, with the placing worker's help, to review the experience and to examine their feelings and reactions. This review serves to put the whole placement in perspective. It may provide a new impetus for the parents to re-examine the need for placement, the goals for placement, and their responsibility and the child's responsibility in placement. Prior to the pre-placement visit, negotiations were largely academic; the parents had only the word of the placing worker to go on. After the pre-placement visit, discussions are based upon the reality perception of the parents and child.

In the pre-placement visit, the placing worker takes the child and his family to the prospective placement resource to have them experience briefly this new setting. The placing worker helps the child and his family "try the facility on for size," so to speak. They meet the people involved, see the physical setting and the general environment—community, school, church, recreational resources, etc.

The child explores the facility, gets acquainted with the foster parents or the staff and children and with the nature of life in that location, and he has an opportunity to consider whether or not he thinks he can survive there.

The family also explores the facility, gets acquainted with the foster parents or staff and with the nature of life in that location and has an opportunity to consider whether or not they can share their child with these people and with this place.

More important than the physical setting or routine personal introductions, however, is the ambience of the resource. The child and his family must have an opportunity to experience, even briefly, the feeling tone of the new setting.

After the pre-placement visit, the child and family return home. There, with the guidance and the support of the placing worker, the child and his family have time to review and think their way through the experience, they have an opportunity to react to a caring and involved person, and finally they can begin to assimilate what they have experienced and what lies ahead. Their feelings are validated and dealt with, and their questions are answered.

PREPARATION FOR THE PRE-PLACEMENT VISIT

When the decision to place the child has been made and a placement resource has been identified, the placing worker gives the family and child a description of the placement resource, with the reasons that this resource appears to be appropriate. She reports as accurately as she can on what the place is like, what life is like there, and what the child and the family can expect in placement. She does not exaggerate the characteristics of the placement, either positive or negative; her words will be confirmed by both child and family when they visit the facility.

The worker makes advance arrangements with the placement resource, foster family or institution, to set a time and date which is convenient for everyone involved. With the institution, the worker must be sure that certain staff will be on campus during the visit and that they will have time to spend with the child and his family.

If the worker uses an institution or foster family home regularly, she may keep pictures in her desk, so that her descriptions can be illustrated. The strangeness of the facility will be reduced when the child and family finally arrive if they have seen pictures ahead of time. The worker can easily take snapshots of a foster home and foster family; some institutions have pictures or videotapes which they will loan. Most agency brochures contain some pictures.

Both foster parents and institutional staff should have some plan for the pre-placement visit. If they are inexperienced, the placing worker may alert them as to particular things she wants to include in the visit. The placing worker has the responsibility for making sure that all ingredients of a proper pre-placement visit are provided for.

The pre-placement visit should be more than a quick stop to see the physical plant and to meet two or three persons on the staff. At least an overnight visit, or, better yet, a weekend or longer visit gives the child an opportunity really to experience life in this setting. He has a chance to size up the children with whom he will be living, foster parents or staff members, the schedule, and the expectations of foster family or institutional staff. After this kind of introduction, he is in a reasonably good position to ascertain whether or not he thinks he can survive there.

For the child, the pre-placement visit is not a "do-you-like-it-and-will-you-stay-there" proposition, for the child may indeed have no alternative. Inasmuch as he is the one who will have to live there, however, his feelings must be recognized and handled.

PRE-PLACEMENT PROCEDURES

Placement procedures will vary in accordance with the age of the child. The older the child, the more influence he may have in structuring the pre-placement process.

A latency-age child may require two or more pre-placement visits. This child has a meager supply of life experiences against which to measure any new experience, and it may take him awhile to get acquainted or feel comfortable with the foster family or institutional staff and setting. A permanent move should not be made until he has some feeling of safety or security with the new caregivers and some feeling of self confidence in the setting.

In the pre-placement visit which almost certainly results in a placement of a latency-age child, it may be helpful to leave behind something which belongs to the child, so that when he returns for placement a little bit of himself will be there waiting for him. One girl left her purse, one boy left a favorite toy he had taken in the car as a kind of security blanket; in one case, the social worker and the child left in the foster home some new clothes which had been purchased for the child. Anything which will reduce, even symbolically, the strangeness of the new setting will be helpful.

The older child can participate actively in the pre-placement experience. Whether or not he will participate depends upon the strength of the relationship between child and worker. The worker does not assume anything; she is thorough and painstaking even with the child with whom she has a strong relationship.

If the placement is in a foster home, the child should be able to meet both foster parents.

If the placement is a group care setting, the worker should check to ensure that the regular child care workers are on duty during the pre-placement visit. If relief child care workers are on duty, it is impossible for the child to form an opinion of his survival chances with the regular child care workers. This assumes that institutional staff can identify at the outset the cottage in which the child will be living, which certainly is to be desired.

The child should have an opportunity during the visit to spend time with children who are already in residence so he can verify the words of the adults involved. No matter how accurate and honest the interpretation of the setting by the placing worker and the staff of the facility, these are adults talking, and, even if they are honest, they may have missed some things of importance to children. If the child talks with children in residence and finds that they say essentially what the adults have said, the adults' words—about the facility or anything else—are given credence.

In an institutional placement, in most cases the placing worker and child will meet first with the institutional social worker. She will give a brief description of the campus and the program and will then introduce the child to another staff member or a resident, who will take the child in tow and start his orientation to the campus, the staff, and the program. The placing worker will plan with the child when she is to leave and when she will return to pick him up.

The pre-placement visit, either in foster family care or group care, should include as many specifics as possible, and the placing worker must ensure that the child gets these specifics. Some of the information will be elicited by questions, some of it simply by observation. The child will be interested in such things as the following:

• Which will be his room if he comes to stay? Who will be his roommate?

• What time does he have to get up? What time does he have to go to bed? Who gets him up? How is he awakened?

• How many rules are there, and how does he learn them? What are the penalties for breaking rules?

• What is the system of discipline?

• Is corporal punishment used in this foster home or institution? Is it used in the local schools?

• What chores will he be expected to do? Who assigns the chores; how often are chore assignments changed?

• In what ways does he have control over his own life and schedule? What decisions can he make for himself?

• Is there a system for him to earn increasing privileges? What is that system?

• Will he have goals to work on? How are those goals determined? What are the benefits for attaining goals?

• How does he get feedback from the foster parent or institutional staff as to his adjustment and progress in the program or progress toward his goals?

• How do his clothes get washed? How does he acquire new clothes?

• Which school will he attend? (Don't tell him—show him the building and walk through it; talk with the principal or some teachers, if possible);

• What time does the school bus leave, and where does he catch it?

• Can he participate in extra-curricular activities in school? What activities are available? What are his chances of getting on the team?

• What happens from the time school is out until bedtime?

• Does he have to go to church, and where? Does he have a choice of denominations? Is there a church of his preferred denomination available? Where is it? Does he have to go to Sunday School? Can he participate in church youth activities? Does he have to? How does he get there?

• What recreation is available on campus or in the community? (Again, don't tell him, show him.) Under what circumstances can the institution gym or recreation building be used, i.e., must a planned schedule of recreation be followed; must a staff member be present during all recreation, or may residents use the gym or recreation room when they please?

• What are the dating privileges?

• Can he bring with him his stereo, his TV, his bicycle, his motorcycle, his car, his dog?

• Where and how does he get spending money? How much money does he get?

• Is a work program available? What kinds of jobs are available? (Don't tell him, show him other children at work on those jobs.) Does he have a choice of jobs? Is he paid for his work? How much? Can he keep the money he earns?

• Can he get a part-time job in the community if he is old enough?

• If he earns money, can he keep it and spend it as he wishes, or is there a required savings program? If there is a required savings program, what is it, who keeps his money, under what circumstances can he spend it, and how is withdrawal of his own funds arranged?

• Can he earn his driver's license? If he has it or gets it, will he have a chance to drive?

• Can he telephone home? If so, who pays the long-distance telephone bill?

• How often can he visit home? How often can his family visit him here?

If the institution provides treatment, additional questions are appropriate, such as:

• Is individual or group treatment used?
• Who will be his therapist?
• How often does he go to treatment?
• Is treatment given on campus or off campus?

Additional questions will occur to the placing worker, based upon her relationship with, and observation of, the child. The placing worker must put herself in the child's shoes and imagine what she would want to know if she were being placed.

Anything she can do, any questions she can ask or help the child ask, which will help the child to get a complete picture of the placement resource will increase the likelihood of a successful placement.

The pre-placement is not a time for speed; it is a time for meticulousness. Pre-placement visits are rarely as long as is desirable; therefore, the placing worker must think through the process ahead of time to make most effective and most efficient use of the time available.

THE PARENTS IN THE PRE-PLACEMENT VISIT

Parents, or a parent, should accompany the child on a pre-placement visit. The parents need to know exactly where and under what conditions their child will be living and who will be taking care of him.

The parents' responsibility during the pre-placement visit includes such things as the following:

• To make their own assessment of the placement resource, including the physical surroundings, the foster parents or staff, and what the placement experience has to offer them and their child;

• To begin a relationship with foster parents, child care workers, social workers, or other staff who will live with the child and with whom the family will be in contact;

• Explore their responsibilities and rights in the placement experience, what they can expect from the foster parents or from the agency staff, scheduling their visits to the facility and for the child's visits home, and related concerns.

• Ask any and every question they have about the foster home or the facility, its program, the staff, the schedule, the expectations which will be placed upon their child and upon them.

The pre-placement visit should provide reassurance to the family that their child will be well cared for, that they are not being cut off from their child, and that they are not being replaced in the life of their child.

Parents may be intimidated by the facility, especially if it is a large institution. Very likely they have never visited an institution before, and the size of the campus, the number of staff, the appearance of the buildings, the offices, and the busyness which attends a normal day in an institution may make them reluctant to ask questions or raise concerns.

The placing worker may need to assist the conversation between parents and staff. From her previous conversations with them, she will know what some of their concerns are; she may observe evidence of unspoken questions during the visit. She has a responsibility for bringing those questions out in the open. She may assist the parent to ask the questions. To the parent, she may say something like, "I remember your being interested in. . . . ; did you want to ask about that?" On the other hand, she may ask on their behalf to see a school room, the work program, the gym; she may ask about washing clothes, responsibilities of children in residence, disciplinary measures, etc.

On the other hand, in their nervousness the parents may be so talkative that the worker will have to come to the rescue of the foster parents or institutional staff, who understandably may be hesitant about interrupting the parents. The parents may talk about anything and everything—except the business at hand. The placing worker may have to intervene and help the parents stay on the subject.

In whatever way is appropriate, the worker will remain sensitive to the feelings of the parents, who are confronting the fact of losing their child, at least temporarily. This cannot be easy for a parent, and the parents' feelings must be recognized and handled.

Parents need to be involved in the pre-placement visit for these reasons for their own sake. Perhaps even more, they need to be involved for the sake of their child. The child needs to know that his parents know where he is and the circumstances under which he is living so that he can never resort to, "If my mother knew where I was living, she wouldn't make me stay here!"

It is preferable for the parents to say to the child, "This is what I want for you," or, "I wish I could keep you at home, but since I can't, this is where I want you to be." This may be beyond the capacity of most parents; however, the very fact that they are present, do know, and do not take action to interfere with placement plans gives the child tacit permission to stay.

FOLLOWING THE PRE-PLACEMENT VISIT

After the pre-placement visit, the child and family are taken home, where the worker, the family, and the child can discuss the pre-placement experience, identify new or continuing concerns, discuss the strengths and weaknesses of the proposed new setting, and plan for what comes next. This may be the same day that they return, or an appointment may be set for a day or two later.

Timing of the post-visit discussion is important: discussion of the visit and their reactions will be fruitless if child, family, and worker are exhausted from the trip; however, the discussion must follow the visit soon enough that impressions, concerns, and questions are still fresh. If too much time elapses, discussion among family members may cloud issues; parents may back away from placement plans entirely.

Evaluation of the pre-placement visit cannot be accomplished while on the visit, for during the visit the child and the family are visitors on someone else's property, and it is unlikely that they will have the internal strength to be honest. They tend to make unrealistic promises and agreements; they may be effusively enthusiastic about everything they see, or, conversely, they may be totally negative.

Evaluation is serious business, and the parents must be able to discuss the situation from a position of their maximum strength. If the parents have power anywhere, it is in their own home, on their own "turf."

The child is interviewed alone; the family is interviewed apart from the child; the family and the child are interviewed together. Not infrequently, fears can be mitigated and confusion relieved through additional explanations, clarification, or by planning some coping mechanisms.

The review of their experience should be relatively wide-ranging, and, as in all casework, the worker is alert as much for what the family does not say as for what it does say. Her prior relationship with them will stand her in good stead at this point, for she knows what some of their fears have been. She helps them think their way through the whole situation.

The worker will assure the child that she is not going to "dump" him in the new location and then abandon him; she will continue contact with him as long as necessary to enable him to settle in and be comfortable.

Similarly, the worker will assure the parents that neither they nor the child will be abandoned; she will be available as long as they need her.

EFFECT OF THE PRE-PLACEMENT VISIT

Despite careful preparation for placement, the effect of the pre-placement visit on both child and family may be startling.

The child may have been threatened with placement so many times that he has discounted its possibility. Seeing the physical facility, he may realize for the first time that placement is an imminent possibility.

Parents, also, may have considered placement as an intellectual exercise until they are confronted with the physical property and the foster parents or staff. Even at this late date, finally faced with the reality of placement, they may find new motivation to make changes which will prevent the necessity of placement. The placing worker must be sufficiently flexible to incorporate this new-found motivation in the planning, but she should also be sufficiently realistic to identify this change of heart as perhaps simply an additional expression of regret that placement is necessary. If the placement is by court decision, of course, there is no alternative.

Families who live in very modest circumstances may be overwhelmed by the appearance of a fine foster home or a large, well-equipped campus, and they may fear the competition for their child's affection. They may feel that he will never want to come home. "What's the use, who can compete with this?" may be a pressing question in their minds.

Conversely, affluent families may be critical of a foster home or of a comparatively modest institutional plant, modest pay scale for residents, or other details, and wonder anew what this place can offer their child which they cannot.

The social worker will have laid a careful foundation by stressing the psychological aspects of the total situation throughout the entire assessment period which culminated in the decision to place.

SPECIAL CONDITIONS

A few institutions have a rule that every prospective resident must make a definite statement, "Yes, I want to come here" before being accepted. This is a questionable practice, because some youth are simply unable to bring themselves to make such a statement.

The child is implicitly pressured to accede to this request. Interviews have been held between parents and placing worker, a decision to place has been made, plans have been laid, he and his family have been transported to the institution, and now he is on someone else's turf, where he has no power. Strangers are asking him to commit himself to a fate he can hardly understand. When confronted by strangers in official positions, the placing worker, and his parents, it is usually unrealistic to expect him to say with conviction that he wants to come. Of course he would rather stay home.

Requiring a child to say that he wants to come to the institution puts the child in a no-win situation. If he says he does want to come, he may feel that he is betraying his family. He may feel that if his parents hear him make this statement, he will be subject to retribution when he gets home—and he may be right.

Conversely, if he says he does not want to come, he may feel that he is letting his family down, since they have spent much time with the placing worker in finding a place for him to live. Thus, he risks the displeasure of parents and placing worker, and he puts himself in jeopardy with the institutional staff, which may haunt him if he is finally placed here anyway. The painful process of placement is prolonged, with no assurance that the next place will be any more to his liking.

Additionally, those children who do not want to leave home in the first place see this requirement as a possible escape hatch. If they refuse often enough, perhaps they will be permitted to remain home.

Whichever the case, refusing to agree to come eliminates this institution from consideration, and it puts the worker and family back at square one, and they have to start anew to find a placement. The time, energy, and paperwork involved in getting a child accepted are enervating, and effective placement resources are not so plentiful that the worker wants to go through the process any more frequently than necessary.

It is always appropriate to give a child, especially a teenager, a choice. With some children, the choice is clear, and it should be presented to them in a realistic and direct manner. "You have a choice: it is this facility or the training school. Which do you prefer?" The training school is not to be used as an idle threat, however. Before the worker lists such an alternative, she must know that the court is prepared to make a training school commitment. An occasional child will opt for the training school, and, if he does, the worker must follow through. The worker may be sure that the one child to whom she offers the training school without the concurrence of the court will be the one who makes that choice. Unless she has the assent of the court, the worker must use some other approach.

LENGTH OF PRE-PLACEMENT VISIT

As stated, a pre-placement visit should be as long as possible, ideally at least several days. The family goes with the worker and child, but returns home with the worker while the child remains at the placement location. The worker will come back to get the child at the end of the visit.

Creative thinking on the part of the worker is needed. If the trip is fairly long, the worker and family may need to stay in a motel overnight, so that the child can have more time than going out and back the same day. Someone has to pay the motel bill, and this must be arranged ahead of time. An occasional institution will have guest space available, which is appropriate, provided the worker and family do not follow the child around.

One worker combined a pre-placement visit with a family visit. She happened to have relatives near the placement resource, so she drove the boy to the institution on Friday, visited her relatives over the weekend, and picked the boy up again on Monday. This was mutually advantageous: the trip was broken in half; the boy had a full weekend in the institution; and the worker had free transportation to a family visit. Such an arrangement requires cooperation on the part of the administration.

EMERGENCY PLACEMENTS

Occasionally a child must be placed without the possibility of the pre-placement visit. The court may order the child to be taken directly from the detention center to the new placement.

The worker should exert every effort to persuade the court to delay placement until proper procedures can take place, but sometimes there is simply no choice. In that case, the worker must be doubly alert to unspoken messages by the child and by his family; she must be ready to spend more time than usual at the placement facility in order for the child to have more time to get acquainted. Her follow-up visits to the child should start sooner, and they should be more frequent than when normal procedures have been followed.

Other circumstances may arise wherein a pre-placement visit is impossible. Care must be taken, however, that these are indeed emergency situations. Oftentimes the emergent nature of a situation is chiefly in the mind of a worker who is overloaded.

COMPROMISE ON PRE-PLACEMENT VISITS

Occasionally the placement resource is so far distant from the child's home, or agency policies or financial status are such that two extra trips for a pre-placement visit (one to take the child to the pre-placement visit and one to get him from the pre-placement visit) are simply not feasible. In such a case, a compromise can be made, but conscious acknowledgment should be made that this is a compromise, and therefore it is second best.

The social worker can describe the setting as fully and accurately as possible in advance, and identify the concerns of the child and his parents.

The placing worker takes the child and parent to the placement location, where they spend as much time as they need, making sure that the child has some time to spend with other children who are in placement. The visit will include as many of the details listed above as possible.

After the visit, the placing worker, child, and parent go to McDonald's for a hamburger and coke, and while they are off the property they discuss the reaction of child and parent to their experience. After a full discussion and airing of feelings, the child is placed the same day.

The guiding principle here is to get the child and parent away from the setting for the purpose of discussing their thoughts, feelings, and reaction. They cannot be candid while on someone else's turf.

Although this is a condensed version of the pre-placement visit, the important ingredients of the pre-placement visit are preserved while saving time, energy, and money. Giving parents and child ample time to react is crucial. Because of the abbreviated nature of this pre-placement visit, the worker must be unusually perceptive in this interview.

SUMMARY

Pre-placement visits are time consuming, and they are inconvenient to work into busy work schedules. However, the time spent initially in proper placement procedures will give the child the best start on a new experience. The pre-placement visit will save time, and perhaps a replacement, in the long run.

The professional social worker will not expect to maintain a 9:00 to 5:00 schedule, for human problems do not occur only between those hours, nor can the solutions to human problems be found only then. The social worker who is involved in placement procedures can plan to be on the road occasionally around midnight. The distress of midnight driving is minor, compared with the distress which children experience when they have to leave home.

Chapter 8

THE PLACEMENT

Placement is a process—this cannot be said too often. In earlier years, social workers hesitated little to go into a home, decide the child needed to be placed, and promptly—the same day or the same hour—removed him. That was not a process, that was an act. A more unconscionable violation of the child's and parents' rights, feelings, and basic needs could hardly be conceived.

We know better today, but we have to be on guard that the pressure of the work load, the complexity of the situation, or the persuasiveness of other parties to the placement do not tempt us to speed up a process which cannot be speeded up professionally. Placement may become somewhat routine for the busy social worker, but it never becomes routine for the child. It should not become routine for the child.

The process begins with the initial request or order for placement or with family work which reveals the need for placement, and it does not end until after the child has returned home or until other permanent plans have been made for him.

The pre-placement visit is one carefully-planned and executed step in this process. The placement itself is another step which is orchestrated by the placing worker.

Placement procedures are essentially identical whether the child is leaving home for alternate care, changing foster homes, leaving or entering an institution—or moving from one cottage to another within the institution.

Too often, in an institution a child is simply packed and moved to a new cottage without thought or preparation. This move can be made for any one of a number of reasons, e.g., his age, his grade in school, tension in a cottage, conflict between child and child care worker, etc. Moving a child from one cottage to another without preparation is unfair to the child. It is true, of course, that he probably knows the residents of the cottage to which he is moving. It is equally true, however, that he has never had to live with them; he has never been part of the group

137

dynamics of that cottage; he has never had to fit into the "pecking order" of any cottage but his own. A substantial difference exists between knowing a person and living with him.

PLACEMENT

When placement day approaches, events begin to speed up.

First of all, the child should know well in advance specifically on what day he will move. He needs time to make his own plans and say his goodbyes. To come home and find one's bags packed and waiting by the front door is not adequate preparation for placement. In one case, this was one institution's announcement to a teenager that he was leaving.

Instead of the placing worker's telling the child what day he will move into placement, she may ask him what day he wants to go. She may give him several alternatives from which he can choose. Either way, she gives him some control in the situation, which enhances self esteem which is badly in need of enhancement.

Even with a well-planned placement, the child's anxiety will mount as the day approaches, and it is not uncommon to have a runaway in the week preceding placement. This nonverbal behavior will be taken in stride and treated as what it is, anxiety, and his anxiety will be acknowledged and handled by the social worker.

The placing worker will help the child conclude his life at his home; for example:

• If money is owed him, it will be paid to him in cash before he leaves;
• If he is to visit Grandma before he leaves, that visit will be made;
• If he is taking his bicycle with him and it needs repair, repairs will be made;
• If books are to be turned in to school or to the library, this will be done;
• He has a chance to say goodbye to his friends;

Whatever other details need to be looked after, either from the adults' perspective or from the child's perspective, will be taken care of; no loose ends will be left.

Details required by the placement resource will be anticipated and taken care of:

• If a medical examination is required within two weeks before or after placement, that physical examination will be obtained before the move, so that he does not have to be poked and prodded by a strange doctor immediately upon his arrival.

• School records will have been transferred. This is perhaps especially important in the case of an institution, which may not have a program during the school year for children who are not in school. Most schools will not admit a new child without his previous school records, and the child may have to mark time until the records arrive. While waiting for the school records, he child will be put to work during the day, often on make-work activity, or he will be bored beyond description, which increases homesickness.

Care will be taken with respect to appearances in making the physical move.

• Clothes will be packed in a suitcase, not in miscellaneous paper bags or carried over the arm except in standard garment bags. (Used suitcases may be donated to the agency, which are quite suitable for this purpose; flea markets or Good Will are likely sources of inexpensive luggage.)

• If new clothes have to be purchased before he leaves, the tags will be removed and those clothes, too, will be put in suitcases, not transferred in bags or boxes with the name of the store displayed on the side, which not only sets the child apart but is an open invitation to thievery.

• Transportation should be provided in the most inconspicuous manner possible, with nothing to mark this child as unusual.

A nine-year-old boy, 85 pounds soaking wet, was accepted into a special education program eight miles away. The official transportation arrived in the form of a GMC Suburban, with a steel mesh behind the driver's seat and a hasp and padlock on the back door; two red lights adorned the roof; a shield of the Department of Mental Health was on the door. The drivers, the shorter of whom was 6′3″, were uniformed and armed.

Logic and common sense did not prevail, the demands of bureaucracy were satisfied, and, to the taunts of all of the other residents, the boy was securely locked in the back of the Suburban, understandably with terror on his face.

• Timing of the placement should be given some attention. If other children are in residence in the new location, placement should be made while those children are absent, in order to provide the child a little uninterrupted time with the new caregiver, either child care worker or foster mother. This is in contrast to the pre-placement visit, which was timed for when other children would be present.

All other details involved in the physical move of the child must be thought through carefully by the worker.

PLACEMENT OF THE OLDER CHILD

Placement day and departure time have been set with the child and his family. More often than not, the worker provides transportation. If more people are going than will fit into the worker's car, the family is responsible for providing additional vehicles.

The worker must be at least on time to pick up the child and his family, if not a few minutes early. Anxiety is high when any trip is imminent, and this trip is more anxiety-producing than most. Timeliness of the worker's arrival will tend to reduce tension, and it will be a role model for subsequent appointments.

If the trip is long enough to require a meal enroute to or from the placement resource, the worker plans in advance for who pays. Normally the placing agency picks up the tab, and the parents are informed of this detail ahead of time so that they will not wonder, worry, or be embarrassed about having to pay a bill. The worker will have cash or credit card available or use whatever other practices are provided for by her agency.

The worker will have given the placement resource an estimated time of arrival so that the people who are involved in the placement will be available. With the foster home, of course, this is at least the foster mother, if not both foster parents. An institutional staff will need to make sure that the social worker, the child care worker, and any other appropriate personnel are on campus.

In the Office

In an institutional placement, worker, child and family will go to the office, where the social worker will have the necessary arrangements in hand. After conversation in the office, which includes identifying the tasks for the day, the child will go to his cottage.

Inevitably, on placement day the placing worker will have some papers to complete with the agency social worker or other business details to look after. Care should be taken that the child and his family are provided for while business is being taken care of.

One visitor to a training school happened through the office lobby where a 14-year-old boy was sitting alone with his suitcase. No other person could be seen. Assuming that the child was ready to leave, the visitor queried, "Planning to take a trip?" The boy replied, "No, I just took one; I just arrived."

Leaving this boy alone under those circumstances was unconscionable insensitivity.

The parents, too, must be cared for during these first minutes of the placement. In a foster placement, this is no problem, for the parents and the placing worker will meet with the foster parents together. Less paperwork is involved in foster family placement, and most of that can be done on another visit by the social worker.

In an institutional placement, the situation is somewhat different, for signing the child in may be more involved. It is easy to overlook the feelings of the parents, and the bigger the institution, the easier it is for them to get lost. The placing worker and the institutional worker do not hole up in an office, leaving the parents to twiddle their thumbs in a waiting room. It may well be that the placing worker and institutional worker have some business to conduct in which the parents need not be involved. The parents should be provided for during this time, however. They may be turned over to someone to get a cup of coffee, they may go with the child care worker to help the child settle in to the cottage—or some other arrangement may be made so that the parents are occupied while business is being conducted.

The placing worker cannot control what goes on in an institution in these first minutes of placement, but she needs to make sure that the caregivers have some plan and that all involved staff are sensitive to the feelings of the child and his family.

Before they leave campus, the parents will be involved in some of the paperwork which must be completed on placement day. The institution's worker will develop a plan of care which will include responsibilities for the family, for the child, and for the agency. The plan should be reviewed in person, signed by all parties, and each party to the agreement should have a signed copy. In some institutions the plan of care is developed at the time of placement; in others, the development of a plan of care is deferred until the child has been in residence for a month or six weeks, in which case an appointment can be made to bring the parents back to review the plan of care.

Some specific details will be taken care of on placement day irrespective of when the plan of care is developed.

How much the parent pays for the child's care and where and when the payment is to be made must be established. Visiting arrangements must be clarified: when can the family visit the child and when can the child visit home; when he goes home, will he go by bus or plane; how does he get to the bus station or airport; and who pays for the ticket. What about mail: can he write as often as he wishes; who pays for the postage; is his mail censored, etc. What about telephone calls: can he call home as often as he wishes to; who pays for the toll calls; can his parents call him whenever they wish to; are there times when it is most convenient to call or times when calls will not be put through, such as during study hall, etc.

All of these details and more must be ironed out while parents are on campus. All arrangements should be put in writing. Most institutions have written policies to cover these issues, and parents should be given a copy, for memories are faulty, and people tend to hear what they want to hear. If arrangements are put in writing and reviewed with the parents, the worker has a reference point when the parents later claim, "But they said. . . ." At that time one cannot be sure whether they misunderstood or whether what they heard has turned out to be inconvenient. Without an agreement in writing, the way is open for a time- and energy-wasting verbal tug of war. The written word does not change; many hard feelings are avoided by putting all agreements in writing.

In the Cottage

The placing worker should know what plans the caregiver has for receiving the child. The sensitive caregiver will have her plans made. Some foster mothers or child care workers prefer to have the bed made up and ready for the new child; others prefer to have blankets and sheets folded at the foot of the bed so that when the new child arrives they can make the bed together. This gives them something to do together initially, it models bedmaking, and it dispenses with the need for speech, if speech is beyond the child for the moment. At the very least, the room, closet, and dresser should be clean to show that the child's arrival was expected and that staff were prepared for him. Specific details of the plan are less important than the fact that there is a plan.

The foster parent or child care worker may help the child unpack, or she may invite the parent to help the child unpack, hang clothes in the closet, and put other things in the dresser. The child care worker may remain throughout this process, she may give the parents a choice of having her stay or leave, or she may just leave, depending upon the atmosphere of the moment.

The child should be given only enough instructions to get through the next few minutes or hours; he does not need now a full set of instructions for all of life in this institution or foster home.

When the other residents come in from school, the new child should be reintroduced (he was introduced on his pre-placement visit), and one resident may be asked to show the new arrival around.

The placing worker will stick around until the child gives her permission to leave. The alert social worker will be aware of when the child is ready for her and the family to go, and they will not go until she gets that message.

In some cases, this permission will be given verbally. The child will not volunteer the information, but if the child appears to be relatively comfortable and the family has done all it can, the worker may ask the child if he is ready for them to leave.

More often, the signal will be in the form of nonverbal communication, which may take one of many different forms, such as the following:

- Initially the child may cling to or linger by the family or social worker, but after awhile become involved with other children or with some solitary activity.
- The child may go off with other children to explore or to play.
- If the child is leaving the building, the worker may say something like, "If you're to be away for awhile, we may have to leave before you get back—is that okay?"

The worker and family will never simply disappear while the child's back is turned. If he is available when they are ready to leave, even if they have alerted him to the fact that they are nearly ready to go, they will seek him out to say goodbye.

Before they leave, the worker will tell the child when she will return—and she will be sure to return on that day and at that time. If she cannot predict precisely when she will return, she may tell him that she will call in advance or drop a note with this information. She will then be sure to follow up with a note or a telephone call.

If her next visit will not take place for more than a week, she may drop him a note primarily to let him know she has not forgotten him.

PARENTS' INVOLVEMENT IN THE PLACEMENT PROCESS

How the parents perceive the placement process depends upon the adequacy of pre-placement preparation and the pre-placement visit.

Who goes with the child on the placement trip?

Everyone who has importance to the child goes on the placement trip. Both parents should go, if both are available. At least one parent is minimum. Additionally, other persons of significance to the child should accompany him. Siblings, grandparents, aunts, uncles, and/or neighbors may accompany him as a support and to demonstrate their continued interest and concern in him.

If the child has been in foster family care, the foster mother or foster parents may go; if he has been in institutional care, a child care worker with whom he has lived or the agency social worker with whom he has a bond may appropriately go with him.

Parents or family members need to be and to feel involved in the process. The family or other relatives may be ignored in the placement process unless the worker is careful. The placing worker needs to be alert to insensitivities on the part of foster parents or agency staff and to intercede for the parents as appropriate. As with the pre-placement visit, parents are powerless on someone else's "turf," and they may be unable to speak for themselves.

In other cases, parents may be very well able to speak, and the worker may need to intercede for the agency staff.

Enroute home (if the placing worker has driven the family to the placement), the worker might well stop for a cup of coffee and give the family a chance to express their feelings.

Responsibilities of the Parents

The parents are responsible for some of the mechanics of preparing the child for placement. For example, the child's clothes must be made ready for the move. The placing agency or an institution may have a basic clothing list, which is helpful so the parents know what to include. Some children will have an adequate supply of clothes; clothes will have to be purchased for other children. Many parents can handle this financially; others will need help from an outside source. The placing worker will discuss this with the parents and assist as she is needed.

Clothing can be a volatile issue. Some mothers try very earnestly, although ineffectively, to prepare clothes to go with the child. In such a case, even though the clothes are manifestly inadequate either in supply or condition, they are taken along without comment. Such parents frequently are unable to distinguish between what they do and what they are. In other words, they may take as a personal put-down any criticism of the clothes they have prepared.

Additionally, if the child has watched his mother painstakingly gathering and washing his clothes, if anyone criticizes the clothes, in his mind his mother is being criticized, and a barrier is erected between that person and the child. The caregiver is well advised to accept the clothes without comment even though they are unsuitable to be worn at the new placement. Comments like "That is hopelessly inadequate here"; "We will have to get you a whole new set of clothes"; much less "What was your mother thinking of when she put these rags together?" are wholly inappropriate. The clothes are carefully put away and left until the child is ready to get rid of them, and in some unobtrusive manner new clothes are obtained for the child. From observation of his roommates or classmates, he will come to the realization that new clothes are more appropriate.

Other parents, of course, make little or no attempt to fulfill their obligations with respect to clothes. The worker will differentiate between those who try and those who do not try. For those who do not try, she may need to become quite directive.

Many institutions utilize used clothes which are donated by interested persons. If handled discreetly, there is nothing wrong with used clothes, provided they fit, they are in style, are in good repair, and are clean. Some institutions have found creative ways of using used clothes which enhance the self esteem of the child; for example, the clothes are displayed in a clothing room and have low prices. As the child learns to handle money, he has a choice of new jeans for $25.00 a pair or used jeans at $5.00 a pair, etc.

AFTER PLACEMENT

The social worker's job is not complete when the child has been placed. In the case of foster family placement, the worker may continue to work with the child indefinitely, which is a real plus. In other agencies, the placing worker must transfer the case once the child has been placed.

In the case of a group care setting, the social worker must stay with the case at least until the child has settled in and has begun to establish a relationship with someone on campus who can take over her function with the child.

The worker's visits with the newly-placed child need to be regular and dependable, especially in the first weeks of the new placement experience. If she has to change appointments frequently or simply fails to show up, the child knows that he really is of little importance even to this person whom he had thought he could trust.

Occasionally circumstances will develop which mean that for valid reasons the social worker cannot, in fact, keep the appointment. When this happens, the worker will telephone the child to tell him of the postponement of the appointment, to set a new time and to give him a chance to talk, even though it is only on the telephone.

If visits must be infrequent, the worker should talk with the child on the phone periodically. If the child himself cannot be reached by telephone, at the very least a message can be left for him so that he knows the social worker has not forgotten him.

One aspect of the child's life in which the worker can make a difference is the lack of continuity of life with his family. Normally, the child and his family have memories of shared experiences, and those experiences were recorded in photographs which are stored in a box which someday they intend to put into a book.

The parents of the placed child cannot share his experiences in alternate care. In later years when the child reviews the pictures, there is likely to be a gap which covers his years in placement. Some workers have done good work in helping the child to develop a "life book" which covers his life and documents meaningful experiences through photographs, among other things.

The placing worker can take her camera with her when she visits the child to take pictures of him, the foster family or his child care workers, his roommates, and the facility. Better yet is to help the child to acquire his own camera so that he can make his own record of his life.

MULTIPLE PLACEMENTS

The pre-placement and placement process are essential in maintaining the placement. If this process is inadequately planned, the child is doomed to replacement, perhaps a series of replacements.

The chief hazard of repeated placements, of course, is the effect on the child, not only in the present placement, but in his attitude toward

toward himself and toward all subsequent placements and relationships. If the child believes that the social worker will be along shortly to move him, why should he exert any effort to fit into the present placement?

One group home operator reported having in care a 15-year-old boy who had been in fifty-six foster homes, which averages 3.2 months per home from the day he was born.

What can this lad think of himself, if adults can tolerate him, on the average, for only 3.2 months? What can he expect of adults generally? Even if things go well for awhile in a new placement, what is the use of becoming involved—he cannot even risk having a buddy, because the social worker will be along shortly to move him, and parting will be more painful for having been involved.

One can surmise that somewhere in this boy's case file is a notation, "This boy has difficulty in interpersonal relationships." Without question, the notation is correct, but this label will stick with him and influence all future placements and the attitude of all future workers. What the case file does not go on to state is that the child welfare system, which moved him every three months, set him up so that he could not relate to anyone.

If, after a number of placements, the child appears to accept placement as a normal part of life, the social worker considers this to be an indication of something that is very wrong which needs prompt, concentrated attention and which may require professional help.

EMERGENCY PLACEMENTS

Emergencies deserve a special word. In an occasional instance, a child's life is in danger, and then, of course, precipitate action is required irrespective of the feelings or rights of parents or child. Only under such catastrophic circumstances is placement as an act acceptable today.

One must be careful about labeling a situation as emergent. If a child has lived under given conditions for six, eight, ten, or fourteen years, a decision that he will be irreparably damaged if he remains under these same conditions for another twenty-four, forty-eight, or seventy-two hours is suspect. A day or two, even some extra hours, may allow for some planning which will ease the trauma for both child and family.

This is not at all to deny that bona fide emergencies do exist, and that in some cases removal must be immediate with whatever trauma that may create. It is to say, however, that some emergencies exist primarily in the mind of the investigating or placing worker whose caseload is too large and who sees immediate removal as a quick solution to a nasty problem, or who is caught up emotionally in the distressing circumstances of the case. If the worker has question as to whether or not a case is truly emergent, she should confer with her supervisor.

SUMMARY

Placement day is the realization of the fears of family and child. Despite careful planning, most families and children hope to avoid actual placement. The social worker must remain sensitive to the possible feelings of separation, loss, and defeat to which the child and his family may be subject.

For the child, this may seem to be the end of the world; the future holds no hope, and in his mind it is now an established fact that he is worthless.

For the parents, this may be the final, visible effect of their inadequacies, real or imagined. If nothing else, placement means separation, and separation almost always involves an element of sadness. The social worker must allot time on placement day to help the family members come to grips with their feelings.

Chapter 9

THE PLACEMENT EXPERIENCE

Placement is an act of protection of the child. It is one element in the process of healing the effects of past experiences, resolving whatever problems led to separation, preparing for final reunion of the child and family or finding a permanent, alternate placement for the child.

Placement has multiple purposes for the child:

• To remove the child from a situation which endangers him physically or psychologically;

• To provide healing from past, negative experiences;

• To meet the child's emotional needs in accordance with his age;

• To provide for the child's care, education, and nurture while he is away from home;

• To foster maturation and self esteem in the child, including specific treatment as required;

• To help the child understand family circumstances and the necessity of placement;

• To prepare for the child's return to his family;

• To provide adoption or other permanent, alternate care for the child when family reunion is impossible;

• For the older child who will not return to his family and is not a candidate for adoption, preparation for independent (actually, in today's world, interdependent) living.

Placement also has multiple purposes for the parents:

• To provide relief from the immediate, stressful situation;

• To identify problems within the family system;

• To develop a plan of action by which the family can strengthen itself and the family and child can be reunited;

• To provide support, counseling, teaching, or whatever else is needed to help the family carry out the plan.

• To provide planned interaction between family and child so that each can practice new insights in their relationship;

• To help parents terminate their rights to the child when reunion cannot be effected.

149

Those are fairly simple and straightforward concepts; the implications are less so.

THE CHILD IN THE PLACEMENT EXPERIENCE

Placement should facilitate growth and maturation despite the child's past experiences and in spite of negative influences of the family. Although placement in alternate care is a response to negative circumstances, placement should be a positive in the child's life. Whatever the placement and irrespective of the duration of placement, the child should be more mature and more self directed when he leaves placement than when he entered. The worker must ensure that placement never becomes a holding action which maintains the child as he is when he is admitted.

Placement is not an end in itself, it is a means to an end. Placement is intended to be a time-limited experience designed to achieve a specific purpose. Irrespective of the type of placement, i.e., foster home, group home, or institution, if that purpose is to be achieved, certain conditions must exist, and the worker must ensure that whatever placement resource is used contains at least those basic conditions. The placement experience must provide for the child at least the following:

Structure

The placement resource must offer structure for the child. Placed children characteristically initially need a setting which contains structure. Structure includes such mundane things as having meals at regular times, regular work time and play time, academic expectations, church attendance, a system of discipline, and caregivers whose word is reliable. A routine can have a healing effect upon a child whose life has been bereft of structure.

Most children who are placed lead disorganized lives prior to placement: the family is disorganized; both parents work and no adequate day care is available; children are "latchkey children"; they are free to roam the streets with the neighborhood gang; or for other reasons parents have been unable or unwilling to place limits on the child's behavior. No one has told the child "No" and meant it.

Every newly-placed child needs external controls. The problem with external controls, however, is that in some placement resources, in institutions, perhaps, more than in foster family homes, external controls never change: the same restrictions which were in force the first week of the child's residence are still in force the week he is to leave a year later. The child has no opportunity to internalize control and no need to assume responsibility for his own actions. When he moves to another placement location, then, another set of rules must be imposed, and the child is perpetually denied the right to learn and practice self control. External controls must diminish during placement in proportion to the child's ability to control himself. The worker must ascertain that a progressive structure is in place.

Reliable Adults

Placement of a child requires meticulous reliability on the part of adults. The child needs the opportunity to learn that the adults who are now in his life mean what they say, do what they say they will do, and what they say will happen will happen. It is always important for adults to be trustworthy, but nowhere is this as intensely true as in placement, where children are unwillingly subject to the direction of strangers. During this process, when external events have taken over his life, the child is the most vulnerable and helpless.

This reliability includes such things as thoughtful preparation of the child for any experience that lies ahead; prompt and timely administration of concrete services; structuring of appointments and routine promptness in appearing for those appointments, being available for help when needed, etc. These are relatively simple matters for the adult, but they are not simple to the child who is waiting.

Empathy and emotional support are important, of course, but they are misleading if required, tangible services are not provided. One can repeatedly assure the child of one's support, but if one does not show up for an appointment agreed upon, the assurances fall on deaf ears. It does little good to support and reassure the child about his new school if, at the same time, school records are not transferred.

Limits

The placement resource must provide limits which are reasonable, understandable, and consistently enforced, limits which do not change even in the face of tantrums, defiance, threats, runaways, or other negative behavior. Limits should be logical, objective, and impersonal; they should be clearly enunciated, and they should be upheld.

Logical limits are those limits which by any rational analysis are demonstrably in the interest of the child. Additionally, logical limits have relevance to the goals and needs of the child. Thus, some limits will vary from child to child. "Equal limits" does not always mean "uniform limits."

Limits are objective and impersonal. Establishing limits is no place for a foster parent or child care worker to express his own biases, to echo the biases of his own parents, or to reflect his own childhood experiences. One child care worker's comment that, "If I had said that, my father would have washed my mouth out with soap" may be interesting as a comparative statement, but it has no bearing on the handling of the child in her care.

Limits are age-appropriate. Attempting to enforce inappropriate limits leads only to controversy and resentment. A 9:30 p.m. bedtime is inappropriate for teenagers, it is impossible to enforce, and such an unrealistic limit justifiably generates resentment in the child. Getting up at 5:30 a.m. when the school bus leaves at 8:15 is equally inappropriate. A needlessly early getting-up time is set more for the convenience of staff than for the good of the child.

The rules and expectations in the placement setting may be quite different from the rules and expectations at home, and it is only fair that those rules and expectations be so clear that the child cannot mistake their meaning. For many children, living in placement will be the first time that limits have been defined, and those limits and the reasons for them will have to be interpreted and re-interpreted until the child can internalize what is being said.

The penalty for exceeding the limits must be clear. As the child tests the limits, which he will, he is not only testing to see how far he can go in his behavior, but, more importantly, he is testing the integrity of the adults.

When the child knows the limit and the penalty, he has a choice: he can abide by the limit and live without the penalty, or he can choose to exceed the limit and pay the penalty. Making such a choice is a reasonable mechanism for growth. For example:

The rule is that the child must be home by 12:00 midnight from a weekend date, or dating privileges for the following weekend are forfeited. John is having such a good time on Saturday night that he does not return until 1:30 a.m. This is precisely the kind of choice the child must learn to make and be permitted to make; whether or not tonight's fun is sufficient to warrant datelessness next weekend.

The following weekend he will want to date again, of course—that is a given. He will beg, plead, wheedle, and threaten to get the foster parent or child care worker to relent. There is nothing punitive or personal about the consequence, however, and this is no time for anger, for a verbal tug of war, personal animosity, personal attack, or ridicule. The rule is upheld in a dispassionate manner: "You made your choice; this is the consequence. You may date again next weekend." The child will not like it, and he may state eloquently his complaints, but he will respect the integrity of the child care worker or foster parent who upholds the rules.

The same principle is at work in more serious situations than staying out late on a date: the use of alcohol and/or drugs, personal honesty, an appropriate relationship between the sexes, choice of a vocation, stealing cars, etc.

Every child should have as many choices as can be offered him. Only through the experience of making poor choices can a child learn to make good choices. A child cannot say "Yes" unless he is also free to say "No." Offering a child a choice when only one response is acceptable is unfair.

Behavioral Control

The object of behavioral control is to develop behavior which is controlled by the child. The foster family or group care facility which relies upon external control as an end in itself has already lost the ball game. The child may very well be able to subordinate his impulses and desires to the official rules while he is in placement, but if he does not learn self control while he is in placement, he is no better equipped to survive outside the facility than he was when he arrived.

The placement resource must be prepared to support positive behavior and to refrain from supporting negative behavior.

When possible, negative behavior should be ignored. Not all negative behavior can be ignored, of course, but more can be ignored than is generally conceded.

Positive behavior of the child should be reinforced. Many children have gone through their short lives without hearing a commendatory word.

The program in the placement facility must adapt itself to the behavior of the child. If the program has a preconceived mold into which the child must fit, the placement will fail. Children do not fail programs; programs fail children. Certainly the program has standards and policies, but those standards and policies must allow for the child's individuality and for his previous experiences without bias.

Behavioral control is subordinate to, and develops within the context of, the goals which have been established with and for the child. In striving to achieve his goals, the child learns that certain behaviors are productive and other behaviors are counter-productive.

Education

The child must have education commensurate with his ability. Because many placed children lag behind in academic achievement and frequently have low motivation for schoolwork, they may need supplementary or remedial academic help. Some children may need special education. The worker should check to make sure that foster children or children in institutions are eligible for special education in whatever local schools they will attend. Some schools do not have adequate teaching staff to accommodate numbers of foster children, and special arrangements must be made for education.

Assistance in Handling Feelings

In placement, the child must have someone who can understand his feelings and will work with him to help him understand those feelings. Some caregivers may encourage children to suppress their feelings, which only exacerbates the problem and prolongs the adjustment period. Symptoms of grief may be ignored or, worse, punished.

Typically, the child may be subject to the "shuns": depression, regression, suppression, repression.

Depression

Many children are seen as settling into alternate care with no apparent conflicts. They do pretty much what they are supposed to do and seem content; they manage to conceal their pain through general preoccupation with activity. Since these children do not appear to be hurting too much, caregivers disregard warning signals that indicate the presence of grief and suffering beneath the surface. Some institutions unwittingly aid and abet this by keeping the children so busy that they do not have time to think or to feel.

Regression

The areas of regression depend to some extent on the developmental stage of the child. The child who has relatively recently achieved speech, bowel or bladder control is the most likely to regress temporarily in these areas. Regression in some areas, such as fear of the dark, disturbances in eating and sleeping, shortened attention span, agitation, may occur at any age.

Suppression

Suppression is a conscious, largely controllable, reaction. Scarlett O'Hara's "I'll worry about that tomorrow" is suppression—deliberately putting aside that which is worrisome. Suppression may be a partial explanation for the so-called "honeymoon period" which is often evident during the child's initial days of placement. During this period, when the child seems to be making a relatively untroubled transition, it is important to remember that the child is likely suppressing the feelings attached to his placement. Eventually, this act of denial will fail, with erratic and difficult behaviors usually following.

Repression.

Repression is more serious, for it is subconscious. When pain is too great, the psyche simply removes it from memory. The mind says, "This is too painful to remember—we will bury it so deep that you won't remember it." Unfortunately, these memories are only buried, not eliminated. Any crisis, or even the normal demands of adolescence, can rupture the defenses, and the earlier pain rages to the surface. Too often, the result surprises the worker and so shocks foster parents or child care workers that replacement, with repeated separation trauma, occurs.

Planned Contact with Important Figures from the Past

The placement resource must provide continuity for the child with his own past. Unless the decision has been made at the time of placement to separate the child and family permanently, a continuing link with the past must be maintained.

Even when the decision is made to separate the child permanently from his family, and the court has so ordered, the child cannot be barred from thinking or talking about the past and about his family.

Whether the parents are present or absent, the child needs to know about his family and where he stands with them. The fact that he does not verbalize this need will not delude the worker into thinking that the child has forgotten his family. The parent will always hold an important place in the child's inner life.

The worker will bring him information about the family. If no information is available about the family, the worker will inform him of this, also, so the child knows the worker has not forgotten the family. To have the family simply disappear is to lay the groundwork for future inner distress for the child.

The child must be able to interact with his family by telephone, correspondence, and visits. The frequency and nature of such interaction will vary from child to child, but in each case the plan for visitation and other contacts will be incorporated into a plan of care.

Family members are not the only people from the past who have meaning to the child. Friends, neighbors, teachers, preachers, and other acquaintances may have continuing meaning to him, and those relationships are to be encouraged and preserved unless contra-indicated for professional reasons.

Significant figures from the past include the social worker who orchestrated the placement process. The child needs ongoing contact with a worker from the agency which has legal responsibility for him. The child often perceives the worker as his only hope of ever returning home.

Useful Activities and Routines

The child may wish to continue activities in which he has participated in his own home. A child may be a basketball player, an artist, a musician, a woodworker, a ham radio operator, or have other talents, skills, or interests. The placement experience should not only provide for continuity in these interests, but should actively explore other interests of the child. Activities other than television should be available.

A Chance to Mature

Any placement should provide a set of graduated learning experiences, the goal of which is that the child will become self controlled, self directed, self disciplined, and self reliant, confident of his ability to function with increasing independence in a manner commensurate with his age and ability.

The child must have an opportunity to earn increasing privileges and to exert increasing control over his life. Because of his placement experience, he should be better able to make reasoned decisions and exercise reasonable judgment when he leaves placement than when he entered placement.

The child must have an opportunity to handle responsibility and to be trusted. A child cannot learn to handle responsibility unless he is given responsibility to handle; he cannot learn to be trusted until he is trusted. As long as someone else protects him from all temptation and from the consequences of his own actions, he cannot learn to withstand temptation or to anticipate the consequences of his actions.

Like everyone else, the child will not succeed the first time. Making a mistake is serious only if those around him treat the error seriously and fail to give him another chance. Through trial and error, if he is encouraged in his attempts, the child eventually will learn to succeed. The process of making a mistake but then picking himself up to try again is what is meant by the eloquent phrase "failing successfully." To criticize him for making a mistake is to demean him; not to allow him to try again is to infantilize him; it is to mark the child, rather than his actions, as a failure.

Goals

A placement plan will be developed for the child which is a part of the agency/family plan of care. The placement plan is specific for the child; it contains the goals upon which he will work while in placement in order to fulfill his responsibility in the agency/family plan. This placement plan of care is the child's "road map" for his placement experience, it shows him clearly where he is headed. In a foster family placement, the placing worker will develop the goals with the child; in an institutional placement, the institutional staff will develop the goals with the child, but with the concurrence of the placing worker.

The goals should be measurable, and they should be measured at frequent intervals so the child can see documentation that he is working in the direction of his goals, has digressed from them, has made no progress, or has regressed.

Acceptance of Testing Behavior

Generally speaking, testing can be described simply as a child's efforts to see how far he can go, what the adult will tolerate, and what controls and limits are reliable. Children want and need to know the limits within which they must operate.

Testing behavior is usually provocative, and it takes such forms as disobedience, excessive demands for privileges, demands for excessive or inappropriate privileges, or other behavior that tests the limits set by the adults.

Children have a remarkable capacity to assess the specific behavior which is most troublesome to each adult, and that is the behavior in which he will specialize when that adult is present.

Implicitly, the child is testing the integrity of the adults. The child is between living arrangements; his own strength, adequacy, and worth are in question, and he knows intuitively that for a time he may have to rely on external controls. It is critical for the child to know that adults will do what they say they will do and that the controls are dependable.

THE CHILD'S TASK

In a definitive exposition of the task of the placed child,[1] Kenneth Watson depicts the placed child as caught between two families, the "family of circumstance" and the "family of ideation." The "family of circumstance" is the family which is currently experienced by the child, foster family, group home or institutional staff, and whoever else is involved in providing day-by-day care, attempting to meet his needs.

The "family of ideation" consists of the child's natural family as he perceives it. This family is based on historical, objective fact, but it is enlarged by the child's experiences in the family, his memories of the family, and it is embellished by his fantasies about the family. Particularly if the child was placed at an early age or a long time ago, he may have lost track of the reality of his family, and his fantasy fills in the cracks as he attempts to explain confusing circumstances or to have the family of his imagination and dreams more nearly serve his needs and purposes.

The reconciling of these two families is the task of the placed child and the challenge of those who work with the child. Included in this task is learning to deal with the pain which separation from one's family entails; learning that one is not disloyal to one's parents if one relates to a foster parent or a child care worker; and learning that it is possible to relate to other family members without being controlled or impeded by them. This task can be enhanced by an appropriate placement resource.

THE FAMILY IN THE PLACEMENT EXPERIENCE

If separation is to be temporary, obviously something positive must occur with both child and family during the temporary separation. If, when left to their own devices, the family was headed for dissolution or separation, separating the child from the family and again leaving the family to their own devices accomplishes nothing.

A plan must be made for and with the family and carried out during the child's placement experience, and they cannot do this alone; someone outside the family must be qualified and prepared to help the family to carry out the plan.

All persons who are legitimately involved with the family may be involved in the plan. This may mean placing workers, court workers, foster family members, mental health workers, physician or medical clinic staff, group home or institutional staff, school personnel, probation personnel, categorical assistance workers, and others.

Whether the worker who performs the family study carries the burden of responsibility for the plan or shares that responsibility with another worker or agency varies from case to case. The original social worker, however, must accept responsibility for ensuring that service is continued both to the family and to the child by whatever means may be available.

All three types of non-family resources, foster family, group home, or institution, must be oriented to a collaborative, teamwork approach among worker, family, child, and placement resource.

To put it another way, any placement resource must be oriented to treatment, rather than to control. "Treatment" in this sense suggests something both less and more than classical psychiatric treatment, although in selected cases that may be included. Treatment in its broader sense suggests a purposeful, therapeutic process of evaluation of and intervention in life circumstances, behavior, attitude, and relationships in accordance with some theoretical formulation of growth and development, remediation of individual problems, and reconciliation of interpersonal relationships.

SUMMARY

The placement experience is more than the process of finding a place for the child to live where he is safe and out of the clutches of a dysfunctional family. The placement experience must provide a mechanism by which the child may grow in emotional stature; its ancillary services must include ongoing help for both parent and child. During the child's placement, parents and child must interact under the guidance of a plan and with the support of a worker. If only the child is considered, during placement the child may grow, and the family may also grow; yet if they do not grow together and have not changed in relation to each other, reunion will fail. If attention is given only to the child, further alienation between child and family will occur.

Placement is one tool in the process of preparing the family and child for reunion. The placing worker is responsible for ensuring that the placement resource selected possesses the characteristics which will support the adjustment of the family and child to placement and to each other and that a process of growth takes place.

Placement is not a holding action; separation in and of itself is useless except as a temporary, emergency expedient in the case of imminent danger to life and limb or to the child's physical or psychological well-being. Placement must be accompanied by concurrent work with the family.

The ideal goal of placement is to reunite the child and his family. When it is apparent that reunion of child and family cannot be effected, the nature of the placement must be re-examined to ensure that the placement is still appropriate while permanent plans are being made for the child.

Endnote

[1]Watson, Kenneth. *Social Work with Families Divided by Placement.* Proceedings of Seventh Winter Seminar for Social Workers, Group Child Care Consultant Services, University of North Carolina, Chapel Hill, North Carolina, 1976.

Chapter 10

VISITATION

Visitation between parents and child is crucial for two fundamental reasons: First, barring a court order to the contrary, parents and child have a legal right of access to each other. Second, visitation is only the arena within which family and a placed child can work together to establish or to re-establish a relationship with each other.

In most cases, ultimately the child will return to his parents whether or not they and he are ready for reunion and whether or not they are better prepared to interact meaningfully than they were when placement first occurred.

Placement is a product of the family system, and if reunion is to be successful, some change must be made in the system. Whether or not the family system is amenable to change is one of the questions to be answered through visitation.

PURPOSE OF VISITATION

The purpose of visitation is at least sixfold:

- To keep alive for the child reality perceptions of his family;
- To keep alive for the family reality perceptions of the child;
- To provide continuity in the relationship between parent and child;
- To permit parent and child to practice with each other the insights gained through the helping process;
- To lay the groundwork for reunion by enhancing the parent/child relationship;
- To assess the likelihood that parents and child will be able to live together permanently.

The purpose is simply stated; the implications are less simple.

Visits help family and child to have a realistic perception of each other. In the absence of visits, both child and parent may forget what life

163

together was like, with all the unpleasantnesses and the conflicts which led to placement in the first place.

One suppresses unpleasant memories and retains the pleasant ones. More accurately, one suppresses the pain of unpleasant experiences. It must be this way: if every pain were retained in its full intensity, the cumulative pain would be unbearable. As a safety device, memory selects out those things which we are able to retain, or it transposes painful experiences into something which can be tolerated. Only visits can correct these skewed memories.

After four years in an institution, Derrick, age 16, still cannot get along with his parents. In the institution he is a model citizen and functions well; he is a good student, he gets excellent grades, and he appears to be well adjusted. But every time Derrick goes home, he gets into trouble.

The fact is that institutional rules permit Derrick to visit home only three times a year even though home is less than sixty miles from the institution. No one can establish or maintain a good relationship, much less overcome past, faulty relationships in only three visits a year.

The placement experience is exactly opposite for parent and child. The placed child has new experiences; he is surrounded by new faces, new rules, and new values. Thus, his life in placement provides a model for him in changing behavior.

By contrast, the parents have the same experiences, rules, and values; they do things as they always have done them. Without outside intervention, the family will remain as it always was, and when the child returns, even though he is changed, he returns to the same environment which gave rise to problems in the first place.

Even if the child and family cannot be reunited, the child must have contact with his family in order to provide continuity in his life and to preserve a sense of his own roots and identity.

Paul, age 16, had been in institutional care for six years, during which time he had no contact with, or information about, his family. He was a good student, well-behaved, and well adjusted. Unexpectedly, Paul's behavior began to deteriorate. He became testy, abrasive, and subject to drastic mood changes; his schoolwork suffered. No apparent cause could be found in school or in the cottage. Finally, after checking Paul's history and record carefully, the executive surmised that Paul was suffering from lack of information about his family.

One morning the executive packed a bag, drove to the cottage, and told Paul, "Paul, pack a bag. We're going to find that family, and we won't come back until we do. We may be back tonight; we may not be back for a week." The executive and Paul set out, and in the town where Paul had spent his infancy they found a grandparent, an aunt, and a cousin. Paul talked with his relatives, then walked around town for several hours steeping himself in the atmosphere of a town which he could no longer remember. Finally he signalled to the executive that he was ready to leave.

Paul returned to campus and reverted to his usual exemplary behavior. Now that he knew where he came from and from whom he had come, he could again afford to be himself.

This executive took a risk that few executives would be courageous enough to take. Paul should not have been allowed to lose track of his family in the first place. Once that had happened, however, specific action was necessary to fill the void in Paul's life.

The point is, that the need of a child for his family which has been lost does not disappear, even though it may be invisible for a time. Finding a lost family warrants some risk-taking.

It is too late to ascertain why Paul was permitted to lose his family. In other cases, the responsibility can clearly be assigned.

Juan, a jovial, contented fifteen-year-old, was a model citizen in the institution. He was a hard worker, did reasonably well in school, and he was a pleasure for staff and other residents to have around. Juan came from a neglectful home which, according to the local social worker, had nothing to offer him. Juan's father would telephone Juan once or twice a year, usually when drunk.

Juan had an increasing need to visit home, and the staff, sensing his growing desperation, supported that desire. The placing worker, who had responsibility for Juan's family, never visited Juan, but she adamantly refused to permit him to go home, even for a short visit.

Finally, Juan's behavior deteriorated to the point that he had to be admitted to a residential treatment center.

One visit home might have enabled Juan to perceive that the workers were telling him the truth, that his home had nothing to offer him. Significantly, no work was done with a father who had to fortify himself before he could even telephone his son; no one explored the distress or desperation which perhaps he felt; no one encouraged — or brought — the father to visit his son.

Visitation may fairly be described as the laboratory, or the practicum, for the new learning of parents and child. A family/child visit is not just a family reunion: it is a planned experience, developed as an integral part of the plan of care.

Placement provides an opportunity for family and child to develop insight into their behavior and its effect upon their relationship. What is cause and what is effect in the family dysfunction; what are the problems of parents and what are the problems of the child; in what ways does the family and in what ways does the child need to change in order to have a functional family? These insights are acquired with the help of the worker.

If the insights are to be more than an intellectual exercise, parents and child must try out their new insights with each other in the crucible of visitation.

BACKGROUND OF VISITATION

Family life is composed of shared experiences, most of them very ordinary: in the traditional family, these include watching the small child learn to walk and talk, eating meals together, going to Grandma's for Thanksgiving, watching Junior play basketball and Susie in a class play, etc.

Other family experiences are less positive, but they are equally formative of the family ambience: watching mother stretch a welfare check, learning to cope with the drug dealers in the neighborhood, or, in some families, having parents share drugs with their children; longing for the products advertised on TV; being truant from school, etc.

Remembered, shared experiences, ordinary, comic, and tragic, go into family relationships.

When a child has been placed, the experiences of the parents and siblings at home and the experiences of the child in placement have no mutuality, nothing to relate them to each other. The longer and the more nearly complete the separation, the more the child and family will be strangers to each other when they get together. Only visits provide experiences in common and can keep the child in touch with his family.

In work with the child and his family, the intention is not to turn out a model family, one which by any standard is deemed adequate and mature. The goal is to help family members gain insight into their own functioning and into their family's functioning and to help them reduce the problem areas to a point where the child can survive and thrive and the child and family can have a meaningful existence together within the framework of their family culture, traditions, needs, and limitations.

For many children, visitation is less restoration of family living than teaching family living both to family and child. The quality and quantity of the child's interactions with his parents are an essential part of the healing process. In placement, these interactions are planned by the placing agency with empathy and understanding for both the child and the parents.

HISTORY OF VISITATION

The history of visiting between family and placed child is not particularly laudable. Families have been at the mercy both of the placing agency and the receiving agency, and they have not always been well treated by either.

The importance of visiting with respect to the likelihood of the child's return home can be seen through research.

In one longitudinal study of children in foster care over a five-year period, children whose parents in the first year visited the maximum permitted by the agency or who visited frequently but irregularly were almost twice as likely to be discharged eventually as those not visited at all or only minimally. Two-thirds of the children whose parents did not visit were still in foster care five years after their entry.[1]

In a study of a stratified random sample of 140 counties, the Children's Defense Fund found that parents were officially discouraged from making contacts with their children. They found the following practices on the part of the placing agency:[2]

• There was a massive failure of agencies to articulate specific policies about parent/child visiting.
• When specific policies did exist, they were often restrictive, implying that the majority of parents could not be trusted with their children.
• Even where state policies specified visiting requirements, they were generally disregarded in practice.
• Perhaps the most widespread disincentive to parental visiting was the failure of agencies to make provision for or reimburse parents for transportation.

In other ways, parents in these counties were treated in a manner which indicated that they were not considered to be important to the child and perhaps were an inconvenience to staff. For example:

- Parents did not routinely receive progress reports on their child.
- Parents were denied other information about their child in placement.
- Parents were not always told when their child is transferred from one placement to another, sometimes when the child was being transferred across state lines.
- Parents were not encouraged, expected, or permitted to participate in decisions about their children's medical care.
- They were not expected to raise questions about what was happening to their children.

Workers are well advised to scrutinize the visiting policies of their own agency.

THE VISIT

Family visits are not simply vacation time; they are an integral part of the plan of care which leads to reunion or a decision for permanent placement. Visits are prepared for, experienced, and reviewed as part of the plan.

The worker helps the family prepare for a visit with the child, whether that visit takes place at home or at the placement resource. The worker raises questions with the family to help them think through what lies ahead. Specific questions depend upon the details of each individual case, but they include such things as the following:

- What does the family want to have happen during the home visit? What will mark the visit as a success, as far as the family is concerned?
- What are transportation arrangements, and who pays for the transportation?
- Will the parent(s) be at home all during the child's visit? If not, is supervision of the child necessary? What arrangements will be made for supervision?
- In view of past experience when the child was at home, what problems might be anticipated during the visit? If those problems arise, what does the family plan to do?
- What plans can be made in advance to ensure that communication will take place between parent and child?
- What can the family do to ensure a visit that is meaningful both to family and child?

• Will specific activities be planned for while the child is at home?

• To what extent can the child be permitted to plan his own activities?

• Does the family have some special treat or surprise planned for the child?

• What method of discipline will be used while the child is home?

• What will they do when. . . . ? (He gets angry; they get angry; he does not come in at an agreed-upon time; he gets drunk and/or gets physical; he runs with his old crowd, uses drugs or otherwise breaks the law—or whatever other problem past experience suggests might arise.)

• What will the family do if the child appears to be out of control?

• What will the family do if their level of frustration with the child escalates?

• May the family send him back early if the situation becomes untenable? If so, what procedures must they follow?

If the child is in a foster home, the social worker will help him prepare for the visit. If the child is in a group home or institution, that agency's worker will help the child prepare. Specific questions for the child will vary from case to case, but they will include such things as the following:

• What does the child want to have happen during the home visit? What will mark the visit as a success, as far as the child is concerned?

• Does the child need to do anything here (in the foster home or institution) to prepare for the visit, e.g., have school work completed before he leaves?

• In view of past experience when the child was at home, what problems might be anticipated during the visit? If those problems arise, what does the child plan to do?

• What will he do when. . . . ? (He gets angry; his parents get angry; his parents get on his case; his parents tell him to come in earlier than he wants to come in; Dad gets drunk and/or gets physical; his old buddies want him to use drugs or otherwise break the law—or whatever other problem might arise.)

• What will the child do if his level of frustration escalates?

• Does he have any particular activities planned for while he is at home?

• What can the child do to ensure a visit that is meaningful both to family and child?

• May he choose to come back early? If so, what procedures must he follow?

After the visit, the appropriate worker reviews the visit with parents and child to assess what went right, what went wrong, what difficulties could have been anticipated or avoided, and what better plans can be made for the next visit.

A summary of the visit assessment should be entered in the record to serve as a guide for the next visit and to contribute to the overall evaluation of the feasibility of reunion.

The most frequent justification for curtailment of visits is the fact that the child is upset when he returns to foster home or institution. Undoubtedly this is true. The fact that a child returns from a visit upset and distressed is no justification for curtailment of visits, however. Fresh separation invariably causes distress, for it reactivates the feelings attendant upon all separations, going back to the original separation. The foster parents, child care worker, and the worker must realize that the distress of the child provides the most fertile opportunity for therapeutic intervention.

With the possible exception of the residential treatment center, where the level of emotional disturbance of the child may require special timing for home visits, visits should not be predicated upon the child's behavior. Even in the residential treatment center, parents should be able to visit their child. The center is well equipped to monitor such visits and to safeguard the child's progress.

Some institutions have a "levels" program, which allows children to earn increased privileges. A levels program may incorporate extra visits as part of the increasing privileges, but every child should be entitled to a basic number of visits irrespective of his behavior unless there is clear and convincing evidence that he will injure himself or others on a visit. The child has a right to his family unless otherwise ordered by the court.

Visits are timed in accordance with the ability of child and family to handle their relationship. As the family and child grow in insight and in their ability to handle a relationship, and as reunion nears, visits increase in frequency and duration. Ultimately, the child who will return home permanently should be able to spend every weekend and every holiday at home.

SUPERVISION IN VISITS

Unstructured, Unsupervised Visits. Ideally, parents simply visit their placed child whenever they want to. This may be possible in an institution; it is not practicable in foster family homes. Foster family care is now used for more disturbed children and families than a few years ago; consequently, unsupervised, unstructured visits are increasingly rare. Visiting by a parent to his child in a foster family home depends upon relative health in the parents and child. The parent who has any substantial degree of emotional disturbance or anger may cause problems for the child, for the foster family, for the relationship between the child and foster family, and, ultimately, for the parent himself. A parental visit without supervision in a foster home may undermine and perhaps destroy the placement.

The Supervised Visit. The placing agency must protect the child, the foster family, the foster placement, and the family. In such a case, the social worker is present at each visit. In most cases, just the presence of the social worker may serve to keep the visit on an even keel.

The supervised visit is not only a monitoring device; it is an educative tool. In advance of the visit, the worker plans with the parent what is to take place and what will be allowed or not allowed. This is terms of actions, what will the parents and child do during the visit, and in terms of communication, what can be discussed and what cannot be discussed. For example, attacks on each other or on the foster parents are not permitted; false statements and promises by the parents may not be made, and various other subjects may be forbidden.

With a plan agreed to by the parent in advance, the worker is prepared to intervene directly in family interaction during the visit. The parents may inadvertently slip and begin to talk about forbidden subjects, they may deliberately try to slip them into the conversation, or they may yield to the pressure of their child to make promises which they cannot keep.

As with words, so with actions. The worker curtails behavior which is provocative or infantilizing; behavior which reverses the role of parent and child, or behavior which in other ways is inappropriate for the child or for the parent.

The supervised visit between parent and child lends itself to any or all of these preventive and therapeutic uses:

- The presence of the caseworker provides emotional support for parent and child.
- Problems in communication can be identified and clarified.
- The worker is available to facilitate communication when parents and child are stymied for things to say.
- Direct intervention is employed when the behavior or words of either the parent or the child is psychologically destructive to the other or to the relationship.
- The worker observes family dynamics and can relate present behavior to past behavior and to growing insights, which facilitates treatment.[3]

Visit in a Neutral Setting. If the parents constitute a physical danger to the foster family or to the child, it may not be possible to reveal to the parent even where the child is living, in which case family visits take place in the agency office or in some other neutral location. Generally speaking, in such a case the worker will consider carefully whether or not foster family care is recommended.

Physical danger is not a myth, it is a reality, and foster families must be protected. One father came armed to a family Christmas party, which was held in the district office of the department. In very short order, two workers and two members of his family lay dead, and four others were wounded, after which the father left and later shot himself.

Creativity in Visits. The worker needs to use creativity in visitation. For example, a 17-year-old girl in one institution was the daughter of a prostitute. Conventional wisdom and mores say that this child should not visit home, lest she take after her mother's ways.

The executive director said that there is something precious between this mother and daughter which must be preserved irrespective of the mother's profession. Where most workers might have considered a brief, supervised, mid-day visit, this courageous executive took another tack. He sent a man along with the daughter when she went for a weekend visit. The man stood by the door for the weekend to turn business away. "Sorry, fellows, business is closed until Monday." No one was fooling anyone: the mother knew why the man was there; the daughter knew why the man was there; customers soon learned why the man was there. The bond between the mother and daughter was preserved; the concern of the agency for that which was good between mother and daughter was demonstrated; and the point was made eloquently but silently that prostitution is not a preferred career for a 17-year-old.

Manifestly, such an arrangement grows out of a good working relationship between executive and parent. Any plans, much less such a novel arrangement, must be made in an open and above-board fashion with the parent.

Similar sensitivity must be used with visits of the family to the foster home or the institution. If a picnic is arranged for foster family and biological family, the biological family, as well as the foster family, should bring part of the meal. If they can bring no more than a package of cookies bought at a store, the family becomes a contributing member of the group, which boosts their self esteem.

When visiting their child in an institution, parents should be encouraged to contribute their talents to institutional life. Almost everyone has something he can do, and the worker needs to discover what it is.

The creative use of visits is limited only by the imagination of the worker.

PARENTS' PERCEPTION OF VISITATION

While social social workers are deriding parents for their refusal to visit, intransigence, lack of cooperation, and obnoxious behavior when they do visit, parents have a concern about official policies with respect to visiting. In one study, 37.5% of the parents were prohibited from seeing their child as often as they wished, if at all, by the social worker; almost 20% of the parents stated that parent-child contact is discouraged by the foster parent.[4]

If visitation rights are not upheld, and the parents are excluded from the life of their child, they are likely to defend themselves through behaviors which are counter productive. The most common maladaptive defenses observed in the parent-child visits are these:

• Some parents simply disappear;
• Some parents ignore planned visiting arrangements or visit on impulse without an appointment. They may feel a loss of control, they may be worried about their child, or they may simply feel lonely.
• Some visit consistently and handle their guilt, fear of loss of love, or competition with surrogate parents by over-indulging the child with unrealistic promises, gifts, or permissiveness;
• Some express their emotional dependence on the child with inappropriate confidences, physical seductiveness, and the like;
• Some subtly or overtly depreciate the child, the foster parents, or the institution.
• Some express competition by setting up a triangular struggle among themselves, their child, and the foster parent or agency;
• Finally, some develop a dependent relationship with the surrogate parents. This may be temporarily satisfying to both, but ultimately, excessive demands of the parent will sour this relationship.

There is no question that a few parents have invited restrictive treatment because of other behaviors. Parents have appeared under the influence of drugs or alcohol; they have brought drugs to their child and shared drugs with other children on campus; they have been abusive to foster families or institution staff; they have allied themselves with their own child and/or other children against the administration, and they have performed or caused to be performed other acts which are unacceptable to even the most tolerant agency.

Certainly, such behaviors cannot be countenanced; the question is how to handle them. If these situations are handled in a way which further diminishes the parents' feelings about themselves, the offensive behavior will continue. Sensitive, professional handling of these parents may succeed in diminishing objectionable behavior.

PROBLEMS WITH THE RECEIVING AGENCY

The placing worker should examine the visiting practices of the placement resource. With a group home or institution, she should check details such as the following:

• Some institutions require a child to be on campus for a specific period, e.g., thirty days, before going home. This should not mean that he is held incommunicado, however; he should be able to talk with his family on the telephone and to exchange letters.

• Some agencies limit visits to official visiting days, which may be impossible for some parents to utilize because of their work schedule. This policy may be designed for the convenience of the staff, rather than for benefit of the parents or the good of the child. This has resulted in some ridiculous situations; for example, one father's business travels unexpectedly took him near the institution where his son was placed, and he stopped in for a surprise visit. Because it was not visiting day, he was not permitted to visit with his son, even though he could see his son across the campus.

• The wording of visiting policies may be objectionable. In one agency, rigorous visiting rules were given in what sounded like infantile detail. The rationale behind the requirements was sound: the rules were designed to safeguard the children from strangers who frequently crossed the campus. The rationale was not given in the policy, however, and the wording of the rules was offensive and belittling to parents.

• On some campuses, parents are not permitted to take their child off campus to have a hamburger or to have time together apart from the campus population. The usual justification for it is that parents might run away with their child. Theoretically, of course, they might do so, but the incidence of parents kidnapping their children from an institution is remarkably low. Most agencies will know if a particular parent is likely to do this, and special arrangements can be made for such a high-risk situation.

• Parents may not really be welcome on campus. In some institutions, parents are not allowed to share any part of the child's campus life; for example, parents may not be able to share a meal with their child, and they may be faced with the uncomfortable situation of waiting in the living room until the child finishes his meal. Also, the parents may be hungry.

• Some institutions require the child to be back on campus at an arbitrary and needlessly early hour after a weekend visit. Usually there is no need for the child to be back from a weekend visit in time for Sunday night supper. If the family wants to get him back by bedtime and then have a late-night drive home, that should be their decision.

• Residents may be required to earn every visit home by good behavior. This penalizes the child who initially has problems with behavior, problems which may be exacerbated by lack of contact with his family. A reasonable number of home visits should be available irrespective of behavior. No staff member should be able unilaterally to threaten the child with curtailing of home visits because of behavior.

• When parents visit their child in the institution, they are not always in the best condition. Some are very poor, and their clothes are not up to the standard of the institution, their automobile may not make a welcome addition the the institution's parking lot. Additionally, not infrequently they have been drinking before they arrive.

Most institutional staffs can handle the disreputable automobile and physical appearance of the family. Fewer are able to handle the parent who has been drinking. Many stand in moral judgment of the parents, and refuse to permit the parents to visit their child if there is evidence of liquor on their breath.

This is an issue which requires careful handling. Without doubt, the child has seen his parents under the influence, so this will be no surprise to the child. Then there is the issue of safety: is the parent in fit condition to be behind the wheel?

Perhaps most of all, the institution staff needs to examine why it is that the parent feels a need to drink before visiting. Is it to fortify himself against previous handling by the staff? Is it a feeling of shame to visit his child in placement? As with all behaviors, drinking before visiting does not occur without a reason, and simply barring the parent from visiting his child because of previous drinking is not an answer. Before an answer can be provided, the problem must be identified.

The worker should check out institutional visiting policies and procedures to ensure that they are consistent with the treatment plans for family and child.

REPORT CARD

Some agencies have formalized the evaluation process by involving the parents and child in a written assessment of the visit. A "report card" is developed, half of which is completed by the parent and half of which is completed by the child at the conclusion of the visit. The report card is tailored to each family situation and is composed of a checklist or a rating scale with respect to specific factors of the visit.

That part of the report card which deals with the child's behavior is completed by the parent. For example, if, before placement, the child had difficulty coming home on time at night, this might be one statement on the report card. Other statements might deal with temper outbursts, completion of chores, interaction with other family members, refraining from stealing, drug or alcohol use, proper use of the family car, or any other behavior which needs changing.

The part of the report card which deals with the parents' behavior is completed by the child. The report card might include such things as reasonableness of parental demands, whether or not the parents listened to the child, whether or not they followed through on what they said, whether the parent told the child what to do or asked him to do something, harmony between parents, etc.

The report card is completed at the conclusion of each visit and is submitted to the alternate caregiver, who shares it with the placing worker. The report card is an additional tool in evaluating progress of family and child.

PRESSURES ON THE FAMILY

One of the problems associated with the placement process for a family of marginal income is that the removal of a child relieves at least some financial stress. The financial stress increases again when the child returns home, of course, for the parent receives no financial help for his child as foster parents do.

Although the parent may want the child home and perhaps is ready emotionally to accept his return, he may dread the reality considerations of accepting the child back into the home. This is just one more financial pressure on a family that is marginally able to get along. Thus, financial considerations militate against the child's return.

Visits by children to their own homes often are difficult to arrange. If the family has no resources to assume additional costs for transportation, food, and other incidentals, such visits are unlikely to happen.

Some institutions are perceptive with respect to the financial implications for some families of even home visits by their child, so they provide bus fare or gasoline money for the parent or child.

Then there is the matter of food. A teenage stomach may be the closest human counterpart of a bottomless pit, and when some children go home to visit they may literally not have enough to eat. Aside from the physical distress for the child, the parent is embarrassed by not being able to provide adequately. Recognizing this, some institutions provide "Care" packages for the child's visit home, packages of food to cover the length of the visit. Needless to say, this must be done openly through negotiation with the parents in order to preserve their self esteem.

As always, when dealing with people, the result cannot always be anticipated. People insist upon being people, and some strange and occasionally entertaining comments may follow. One family, which received a Care package regularly when their child returned home, notified the agency that "We're tired of sausage, send bacon next week instead."

SUMMARY

When placement occurs, parents and child have altered roles. Some of the authority and some of the decisions of the parents are transferred to an agency, either the placing agency, the institution, or, in a somewhat limited sense, the foster family. The child is guided and taught by adults unrelated to him.

In the early months of placement, adapting to these changed life circumstances can perhaps best take place within the structure of visitation. Both parents and child are going through a process of adaptation, which provides a common base of experience—perhaps the first time in years they have shared anything. Also, for perhaps the first time for either, they do not have to face a perplexing situation alone: the agency is in the background of every visit as a guide and a safeguard.

Placement affords relief from stresses of life in a dysfunctional family, and provides family and child with assistance in identifying the causes and cures of dysfunction.

Visitation is an integral part of the plan of care for parents and child. As parents and child gain insights into their own behavior and attitudes, visitation offers a planned process of interaction within which parents and child can practice their new learnings together, and so lay the groundwork for workable relationships and eventual reunion.

Visits are prepared for, experienced, and assessed with the help of the worker. Visits are tailored and timed to the growing insights of parents and child, and they become more frequent and of greater duration as the relationship heals.

The size of caseloads, turnover of social work staff, or other circumstances beyond anyone's control help children "fall through the cracks" of the system. Somehow the worker must work around these obstacles to ensure that visitation between family and child takes place as frequently as is appropriate for their ability to interact meaningfully with each other.

The worker has the responsibility for all aspects of the visitation process, including scrutiny of her own agency's visitation policies and the policies of any institution in which a child is placed.

Endnotes

[1]Fanshel, David, and Shinn, Eugene B. *Children in Foster Care: A Longitudinal Investigation.* New York: Columbia University Press, 1978, p. 96.

[2]Knitzer, Jane, Allen, Mary Lee, and McGowan, Brenda. *Children Without Homes.* Washington, D.C.: Children's Defense Fund, 1978, pp. 22–23. Used with permission.

[3]Kline, Draza, and Overstreet, Helen-Mary. *Foster Care of Children.* New York: Columbia University Press, 1972, p. 182.

[4]Fanshel and Shinn, op. cit., p. 96.

Chapter 11

RETURNING THE CHILD TO HIS OWN HOME

The most important decision after the decision to place a child is that of returning him home. This decision is as grave and complex as the decision to place.

Parents do not have an inalienable right to their children; biology is not a controlling factor in the decision to return the child. Rather, the parents' treatment of the child over time, their willingness and ability to demonstrate substantive change, the length of the separation, and the extent of the attachment of the child to surrogate parents all figure in the decision to return the child.

This chapter is concerned with the child for whom the decision to return has been made.

The process of returning a child to his own home approximates the process of placing the child in alternate care in the first place. Whether moving the child from home to alternate care or back home, the purpose of the process is to provide continuity in the child's life. The dynamics of any move are essentially the same, because any change of living arrangements means an uprooting from one location and an adjustment to the new location.

It is true, of course, that the child knows the people in his home, but he does not know—he cannot know—what his reception there will be.

The child's life in alternate care is more orderly and dependable than was life in his own family. In alternate care the child found orderliness and dependability and people to whom he could become attached. In returning home, the child must sever those relationships.

FOR THE CHILD

When the child returns home, he faces two problems: (1) Separation from those who have come to have meaning to him, and (2) Return to parents whom he may or may not feel he can trust, who may or may not have changed, and who may or may not acknowledge or validate the

179

changes he has made. Even though he is returning to his own home, then, he is going into the unknown.

Let us examine briefly this new separation. In alternate care, the child has caregivers who helped him to find himself and to value himself; who helped him to perceive the reasons for his placement and to understand the nature of his family and his relationship with his family.

In placement, perhaps for the first time, the child was treated and respected as an individual; he learned to assume responsibility for his own actions; he was permitted and encouraged to make decisions for himself, and he learned that negative experiences can be survived. In alternate care, the child should have learned to "fail successfully," i.e., that it is possible to recover from error and go on, and that he is not diminished as a person for having made a mistake.

He can hardly fail to have some positive feelings toward those persons who helped him learn these things. Now, in returning home, he is separating from the persons who helped him.

Separation from those who have had meaning to us is always painful. When separation also threatens one's personhood, when it threatens to take away that which one has struggled to become, it takes on special pain. One should not have to choose between losing one's family and losing oneself.

The fact that the child knows the people at home is the second problem. He lived at home before and then had to leave. He knows the disorganization of his family prior to separation, he knows how he was treated there, and he remembers the pain and confusion which attended his leaving.

He knows the work he has done in placement, and he knows what his parents are supposed to have been doing while he was in placement. He may be suspicious—or he may know—that his parents have not discharged their responsibility under the plan of care, and it is only natural for him to wonder if they will fulfill their responsibility to him when he returns.

Will his newfound strengths, capabilities, and insights hold up when supportive caregivers are not available, or will he be expected to revert to the behaviors, attitudes, and feelings about himself which he had when he left home?

In alternate care, the child measured the values and practices of foster family or institutional staff against the values and practices of his family, and he learned that these new values and practices enabled him to be himself without depriving him of the protection and support which he needed.

The child has observed his family only during visits, and even if parental behavior was exemplary during those visits, visiting is one thing, while living together day in and day out is something else. He cannot be sure that his parents' exemplary behavior on visits will endure after the novelty of being back together has worn off.

This is a real dilemma, for every child intuitively knows that he should be at home, almost every child wants to go home, and yet growing maturity in itself is attractive, and he does not want to give that up. The older the child, of course, the more intensely is this true. Adolescence, with legal adulthood immediately ahead, is intimidating enough without being pushed back toward childhood by one's family.

Unspoken questions of the child who is preparing to return home are, "Am I now good enough that my family will take me back and keep me?" "Can my family understand and accept what now I am, know, and can do?"

The child who is preparing to go home legitimately has a variety of concerns, then, including such things as the following:

• He has no assurance that the conflicts at home which resulted in his placement have been permanently resolved.

• He cannot be sure of his reception; his family kicked him out once (in his opinion); he has no assurance that they really want him back now.

• He and his family are somewhat strangers to each other, for they have had different experiences, unshared by the other; what will they be able to talk about?

• The family and family circumstances have changed in his absence; can he find a place for himself within this changed family.

• The child is not the same person he was when he left; he is more mature and more responsible than when he left home. Will the family accept him as he is, or would they like him better as he was? What will he do if they reject what he now is?

• Will communication with his parents continue? Will the worker be available when communication breaks down?

• How will his siblings treat him?

• Can he continue contact with his alternate caregivers? If things do not work out at home, can he go back to them?

• He was placed once, how can he be sure that he will not be placed again?

FOR THE PARENT

There is some question as to who is more apprehensive about reunion, the child or the parent. Almost without exception, the parents view the child's return with mixed feelings.

From a social point of view, having the child home again mitigates the stigma the parents felt when the child was removed and puts closure on a disagreeable situation. The parents can lay their guilt aside, and inadequacies in other areas of life temporarily take on secondary importance to the child's return.

Other feelings, however, are enhanced. The parent recalls the conflicts which existed in the family prior to placement, the arguments, the tension, the problems of the child, and especially their own feeling of helplessness in a deteriorating situation.

Return of the child reverses the process of placement. When the child went into placement, the parent relinquished much of his parental authority, and the child had to learn to accept the authority of unrelated adults.

In the return home, the reverse is true: the parent resumes the authority he had given up, and the child must learn to look again to the parent for that authority. Both parent and child have to adjust to this change.

While the child was in placement, the parents were spared day-by-day conflict. Now, when the child returns, will things be better? Will the parent now be able to control the situation; will the child have been "fixed" so that negative situations will not arise again; will there be more conflict or less conflict among family members, etc.? Understandably, the parent may have real ambivalence about risking confrontation, lest it precipitate another placement.

Thus, the parents have a variety of concerns, which include the following:

• They may still have guilt about having allowed or caused the child to be placed.

• They may labor under a sense of failure because of the need for placement.

• They may be angry at the child for having put them through the pain and embarrassment of placement.

• They may realize the child's anger at having been placed, and wonder whether or not they can handle his anger in addition to their own.

- They cannot be sure that they will be better able to handle the child now than before placement.
- They may be apprehensive as to whether or not the child now will accept their authority.
- They may wonder where the child's primary loyalty will be—to them or to the alternate caregivers.
- The family stability, financial and/or emotional, may be fragile, and they may wonder if it can withstand the return of the child.
- They may have become comfortable with their life in the child's absence and be worried that this comfort may disappear again.
- They may be aware that the child has been living in more substantial physical circumstances than they can provide and wonder if he will look down upon them for not providing so elegantly for him.

All of these concerns are legitimate. They serve to underscore the need for consistent work with family and child during and following placement.

When the child goes home, some change must have been achieved in the total family system so that the conditions which led to placement no longer exist or at least are under control.

With the support and guidance of the worker, parents should now understand the nature of the family problem; their self esteem should have been enhanced; they should have learned new ways of interacting with each other and with their children; they should have increased or relaxed the limits they set for their children; they should have learned to listen and to understand someone else's point of view, and whatever other problems existed should have been brought at least partially under control.

The child should have gained insight into his own behavior; he should have learned new ways of interacting with his parents and siblings; he should have learned the value of consistent, reasonable limits; he should have learned to listen and to understand someone else's point of view.

Whatever the problems within the family system which led to placement, both family and child have made progress, with professional help, in dealing with those problems.

The fact that return of the child is now possible does not mean the problems are solved. Rather, it means that family and child have grown to a point where they can have a fresh start with each other.

Return home, like placement, is a process. There is nothing magical or dramatic about the return home; it is a carefully orchestrated process which capitalizes upon and coordinates the growing strengths of family and child and handles the feelings of both child and family.

REQUIRED RETURN HOME

In some cases, return home is nearly automatic; circumstances develop which put the child's return home beyond the control of the placing worker. Conditions of the original placement contract have been met, and there is no alternative to returning the child, e.g., separated parents have reconciled; a widow, widower, or divorced parent has remarried; the mentally ill parent has recovered to the point where he or she can resume care of the child; inadequate living arrangements have been replaced; or other conditions, which led to placement in the first place, have been ameliorated. The court may order the child returned.

When the conditions which led to placement have been eliminated or substantively modified, the child must return home, even though the resulting conditions hold little promise of real stability. Ideal family functioning is not a prerequisite for the child to return home. What is needed is at least minimally adequate family functioning by which the child has reasonable assurance of a chance to grow, to mature, and to have emotional support.

The worker cannot change the rules in the middle of the game. That is, if the child was placed because the mother had to enter a mental hospital, when the mother has been declared well enough to return home and resume parental responsibilities, the worker cannot then decide that the child will not receive adequate nurture and must remain in placement.

Occasionally a parent who has voluntarily placed his child will suddenly demand his immediate return, and the worker has no legal ground to defer the child's return. Here the worker may have some room for negotiation.

If the parent has made a sudden decision to bring the child home, more than likely the decision is based on something other than the good of the child, and the worker needs time to gather information as to the real cause. If she has a working relationship with the parents, she may be able to delay the child's return.

This delay may be predicated upon the need for the parents' adjustment to a new life, either the demands of a new job, the adjustment to a new spouse, or an adjustment to life outside the mental institution.

When the parent's life has been in disarray, it is prudent for the parent to achieve some personal stability before adjusting to a returned child. In the long run, the parent can best help his child by first finding security for himself, and the parent may accept that rationale. The parent is not only a parent; the parent is also an individual, with certain rights and expectations for himself/herself.

The parent may be willing to postpone the child's return home until the end of the school year. If the parent cannot wait until the end of the school year, he may be willing to wait until the end of the semester. If he cannot wait until the end of the semester, he may be willing to wait until the end of the current grading period. Dual goals are at work here: first, the child should be able to retain credit for school work completed, and he should have continuity in his school work; second, the worker needs time to help the parent consider the ramifications of the child's return at this time.

THE RETURN PROCESS

The object of the process of returning a child to his home, like the process of placement of the child, is to provide continuity in his life. The child is not simply "dumped" on the family. Both family and child are prepared for visits and for his return.

The expectations of the child in contemplating his return home must be taken into account. He should not be allowed to return with the idea that life at home is going to be perfect and without stress and strain. During his placement, frequently he will have idealized life at home, and, living under the rules of the placement facility, imagined that life at home would be devoid of restrictions or requirements. If he is allowed to keep those fantasies, he will be disappointed, and his relationship with his family will be strained. Graduated visits home should help dispel these myths.

The parents' predictable fantasy that the child will be cured and that henceforth he will be tractable and obedient and that they can all live happily ever after also will be dispelled.

When the child returns to a home which kicked him out once; he has little reassurance that this will not happen again, requiring him to go again through the pain of separation. Testing behavior may very well take place, as he seeks the limits of home. If he is going to be kicked out again, he might as well go ahead and get it over with. The worker will prepare the parents for this.

As return approaches, home visits should increase in frequency and duration to enable family and child to practice together their growing insights. Supervised visits may be necessary initially, but these must give way to unsupervised visits. Early unsupervised visits are carefully assessed, but that assessment becomes less detailed as family functioning improves.

After each early visit, the worker will discuss the visit with parents and child to help them plan for future visits and to help her plan her interventions. If the child is in an institutional placement, work with the child will be provided by the institutional social worker, with whom the placing worker coordinates her efforts.

Thus, the child is moved home in stages, so that both child and parent can adapt to living together again and to the parents' resumption of parental authority.

As a general rule, plans for return of the child will take place over a period of months. The actual move should take place when both parents and child are ready for his return. As with placement, the feelings of the parents and the feelings of the child are dealt with throughout the process.

Certain practical steps can be taken as the child and family prepare for reunion.

• The child must be entered in a new school. This is something the parent can and should do. This is a tangible and impersonal act, and it may help to get the parent reinvolved with his child. If the child has been in foster care, and the name of the foster parents has appeared on school record as guardian, the new school may need some interpretation, which the parent should give.

• The child should be taught that wherever he lives, there will be rules and limitations. Parents and child must be reminded that part of parental responsibility is to see that appropriate rules and limitations are established and enforced.

• The social worker can transmit to the parent any need for medical or dental follow-up for the child.

• The parent should receive information with respect to the child's eating habits, hygiene, or other normal habits in alternate care. If these are different from practices at home, at least the parent can understand what the child is doing when he does it.

• Parent, child, and worker can discuss rules, limits, discipline, and communication techniques.

AFTERCARE

Service to the child and his family does not terminate when the child has been returned home. In a foster care research project in Massachusetts, in cases where the child had been in foster home care prior to the placement in question, the parent was asked whether or not she had seen a social worker during the interim. About half of the parents of children who had been placed more than once replied in the negative. If there had been more adequate follow-up on discharged cases, at least some of the subsequent placements might have been avoided.[1]

Aftercare will be tailored to the abilities and needs of family and child; it will be governed in part by the child's chronological age, stage of development, and prior experiences.

Immediately after the child returns home, the social worker must be available to the family on a fairly immediate basis. Just as she was available to the newly-placed child until he could settle in and find his primary support elsewhere, so when the family and child are newly reunited, the support of the social worker is imperative until family and child can establish their own balance and perhaps develop their own support system.

As the family demonstrates increasing confidence in their ability to function as a family, supportive services will diminish and eventually be put on a "you call me, I won't call you" basis.

It may well be that the child, once feeling himself emancipated, will not want further contact with the agency. On the other hand, the child may bring to the worker problems about his job, questions about dates, courtship and marriage, for advice on how to deal with a parent. The worker will respond to these requests, even though time does not permit resuming a full casework relationship with him.

Many agencies refuse to give post-placement service to children and their families on the basis that courts and departments of social services will not pay for aftercare. In most cases, this is a cop-out. Aftercare need not be expensive or excessively time-consuming. An occasional telephone call can reassure child and family that the worker and the agency have a continuing interest in whatever happens to them. In the aftermath of placement, this is a reasonable expectation.

SUMMARY

Returning home is a test for both parents and child. For the parent, the child's return means vindication—the parent's "badness" as a parent has been erased, and he is a "normal" parent again. For the child, return means that he is back where he belongs, he has been forgiven by his family, he has achieved in alternate care what he was supposed to achieve, and he is "normal" again. If the child and his family pass the test, they can stay together; if they fail, another placement, with all of its attendant pain, awaits.

In appraising the readiness of the parent to provide adequate care for the child who has been placed, the questions pertinent to the decision-making process are:

  • What changes have taken place in the parents, the children, and the situation since the separation of the family?
  • What is the evidence?
  • What can be anticipated on the basis of this evidence?

Such an evaluation can be structured around the following:

  • The current ego status of the parents, their adaptiveness and capacity to absorb and cope with stress, as differentiated from the conditions at the time of placement;
  • The child's condition;
  • The interpersonal relationships among the family members;
  • The current family organization and stabilization;
  • The environmental situation.

Endnote

[1]Gruber, Alan R., *Children in Foster Care.* New York: Human Sciences Press, 1978, pp. 140–141.

PART THREE
DIFFERENTIAL USE OF
PLACEMENT RESOURCES

Chapter 12

SUPPLEMENTAL PARENTING

INTRODUCTION

When placement of a child has been decided upon, additional decisions are required. What kind of placement resource can most effectively meet the needs of a specific child? Will one type of placement resource meet all of the child's needs during his placement experience? What should be the nature of work between parents and worker?

Selecting a placement resource ought not to be a casual or haphazard process. The worker must assess the strengths and weaknesses of each type of resource for each child. Additionally, needs of children are not static, they change as the child grows older and more mature. One type of placement resource may not be able to meet the needs of a growing child child over time, so the worker must determine when a child needs a change of placement type. When, where, and to what kind of placement to move the child, or what should be the progression of placement types are continuous questions for the worker as the case unfolds. The worker also must have clearly in mind the nature of her ongoing relationship with the parents.

This section deals with these matters, starting with the relationship of worker and parents. It then describes a range of services and their linkages. Finally, it considers the uses, strengths and weaknesses of the different kinds of alternate care.

SUPPLEMENTAL PARENTING

The concept of "supplemental parenting" has been coined to reflect today's philosophy of helping families and children. "Supplemental parenting" is a replacement for the phrase and philosophy of "substitute parenting," which has now been retired except for special circumstances as noted below.

Substitute parenting was the rule for many years in providing service to children. In substitute parenting, children were taken out of their homes, and parents were permanently replaced by unrelated caregivers, first in institutions, and later in foster family homes. In either case, parents were discouraged or prohibited from seeing their children, and they certainly were not expected to have further interaction with them. Parents were written off as unfit, ineffective, undesirable, or all three. It was believed that the new caregivers' ministrations would demonstrably be so superior to those of the parents that the children would forget their parents and bond to the new caregivers. This was fine as a theory, and it was the best that was known at the time, but it was wrong.

As has been seen in previous chapters, practice, study, and observation have demonstrated that no one can take the place of a parent in the life, mind, and emotions of a child. Irrespective of the nature of the treatment of the child in the family or the duration of the placement, children maintain a life with their family either in reality or in fantasy.

Further, it has been discovered that parents are not necessarily permanently unfit, ineffective, or undesirable, regardless of the lifestyle of the family or of the nature or extent of the problems within the family. Many more parents than was previously believed possible are receptive or can be supported in becoming receptive to help for the sake of their families and for their own sake. Children, parents, and the family are more than simply a collection of problems; they are entities with aspirations, hopes, fears, and potential that can be worked with, motivated, and guided if sensitive, persistent workers are willing to take the time and energy to provide support, guidance, and treatment.

This realization has brought about the fundamental change in working with children and their families which is reflected in the foregoing chapters. The goal now is not to eliminate families of children in care, but to recognize them; it is not to exclude them, but to involve them; it is not to do something *to* them, but to do something *with* them.

Supplemental parenting has evolved in recognition of the complementary roles played by parents and worker in the attempts to restore family functioning. The term "supplemental parenting" suggests an "adding to"; in this case, someone adds to the parents' ability to parent. Parents carry the responsibility as far as they can, but when they come to the end of their strength or ability for any reason whatever, someone else completes the task. In supplemental parenting, the aggregate nurture of the child is provided a team composed, first, of the parent(s) and the worker.

From their combined input, the child receives total nurture, albeit not in the traditional pattern.

For example, in one case (Family A below),[1] the parents and family are so severely disorganized that they can do little for the child. They are barely able to keep in touch with him, and they have little or no emotional support to offer him. In this case, the worker provides the major portion of the nurture. She is assisted by other family members, foster family, or institutional staff as appropriate, according to the details of the specific case.

In another family, the problem is less pervasive, so the parents provide the major portion of the nurture of the child (Family B below). In this case, the worker, foster family, and institutional staff provide relatively little nurture.

All families and their workers are situated at some point on this continuum.

The key to supplemental parenting is the fluidity of the line demarcating family and worker input. Supplemental parenting recognizes that parents vary widely in their capacity to meet their child's needs, and requires that the role of the worker vary proportionately. Wherever the line of demarcation exists at the outset, as the parents' relationship with the worker strengthens and parents gain insight and ability, the line moves to reflect expanded work by the family and diminished activity by the worker. Initially, the demands on the worker may be great, but as the parents grow in their abilities, the balance in parent/worker activity changes, for the worker transfers her activities to the parents as rapidly as they can absorb them. Thus, the line moves toward the worker, indicating diminished activity on her part. The line must keep moving.

In her own defense and for the good of the family, the worker is well advised to step back from the case periodically and assess what she is doing and whether or not she must continue doing it. Because caseloads are heavy and the worker wants—and needs—to save time, her temptation will be to do much of the work for the family—and to keep doing it. This is certainly more efficient, for new learning comes slowly, and parents are struggling with more than new learning—they are struggling with perhaps a lifelong sense of inadequacy. For the worker to do that which the family may be able to do is counterproductive in the long run, for it prolongs the helplessness and defeatism of the family. The worker will have to take some calculated risks in transferring new responsibilities to the parents.

Total Nurture of Child

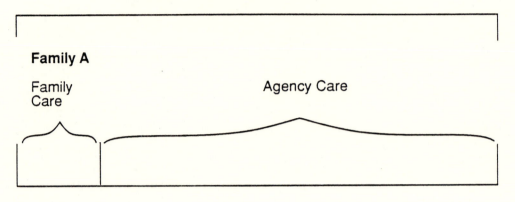

Family A

Family
Care

Agency Care

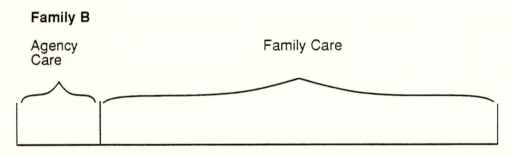

Family B

Agency
Care

Family Care

Figure 5.

This may be an appropriate time for the worker to seek counsel from a supervisor in order to obtain an unbiased analysis of the movement of the line of demarcation.

It must be acknowledged, of course, that some parents are unable to carry even partial parenting responsibility. Where parents are irredeemably ineffective or resistant and parental rights cannot be terminated, substitute care is the only recourse. When the parents are not available or even with support choose not to be involved, substitute care may be necessary whether or not parental rights can be terminated.

Adoption, almost by definition, is substitute parenting, although changes in the adoption field in recent years has provided for open adoptions, which really constitute a form of supplemental parenting. Substitute care may be appropriate for the adolescent who knows well the impossibility of reunion with his family, but is not interested in being adopted.

SUMMARY

The genius of supplemental parenting is assuring the child of adequate nurture through the combined efforts of family and worker while the family gathers its strength and capability to parent. As the case progresses, the worker gradually relinquishes to the parents responsibility for action. This is a gradual process, and the worker must be constantly alert to diminish her input as rapidly as possible, even though this entails some risk.

Endnote

[1]Plumer, Erwin H. *Direction and Management of Children's Institutions and Agencies.* Springfield, IL: Charles C Thomas, 1989, p. 103. Used with permission.

Chapter 13

CONTINUUM OF SERVICES

One of the pressing needs of the human service delivery system vis-a-vis a child who is to be placed is a continuum of services. A continuum is needed for two reasons: (1) so that within the framework of all services, initially the child can be slotted into the service which most nearly meets his needs, and (2) so that the child can be provided with a different service in a logical way with minimum disruption as his needs change.

The concept of a continuum of services has evolved to overcome gaps in service in practice. The whole service delivery system has been cumbersome, and some state services have been fragmented both intra-departmentally and inter-departmentally, with no coordination of effort within or between departments. Additionally, when services have been provided to a child or family by separate agencies, public or private, coordination of services has been left to the initiative and creativity of individual workers.

The result has been that services often are provided by default, and in default they become unproductive, if not damaging: a temporary placement unwittingly turns into a permanent placement; an institutional placement, initially appropriate, inappropriately becomes a terminal placement; a child languishes in foster family care which is increasingly unable to meet his needs.

In the absence of an identifiable schema, the worker, faced with a heavy caseload and a dearth of resources, understandably is relieved once the child is placed in a safe, constructive environment, and goes on to other cases. As a result, children have been left in placements which they have outgrown, or which for other reasons no longer are appropriate.

The fact is that children change, and their needs change. The adjustment of children in placement does not stand still—it either progresses or regresses. When a child "tops out," i.e., has derived maximum benefit from a placement, nothing is left there for him, and his behavior, attitude, self esteem, and achievements go into a decline. Leaving him in a placement which he has outgrown is counter-productive at best, disastrous at worst.

It must be acknowledged that during his total time in placement, one child may require several different kinds of resources. At one period he may need institutional care; at another time he may need placement in a community-based group home; at still another, foster family care may serve him best. When a move is required, it is crucial that the worker have clearly in mind the full panoply of services from which she makes a selection.

The continuum of services helps the worker to perceive all placement resources as part of a systematized array of services. The diagram which follows[1] depicts a continuum of services which ranges from least socially restrictive to most socially restrictive.

As can be seen, the least socially restrictive service is service to a child and his family in their own home. Moving down the continuum, social restriction increases until at the other extreme one comes to the most restrictive setting, the locked ward in a psychiatric hospital.

All services are family oriented, i.e., the family is involved in the child's life to the maximum extent possible irrespective of his placement. It should be noted also that more than half of the settings are community-based; that is to say, as many services as possible are derived from the community rather than provided on campus. Children in residence attend community schools and churches, they hold part-time jobs in the community, they swim in the community pool, if they need therapy they go to community counselors, etc.

Increasingly as one moves in the direction of social restriction, placement resources which are not community based provide services at the placement setting because the services are not available in the community, because they can be provided more efficiently on campus, or for various other reasons.

By conceptualizing the continuum of services, the worker can make a selection of a placement resource within the framework of all available services, which tends to make the selection more precise than if one or two discrete placements were considered.

A CONTINUUM OF SERVICES FOR CHILDREN, YOUTH, AND THEIR FAMILIES

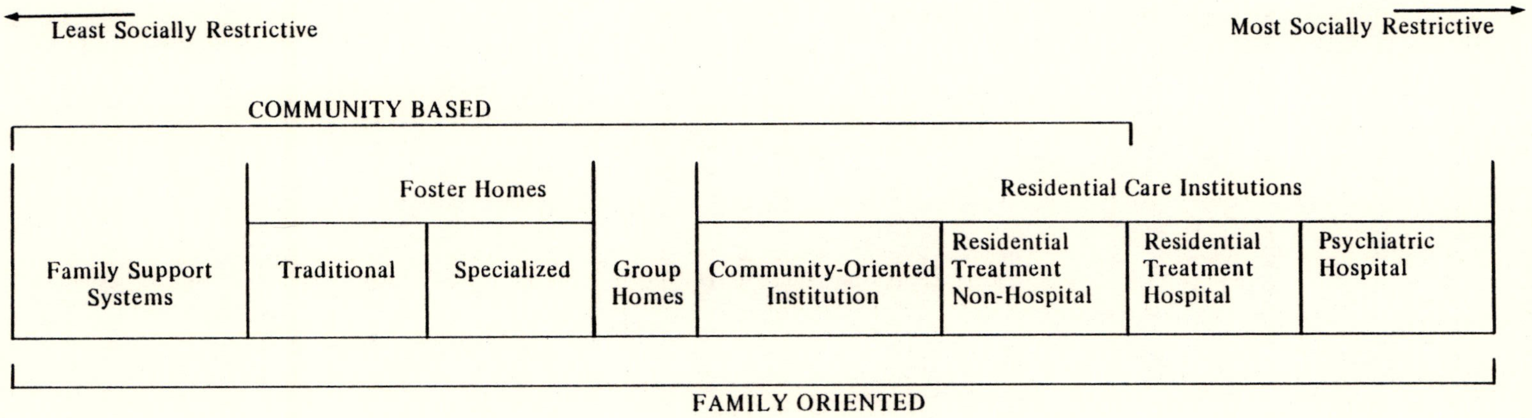

Least Socially Restrictive ← → Most Socially Restrictive

COMMUNITY BASED				Residential Care Institutions		
	Foster Homes					
Family Support Systems	Traditional	Specialized	Group Homes	Community-Oriented Institution	Residential Treatment Non-Hospital	Residential Treatment Hospital	Psychiatric Hospital

FAMILY ORIENTED

Figure 6.

USE OF THE CONTINUUM

A continuum must have fluidity among its component parts. That is, a child must be able to move from one component of the continuum to another with minimum disruption.

Some children will need only one type of service. Others, however, may need a series of placements of different types: institution, group home, then foster family home; institution then foster family home; foster family home, then group home, then institution, or any other combination of services which may best serve the child's changing needs.

Generally speaking, initially the worker would move the child to the point of greatest social restriction needed by the child, then help him to move back up the continuum toward family-centered care — his own, preferably. In placement, the goal always is to keep the child as close to family-type living as possible, or to move him toward family-type living as quickly as possible. Because of the previous disorganization of most placed children's lives, they are likely to need greater structure at the outset of placement than later on. It is less desirable, in most cases, to attempt a family-based placement for a child who has limited capacity for exerting the self control required in most family settings and then have to move him to a more structured setting, for this has the connotation of having "flunked" family living. By comparison, movement from a group setting into a family setting has the connotation of promotion.

Ideally, the entire continuum of services would be offered under the aegis of a single agency, so that a single administration would be involved, staff would have an ongoing working relationship with each other, and coordination and communication would be eased. In such a case, the child can be moved from service to service with a real sense of continuity and stability, and, for the worker, with a minimum of paperwork.

Unfortunately, the ideal is rarely the real. The worker usually must secure one service from one agency and another service from another agency. This puts the onus on the worker to develop her own continuum of services. She must establish communication and a working relationship with agencies which offer discrete services and ensure that she has access to all component parts of the continuum.

TOTAL TRANSFER

One of the unfortunate side effects of changing placements is what has been called "total transfer." When a child leaves one placement for another, too often he is required to sever all relationships with his old placement—he is "totally transferred" to the new location.

No one but children in alternate care is required to fragment his life when changing living arrangements. No one should be compelled to sever one relationship to start another. It is to be hoped that wherever the placed child has lived, he has formed friendships and has had adults whom he has learned to respect, if not love. As the child cannot forget his family just because he has been ordered into placement, so he cannot forget friends or caregivers when he moves from one place to the next. To require the child to sever such relationships is to diminish his self worth and to cause him to be suspicious about entering meaningful relationships in the future.

When the child moves from one place to another on the continuum, he should be accompanied by those who have meaning to him. His parents accompanied him on preplacement and/or placement days; they should accompany him when he moves from one placement to another. If he has been living in a foster family home, the foster family may accompany him. If he has been living in an institution, a child care worker or the institution's social worker may accompany him. If worker, parents, and foster parents, or worker, parents and child care worker accompany him to his new placement, he can hardly avoid feeling a sense of support.

SUMMARY

One method of conceptualizing the variety of services is to place all services on a continuum ranging from least socially restrictive to most socially restrictive. Such a continuum will assist the worker in the type of resource appropriate to the needs of a specific child.

The continuum is more than a list of services. It is a dynamic framework for meeting the progressive needs of the child. Therefore, fluidity must exist between the component parts of the continuum so that when a child has derived maximum benefit from one service he can be moved to another service in an orderly, expeditious manner and with minimum disruption both emotionally and administratively.

The preferred initial placement is at that point on the continuum as far in the direction of most social restriction as his needs require, but not beyond that point. A child who can thrive in foster family care does not need group care; a child who cannot use foster family care, but can utilize the program of a community-based group home does not need institutional care, etc. The goal is always to keep the child in as nearly a family-type situation as possible. As soon as he has mastered the tasks in one placement, he can start back up the continuum in the direction of less social restriction, or, to put it another way, in the direction of family-type living. Movement from more social restriction to less social restriction has the connotation of a promotion, and indicates progress on the part of the child.

The worker must monitor the case closely enough to ensure that the child is progressing in his placement. Once he has reached the peak of his adjustment in any placement situation, his adjustment will begin to deteriorate. It is time to move him to the next effective service before that happens.

Ideally, all parts of the continuum are offered under the aegis of a single agency. Rarely is this feasible, so the worker must develop her own continuum, which will consist of developing a working relationship among agencies which provide the different kinds of services.

Endnote

[1]Plumer, Erwin H. *Direction and Management of Children's Institutions and Agencies.* Springfield, IL: Charles C Thomas, 1989, p. 116. Used with permission.

Chapter 14

PERMANENCY PLANNING

One of the concepts to which every worker must give serious attention is that of permanency planning. Permanency planning is designed to provide permanence in a child's life and to ensure from the outset of the case that plans are constantly monitored and updated with respect to the child and his family. Permanency planning is an established mechanism for reducing the number of children who have been "lost in the drift" of alternate care.

"Lost in the drift" refers to children whose placements were intended to be temporary but became permanent by accident; to the children who fell through the cracks of heavy caseloads; to children whose families disappeared but no action was taken to terminate parental rights; and to all children who for any reason whatever have continued in alternate care simply because they were in a safe placement and no one noticed what was going on. The children bothered no one, and no one bothered them; they simply drifted along, sometimes moving through an unending series of placements, until finally they reached their majority, when the computer declared them ineligible for further services. They were subject to the vagaries of the system and of the workers, and their future was filled with uncertainties.

The emphasis of permanency planning is on family living; permanency planning recognizes the primacy of the parents' claim upon their child and makes every effort to help the family stabilize itself. Permanency planning also recognizes, however, that a child cannot wait indefinitely for adults to get their act together. Therefore, when it becomes evident that family restoration cannot be effected after a time-limited effort has been made to restore the family, permanency planning moves to provide another permanent family for the child.

Some sense of permanence is crucial to the development of a healthy personality. At the time a child and his family are referred for service, a carefully orchestrated sequence of activities is activated, the end result of which is that the child knows where and with whom he will be living and what the future holds.

Permanence has several identifiable characteristics:

• Intent. The intention of permanency planning is that a child shall be placed in a permanent living arrangement at the earliest possible moment. No one can guarantee absolutely that a foster placement will last forever, but if a child is placed in a foster family home under permanency planning, the intention is that he shall remain there as long as he requires alternate care. If the foster home is denominated a temporary arrangement, the worker will keep alive a plan for permanence and work to implement that plan.

• Relationships. Permanence requires commitment and continuity for child and his caregivers. Whatever the vicissitudes of life, permanent caregivers and child share them. In other words, the child is more than a paying guest in the foster placement; he is an integral part of whatever relationships exist in that place.

• Social Status. Permanence means a respected social status. Temporary placement is acceptable because it has a time-limited purpose. A temporary arrangement which slides into permanence, however, is not acceptable, for it pretends to be that which it is not.

PLANNING

When placement is necessary, a plan of action must be developed. A plan can be developed most effectively as soon as placement has been made, if not before, for the parents' pain or embarrassment regarding placement is a motivator for them to participate in planning. The plan will proceed naturally from the intake study which preceded placement. Especially if there is reasonable hope that the family can be reunited, the need for speed is urgent.

Several factors emphasize the need for promptness in developing the plan:

• Involving the parents confirms their importance and reinforces the worker's assurances that the family remains vital in the life of the child.

• Involving the parents immediately may prevent them from disengaging themselves from the healing process, or, worse, disappearing.

• Parents and worker may be able to agree upon the need for action while the placement experience is fresh. Six months later, after the parents are used to having a child in placement, their need for action may be less importunate.

• At the time of placement, the facts of the situation are fresh in the minds of the parents and in the mind of the worker, who has many other cases to handle.

• If the parents have disappeared, they can be located more easily than would be possible a year later.

• If the parents turn out to be incapable of resuming parenting, the sooner this is confirmed the sooner the child can be freed for adoption or other permanent placement, with resultant less damage to him.

• The child hasn't settled into a relationship with his foster parents. If the foster placement has been successful and the foster parents want to adopt, an early adoption in that setting is better for the child than the status of foster child. If adoption in another home is indicated, the move for the child is easier, because he spent only a brief time in foster care.

• If the restoration plan is unsuccessful, the documented effort to treat and the failure of the parents to respond become part of the case for terminating the parents' rights so that the child can be adopted.

In addition to the family plan of care, a separate individual plan of care will be made for the child. If the child is in foster family care, the worker has responsibility for developing that plan with the foster parents. If the child is placed in a group home or an institution, the staff of that facility will usually develop the plan, with a copy to the worker.

CONTINUITY

Permanency planning focuses upon the end result of a case. Prior to final resolution of the case, however, the worker is responsible for providing for continuity in the life of the child. Providing for continuity includes such things as the following:

• Visits between family and the child are the natural, and most important, elements of continuity.

• The worker must encourage, and, where necessary, gently compel the parents to remain actively involved in the life of their child(ren).

• Communication lines must be maintained among parents, child, foster parents or institutional staff. The worker must ascertain that communication is accurate.

• The worker must ensure that foster family or institutional staff maintain a professional stance with respect to the child, i.e., he is not "their" child. Human tendencies to "possess" the child or to "protect" the child from the misdeeds of parents must yield to professional considerations, no matter how laudable the intent.

• The worker will ensure that a harmonious working relationship exists between parents and foster family or parents and institutional staff. This includes allowing the parents to perform as many parental functions as are within their capabilities, e.g., taking the child clothes shopping when the parents are in town, signing report cards, etc.

• In the case of an institution, the total institutional staff must function as a team, each member of which is trained in the philosophy and techniques of child care and oriented to being supportive of all other staff and of parents of children in care.

• The worker will encourage foster parents or institutional staff to keep parents informed of high points in the child's life when the child is in residence and the parents are far away, e.g., sending letters or postcards to announce the child's participation in a school play, his/her first A (or, in some cases, the first passing grade), selection for the basketball team, etc., sending the parents pictures of the child periodically, etc.

The worker is limited only by her own imagination in providing for continuity in the life of the child. Despite her work load, she is well advised to give continuity careful attention.

PERMANENCY PLANNING IN ACTION

Briefly stated, permanency planning works down the continuum of services reviewed in the previous chapter. When separation and placement are threatened, services are introduced into the family home in an effort to preserve the family intact in their own home. As was stated in the chapter on Intake, a careful assessment is made with respect to the likelihood that parents will be able to resume full-time care. Services are then introduced into the home to effect family rehabilitation. The decision to place the child is made only after these efforts have indicated that family stabilization is impossible or that it will require a disproportionate amount of time, considering the age and speed of development of the child.

If, by eighteen months after placement, family restoration cannot reasonably be predicted, parental rights are terminated so that the child can be moved into a stable, permanent living situation.

The general sequence of activity in permanency planning is as follows:

• Provide services to the family and child in their own home.
• If separation is necessary, place the child with relatives.
• If the child cannot be placed with relatives, terminate parental rights and place the child in adoption.
• If adoption is not feasible, place the child in a foster family home.

• If a foster family home is not appropriate, place the child in a community-based group home.

• If a community-based group home is not appropriate, place the child in an institution.

As can be seen, this sequence properly seeks to keep the child as close to family living as possible. The sequence is not to be taken as a rigid prescription, however. If the child cannot remain at home or with relatives, the needs of the child and the relative merits of the total case must determine the type of placement. It would be ludicrous to work the child mechanically down the sequence of placements, moving him gradually away from family-type living after each placement type fails.

One part of the issue of continuity involves moving the child back home. No specific criteria can be listed for making this decision, but guidelines can be given.

The child probably can go home if:

• The parents have no diagnosable, irremediable condition that prevents them from caring for the child.

• The parents can now, or soon will be able to, provide a minimum sufficient level of care.

• Even if the parent cannot provide a minimum sufficient level of care, the child may be able to return if an adequate support system can be arranged to help the parent.

• The child wants to go home. The child feels that he belongs with his parents, and his stay in foster care is simply a temporary sojourn until he can return to his family. The child has formed no psychological ties to his foster parents that will cause pervasive and long-lasting trauma if he is removed from their care and returned to his parents.

The longer the child is with a foster family, the stronger his ties to them grow. Some children seem to transfer their affections to foster parents rather quickly; others do not. In general, the younger the child, the more quickly he will transfer his attachments; therefore, infants and toddlers in particular need permanent homes as soon as possible.

The child probably cannot go home if:

• There has been no contact between parent and child over a period of time, usually at least a year.

• The parent has a condition that is diagnosable and irremediable and prevents the parent from caring for his child;

• The parent cannot provide adequate nurture without help, and no support system is available.

    • There is observable behavior of the parent which indicates inadequacies in parenting ability.

The child should remain with his foster parents if:

    • The parents have had little or no contact with the child for a long period of time, and
    • The child has been in foster care so long and is now so thoroughly a part of his foster family that his ties with them cannot be broken; he has completely adopted his foster family as his own.

Workers must accept the fact that parents do not have an automatic, inalienable right to their own child. When parents have abrogated their parental responsibilities through abuse, neglect, desertion, or other profound behavioral aberration, they have effectively abdicated their parenthood. When their child has been cared for by foster parents and he considers them his *de facto* parents and wants to continue living with them, the child's good supersedes the parents' rights. In such a case, if the foster parents wish to adopt the child, all other things being equal, they should be permitted to do so, for permanence is thereby assured for the child. If adoption is impossible, guardianship or formalized long-term foster care can be arranged.

    The caveat in this situation is that genuine efforts have been made to help the family strengthen itself. One cannot deprive parents of their children because of neglect by the system. At the same time, if the system has been unsuccessful, despite sound, professional efforts, the parents cannot be allowed to continue to underserve their child simply because of blood ties.

EVALUATION OF PARENTS

    In an occasional case, the worker may feel the need for professional help in evaluating a family. The evaluation may indicate the parents' underlying ability to parent, it may assess the parents' potential for treatment, it may indicate the need of one or both parents for therapy by a mental health worker, or it may simply give the worker guidance in her own work with the family.

    The worker is well advised to select the evaluator with care. The focus of the evaluation should be on the parents' present and potential ability to care for their child. If the evaluation focuses upon the parent as an individual rather than as a parent, the findings may be skewed, insofar as the worker's need is concerned.

The evaluation may be used in a termination hearing, if the evaluator is available to testify and the parent has signed a consent for the release of information. Therapy records may be ruled confidential, and thus be inadmissible in a termination hearing. Thus, the evaluation should be performed by a professional who will not provide therapy, if therapy is needed.

ONGOING CASEWORK SERVICES

The worker will provide the usual detail work in the case, such as the following:

• Modify the plan of care as necessary. The plan is not cast in stone; it should be a dynamic tool for both worker and parents. As capabilities, conditions, or circumstances change, so should the plan change. Rigid adherence to an outdated plan guarantees failure.

• Keep in close contact with the parent so that the parent is not inclined just to disappear.

• Provide reasonable support for the family. The degree of involvement by the agency is indicated by the capability, resourcefulness, and sophistication of the parents.

• Use community resources to the maximum extent possible. Community resources are usually located closer to the parents than the agency office. Additionally, whatever services the family can obtain from the community saves the worker time and energy.

• Follow up on all appointments without fail.

• Document everything. Put all agreements in writing, get agreements between two parties signed, and keep a copy in the record.

SERVICE TO FOSTER PARENTS

Foster parents are an integral part of the permanency planning team, and they deserve to be treated as such. The worker may have to help foster parents keep their perspective. Especially if the child is not visited by the parent for long periods of time, the foster parents may begin to believe that the child is theirs and be resistant to later efforts by the agency to arrange visiting or make other plans.

Clearly, it is unfair to all parties, child, parents, and foster parents, to allow foster parents and child to think that this placement is permanent when such is not the case. It is incumbent upon the worker to keep the parent involved with the child if that is possible, irrespective of the parent's condition.

Foster parents may have a difficult time with the child after visits with the parents.

- Provide continuous support to them in their difficulties.
- Remind them that parents have the right to see their children, even though the visits may be disruptive. Child may return from a visit wet, dirty, sick, and disturbed.
- Point out that the worker and the foster parents share a common interest in the child: they both want what's best for him.
- Refer the foster parents to foster parent associations and agency-sponsored training sessions for foster parents.

FORMALIZED, LONG–TERM FOSTER CARE

When termination of parental rights is not possible, the goal of permanency planning can be satisfied through formalized, long-term foster care. This plan formalizes a foster care arrangement already in existence by making a formal, non-legal, written agreement between the foster family, the child welfare agency, the biological parents, and the child. It gives the foster family more autonomy in planning for the child than is customary in regular foster care.

Foster parents are protected by the agreement from fear of losing the child, as the agency agrees to maintain the placement until the child is grown, unless new circumstances arise in the foster home which demand a reappraisal of the placement.

Foster parents often worry when there is a change of worker, since the whole question of whether the child will return to his parents can come up again at that time. This agreement ensures foster parents and the child of placement continuity. Biological parents may find this plan less threatening that guardianship and be willing to sign an agreement and abide by its provisions.

Questions with Respect to Permanence[1]

One of the national leaders with respect to foster care has developed a list of questions each worker should ask to ensure that the philosophy of permanency planning has been fulfilled.

1. Are parents involved in the decision to remove the child? To place the child? Where to place the child?

2. Are children placed close enough to their families for ongoing family contact?

3. Are children (normally) placed within the State?

4. Are children (normally) admitted into care only from within the State?

5. Does the case plan include ongoing family contact?

6. Does the case plan include ongoing contact with any person who is important to the child?

7. Does the initial case plan have family reunification as a goal?

8. Is the case plan direction clear within three months?

9. Is the case plan always subject to modification?

10. Are the case goals clear and understood by child, by the parents, by the placement agency worker, by the foster parents or the institution caseworker and child care staff?

11. Do the parents understand their part in the case plan?

12. Is it clear who has primary responsibility for helping the family, the placement agency, or the child care institution?

13. Are the placement agency's case plan, and the child care institution's service, or treatment, plan synchronized?

14. Are case reviews attended by staff of both the placement agency and child care institution? By foster parents?

15. Can parents count on the threshold for removal and return being the same?

16. Are there pre-placement visits?

17. Do parents participate in the placement?

18. Are parents encouraged to visit as soon as possible after the placement?

19. Does the placement agency worker visit children in child care institutions at least quarterly,-monthly in family homes?

20. Are the parents' feelings about the separation discussed with them?

21. Do staff (or foster parents) help parents to feel welcome?

22. Do staff (or foster parents) uphold the parents to the child, and the child to the parents?

23. Are parents encouraged to visit in family foster homes?

24. Are life books encouraged and updated?

25. Are group homes or child care institution living units limited to ten or fewer children?

26. Administrators, do you treat your staff as positively as you want them to treat the children?

27. If children move from one foster home to another, can they maintain contact with any previous ones?

28. If children leave foster care to adoptive homes, can they maintain established relationships?

29. When children move are they given names, addresses and telephone numbers of past caregivers?

30. When "permanent" family foster care is used, does it convey the concept of lifetime family relationships?

31. If children are adopted after infancy, is further contact with their birth family ever permitted?

32. If families drop away and adoption is not feasible are children linked up with foster grandparents?

33. Are children given sufficient lead time before they are released from care to work through the change in their lives?

34. Do staff attempt to locate relatives of children scheduled for release, to give information about them to the children, and to inform the relatives of the children's status?

35. When it is expected that children to be released will re-enroll in school, do staff contact that school and be sure that school receives a report of the child's school progress?

36. Is after-care service always provided?

37. Does the agency give preference to readmitting children who have been there before, when they need it?

38. Are children permitted to return for visits after leaving?

39. Do staff respond, as able, to children who want to stay in touch with them?

CONDUCTING A SEARCH FOR ABSENT PARENTS

Searching for lost parents can be a time-consuming and frustrating task. The following may give the worker some suggestions as to how to start.[2]

• Send a registered letter, return receipt requested, delivery to addressee only, to the parent at all previous addresses known, even if you feel sure that the parent is no longer residing there. Include letters to the parent in care of all relatives, friends, or employers whose addresses are known.

• Write to the public utility companies — electricity, gas, water, telephone — in the city where the parent was last known to reside.

• If a parent is of Indian heritage, and you know what tribe, contact the Bureau of Indian Affairs.

• In some states, the welfare department, attorney general's office, or other agency maintains a central information unit to collect support from separated or divorced parents. Find out if they have an agreement with your agency to share information about absent parents.

• Call or write to the state department that registers motor vehicles. It may provide addresses for all licensed drivers within the state. It helps greatly if you can supply full name and date of birth.

• Request in writing a records check from the state police and appropriate county and city law enforcement agencies. Also contact the FBI, Records Department, Washington, D.C.

• If you have the parent's social security number, write to the state unemployment office.

• With or without a social security number, you can address a letter contained in an unsealed envelope to the parent, enclosed with your request that it be forwarded, and mail it to:

Social Security Administration
Bureau of Data Processing
Baltimore, Maryland 21232   and they will forward

• If the parent has been in prison or you believe that he might be, call or write the state prison.

• If the parent has a history of mental illness, contact the state hospital.

• If the parent has gone to a community college or university, write a letter to the parent in care of the school, and the school will forward it.

• If you have reason to believe a parent has ever belonged to a particular labor union, call or write giving the name of the last known employer.

• Within the local community — especially if it is a large one — check the telephone directory and the city or county directory. Also try directory assistance for new listings and cities out of state.

• If the parent has been on public assistance, and you have reason to believe he is residing in a particular city, check the Micro-Fiche and/or contact the local public assistance agency.

SUMMARY

Permanency planning is perhaps the single most vital tool in planning for children who must be placed. Permanency planning ensures that the child's life has continuity, that he does not get lost and that he has a future.

If workers adhere to the principles of permanency planning, they will be saved much time and energy, and, most of all, children will be well served.

Endnotes

[1] Unpublished paper by Jake Terpstra, Specialist in Foster Care and Residential Care, Children's Bureau, Dept of Health and Human Services, Washington, D.C. Used with permission.

[2] *Permanent Planning for Children in Foster Care: A Handbook for Social Workers.* U.S. Dept of Health, Education and Welfare, 1977. DHEW Publication No. (OHDS) 78-31024.

Chapter 15

FOSTER FAMILY CARE

After services to the child and his family in their own home, placement in the home of relatives, or adoption, foster family care is the preferred placement for the child because this replicates the family construct.

The agency seeks foster parents in order to achieve two major objectives for the child who can use family care, as distinguished from group care:

• To provide individualized, close, supplemental parental relationships for the child as a context for healthy emotional development and as a model for family living.

• To provide a family environment in which the child can learn social skills and techniques for living as a member of the community.

Foster family care is based on the same reciprocal dynamics as exist in a family. The parents do something for the child, and he does something in return for them. This is not always a formal response, a tit-for-tat reaction, of course. The response parents get may be a smile or laugh from the child in response to their actions; it may be the child's willingness to play contentedly by himself or with other children; it may be a good-night hug; it may be the delight visible on the child's face when the parent picks him up from the babysitter, etc.

The parent's response to the child may be kissing a hurt finger, stopping to listen to what the child says, following through on a promise, returning when the parent said he would return, etc. These details of ordinary family life are replicated in the relationship of foster family and foster child.

Whatever the details in the life of a family, adults and child find satisfaction in their mutual life, and they plan to stay together no matter what the future holds for either. This, too, is replicated in the foster family situation. Although foster care is intended to be temporary unless otherwise defined, until the point arrives for natural termination of foster family care, the foster family and the child will stay together.

215

Unfortunately, it doesn't always work out that way. Various actions on the part of the child can prompt a request for his removal. Perhaps most frequently, foster family care works fine until the child turns 13 and moves into puberty. Unable to face the pubertal roller coaster, sometimes even with a child who has been in care for some years, foster parents have demanded that the child be removed.

Other foster families are able to take many kinds of acting out, but balk at specific kinds of acting out. One foster family can accept acting out, but not profanity; another can accept profanity but not sexual remarks or innuendoes; one family, in which the foster father was a policeman, could not accept even the appearance of stealing, although no stealing had taken place.

Much is asked of foster parents. They are asked to take into their home a child who is a total stranger, who has grown up in a household that may have had quite a different life style from that of the foster parents and who may have values or habits or speech that are quite different from those of the foster family, but treat him as if they were a part of the family, knowing all the while that if things go at all well for the child and his parents, some day he will leave. Just on the surface of it, then, foster parents are asked to expose themselves to pain by becoming emotionally attached to a child who later will leave.

One foster mother said, "Every time they take a child, I bawl my eyes out and swear I'll never go through that again. But the next day I'm ready for the next child." This is exactly the maturity and involvement which foster parenthood demands, for if foster parents do not become emotionally involved with the foster child, they cannot be adequate foster parents.

Foster parenthood means putting the need of the child and the pain of the child ahead of one's own pain. Adults can understand the situation, at least to some degree, and they are better able than children to undergo the pain.

MOTIVES OF FOSTER PARENTS

Why do foster parents expose themselves to the pain of constant separations?

The motives of foster parents include such things as the following:

- They just like children.
- They have love to spare and want to do some good in the world.
- They want the experience of parenthood without a lifetime commitment.
- They had such a pleasant childhood that they want to help others to have a similar experience.
- It is their religious duty to help the less fortunate.
- They need the money.
- They wish to have a larger family but can't afford to have more children of their own.
- Less honorably, they want to have control over someone, to have a resident laborer/slave, sexual partner, etc. These motives are not stated, of course, and it is to be hoped that they will be discovered and weeded out in the foster home study.

The underlying motivations are usually multiple and are not manifest. In any event, in becoming foster parents, they make two deliberate choices:

- They choose foster care rather than adoption or enlargement of the natural family as the means of expressing their wish for more children.
- They choose to carry out this wish under the auspices of an agency in preference to private or independent foster care.

STRENGTHS OF FOSTER FAMILY CARE

Foster family care has specific and identifiable strengths.

Family Setting

A family environment is the natural setting for growing children. The best training ground for adulthood is in the interaction among family members. The art of negotiation, sharing, problem-solving, limitations on behavior, consequences for behavior, budgeting, paying of bills and matching outgo to income, learning how to fail successfully, and learning the give and take of interpersonal relationships are best taught within the family. Through all these things, the child gains a sense of his own worth and learns how to cope with the world.

Reciprocal Relationship

Foster care is predicated on the same reciprocal relationship that exists in natural families: the foster parent gives to the child, and the child responds; the child gives to the foster parent, and the foster parent responds.

The child must be able to enter a meaningful relationship with at least one foster parent, and preferably both, if there are two, if he is to benefit from foster family care.

Foster parents have a right to expect a reciprocal relationship—that is their primary reward in serving as foster parents. If a child cannot engage in this type of relationship, and some cannot, he needs some other type of care.

The exception to this general rule is the specialized foster home. Some foster parents are specifically trained—and paid—to provide care for children who cannot reciprocate.

Personality Development

Personality has a better chance to form naturally in a family setting. Individual talents and preferences can be realized more readily than in group care. Foster parents are more likely to be involved in school and able to follow up on schoolwork with the child on a personal level than can staff in a group care facility.

Expense

For the placing agency, foster family care is cheaper than group care, and this always has an appeal to administrators.

WEAKNESSES OF FOSTER FAMILY CARE

Family foster care contains complications and deficiencies both in the system and in practice.

Weaknesses in the System

In the system, for example:

- The quantity of good foster homes is limited in most agencies.
- Planning is often indefinite. Placements originally conceived of as

temporary in nature turn out to be long-term. Most of the child welfare personnel employed in public agencies have not had a graduate social work education, and, even if they do, many schools of social work give cursory attention to matters of placement.

• Agency personnel tend to have a high attrition rate, especially in the public sector.

• Some individuals feel a conflict between personal or professional values and bureaucratic requirements, which results in further turnover.

• Because of limited numbers of staff, children are often under-supervised in foster homes. Neither natural parents nor foster parents receive sufficient support.

• The agency may have no plan for regular visits by a social worker with the child or his parents or foster parents.

• When the agency ceases to be actively involved, the child develops a sense of being of no consequence and of being abandoned.

Weaknesses in Practice

Family Setting

The fact that foster family care is a family setting may be too perplexing for some children. The foster family may be too sharply reminiscent of what they have lost. If they were abused, it may be too sharply reminiscent of what they have gone through. The pain of separation may be so acute that they cannot at this time enter a family setting.

Reciprocal Relationship

The fact that one or two adults are available for an intense, reciprocal relationship may be overwhelming for some children. They may be too close to the separation from their own parents to be able to accept surrogate parents, at least for the time being.

Natural parents may be unable to accept another couple (or individual) who function in a parenting role for their child, and consequently undermine the placement.

Siblings

If foster parents have children of their own, the risk of favoritism or of exploitation of the foster child by the foster parents' own children is always present. Additionally, the possibility of the foster child's taking revenge upon the foster parents' own children for real or imagined slights or for the injustice of placement is always present.

Disruption

A foster home is more easily disrupted than a group care placement. Foster care is subject to sudden and unexpected changes in the life of the foster family: the father gets transferred out of state, and in most states foster children cannot move across the state line; Grandma has to move in with the foster family, and the only room available is the foster child's room; foster parents are divorced or one dies, etc.

Training

In most agencies, foster parents receive less training than staff in group care. In an earlier age, this was not so important, for foster children needed more than anything else love and a place of safety in which to live. As children going into placement have increasingly complex sets of problems, lack of training is increasingly serious. Additionally, as it has become apparent that much more work can and must be done with natural families than was formerly realized, foster parents need help in dealing with the natural families of children in care.

Supervision

Supervision of a foster family cannot be as close as supervision in group care, for there simply is not enough time. In a sense, foster families function largely on their own.

As can be seen, the strengths and weaknesses are identical in many ways. This means that foster families cannot simply be lumped together and a foster family name picked out of the hat for a new child. The foster family must be selected with precision in order that the strengths of the family will meet the needs of the specific child.

CHANGING NATURE OF FOSTER FAMILY CARE

Foster family care has undergone a substantive change in recent years. This change has been caused partly by the nature of foster families available and partly by the type of child who is referred for foster care.

A few years ago, the typical foster family, if there ever was such a thing, consisted of a married couple in which the wife was a homemaker and the husband was regularly employed outside the home. In many cases, this couple had raised their own children and had available space in their home and in their hearts for a foster child. Remuneration was relatively unimportant; the goal of remuneration was to avoid having the foster parents have to put money out of their own pockets for the benefit of the foster child. For infants and toddlers, this may have worked out as planned; for adolescents, rarely did remuneration pay the full cost of care.

The foster family in those days was a stereotypically average family, with family vacations and mutual activities being a normal part of family life. Foster families were immersed in the life of their community and usually of their church, and they were what was known as "solid citizens."

The foster child in those days came from a family which was breaking down or had broken down, and the greatest problem he had to deal with was the fact of separation from his own parents, who had one or more of a variety of problems which interfered with rearing their children. The child was essentially "normal"; except in rare cases there was little question of underlying emotional disturbance; his main problem was that he could not live at home. Whatever disturbance was recognized was attributed to the trauma of separation.

The concept of foster care was equally simple in those days: the foster family took in the child, treated him as if he were their own, and relinquished him to his parents when time for reunion arrived. Foster parents and natural parents frequently were acquainted; the natural family visited in the foster family home on a schedule developed with the social worker or by direct negotiations between natural and foster families. In rare cases, family visits took place in the agency office. Foster parents were taught to respect and understand the natural parents, but no one assumed particular responsibility for helping the natural parents to gain or regain parenting skills and capability. Emphasis was on the child.

It was not unusual in those days for children to grow up in foster family care; no determination was made either to reunite the family or to release the child for adoption or other permanent living.

Today, the foster care situation is substantively different. Single foster parents today are quite acceptable, and almost without exception those single parents have full-time employment. When foster parents are married, more than likely both are employed. Despite the double income, remuneration for the care of a foster child may be more important today than ever before.

Children coming into foster care today have more complex sets of problems than previously; they have been subjected to life styles and life experiences which are not conducive to healthful growth and development; like all children, they have been exposed to the drug scene, and they may have had less internal strength and no support from home to avoid this temptation; many have been introduced to and supplied with drugs by their parents, who may attempt to continue this service while the children are in foster care. Fewer foster children today have had any experience in stable family living; many are streetwise and aggressive; more come from families where education is not valued, and the school experiences of the children have not been successful, etc.

Additionally, emphasis in foster care today is upon the family. As has been stated, aggressive efforts are made to reunite the child and family, which casts all of foster care in a different light. Foster parents are expected to become part of a treatment team.

With these complicating factors, the need for training and supervision of foster parents is greater than ever, for foster parents need all of the help and support they can get. Unfortunately, budget cuts and stringent economies especially in the public sector have precluded an increase in training and supervision. Rather, the reverse is true, for one of the first items to be cut in any economy drive is training funds.

The practical implication is that the social worker must be especially sensitive to the needs of foster parents and creative in her approach both to foster parents and to foster children.

CONTRA INDICATIONS FOR FOSTER FAMILY CARE

It is axiomatic in work with children in our culture that sound personality is developed during childhood through healthy relations in family life. Therefore, it might follow that the child who cannot live with his own family could have most of his needs met by a substitute family, since there are definite qualities of personality developed through this usual mode of rearing children in our society.

In the appraisal of the child's needs, it is necessary to look for the subtle possibilities that exist which would contra-indicate caring for the child in the community.

For instance, there is the child with a schizoid personality, who has no manifest disturbance as in the schizophrenic child, but who makes only a thin emotional investment of himself in interpersonal relationships.

There is also the child with the narcissistic character, comprised of a shell to cover deeply underlying pain and anxiety, beyond which is an emptiness resulting from the child's early hardlearned resolution not to invest in people except for self-aggrandizement for security.

These children make an appeal to adults for these purposes, only to frustrate the adults thus involved by offering little or no response. Both these types of children are frequently unacceptable to foster families, who request their replacement.

For some emotionally disturbed children, even the most favorable foster family cannot provide the expert kind of environment which the degree of their disturbance requires. Relationships within his own family may have been so damaging that the child cannot tolerate the facsimile of family life with its intimate relationships, and a foster family can neither help him nor accept his disturbed behavior, which he may also show at school and in play.

The disturbance he displays arises not only because he is enraged at the world, especially at adults, but also because he feels guilt over disloyalty toward his own parents when drawn to a parent substitute, in spite of what he suffered from his own parents.

This sense of guilt stemming from a conflict of loyalties or from fear of relating to others out of a belief that this would cause him to be alienated from his parents, will erect an insurmountable barrier in some children to making new ties in foster families, especially if the natural parents fan such feelings.

These are psychiatric kinds of diagnoses. On a less intense level, sometimes, without psychiatrically diagnosable conditions, that is, without being formally diagnosed as emotionally disturbed, the child has been so hurt by the experiences within his own family that he is not able to make use of the experience with a substitute family. This may be true for a brief time immediately after the family's dissolution, or it may continue for an indefinite period.

Some experts suggest that an institution should be used as a first placement for every child to allow him some decompression time before going back into family living. This is probably overkill: some children are quite able to move into foster family care from their own homes. The appropriateness of initial group care should be remembered, however, and the decision should be made on a case-by-case basis.

Other kinds of behaviors which may contra-indicate foster family care are as follows:

• The withdrawn child. For the withdrawn child, placement in a foster family can stir such painful memories of his old family life that he may tend to withdraw even further, with consequent diminished investment in the foster family and in the world about him.

• The destructive child. Some children are so destructive or bizarre in their behavior as to be totally unacceptable in a more or less normal environment. If they are placed in a foster family, their unavoidable rejection—by foster family, by neighbors, by school personnel, etc., —will serve only to reinforce earlier unfavorable life experiences and will be just another rejection for him. Protecting children from a certainty of failure is an important issue.

• The adolescent who is going into alternate care for the first time. Placement of an adolescent in a foster family runs counter to his stage of development, in which he is involved in freeing himself from the control of adults. Here the difference between chronological age and functional age must be kept in mind. If the child is chronologically an adolescent but functionally preadolescent, foster family care may be appropriate.

• The child whose parents are so attached or else so guilty that they cannot tolerate seeing another couple—a man and a woman—or even a single foster parent serve in a parental capacity and would destroy the placement.

• The child who is so attached to his family that he cannot accept another person or couple in a parenting role.

• The severely acting-out child, especially an adolescent.

• The child who is so primitive in his personal life, habits, hygiene, that no foster family could tolerate him.

FOSTER FAMILIES VIS-A-VIS NATURAL FAMILIES

The first task of the foster parents in relation to the child's natural family is in understanding and managing their own feelings about the natural parents and their reactions to the child's feelings about his parents and siblings.

The social worker must recognize and deal with the foster family's feelings about the natural family. These may include the same feelings the worker had to confront in herself, which were listed as including the following:

• Anger, that parents could treat a child the way this child has been treated;

• Morality, if the natural parent smokes, drinks, or uses drugs and the foster parents do not;

• Piety, if the foster parents are churchgoers and the natural parents are not;

- Confusion, when the child openly prefers his own parents to the foster parents;
- Hurt, that their efforts are not recognized and validated by the child and his parents;
- Anguish, at seeing what the parents continue to do to their child;
- Pride, that they are not like the natural parents;
- Judgment, that the foster parents feel that they are better than the natural parents.

The child's feelings about his parents are likely to be an ambivalent mixture of longing, rage, shame, and guilt, but those feelings are often hidden. If the foster parent is to achieve empathy with the foster child, one of his tasks is to be in rapport with these feelings and to open the doors of communication, freeing the child to talk about his family when he feels so inclined.

Foster parents need help in learning to deal openly with the child's feelings. The foster parent who responded to a child's distress by saying "Don't think about that; think about the happy times we can have here," the foster parent who tried to divert the child's tears by saying, "You might as well sing the song 'My Heart Belongs to Daddy,' " and the foster parent who said, "You shouldn't feel that way" have lost the battle.

SUMMARY

The nature of the agency's responsibility for a placed child's welfare is a primary factor in determining the role and functions of foster parents and some of the components in their relationship with the agency.

The agency's defined function, professional commitments, and legal obligations combine to make the agency responsible and accountable for the child's welfare for as long as he remains in placement under agency care.

The agency cannot delegate its primary responsibility; it can and does utilize foster parents as an instrument for discharging certain aspects of that responsibility. Hence, regardless of interest, investment and parenting abilities, as long as the foster parent is not the legal parent, she remains responsible to the administrative agency that represents the legal parent or the state.

Consequently, the agency must exercise a supervisory function as one component in its arrangements with foster parents in order to ensure that they perform in a manner consistent with agency goals and procedures, to protect the foster parents, and to coordinate treatment of the foster child and his family.

Foster family care is the placement of choice for many children who must be separated from their families, cannot live with relatives, and are not immediate candidates for adoption. Foster family care replicates family living in that a reciprocal relationship exists between foster family and foster child, and thus it is the alternate environment within which the child can most efficiently develop self esteem, learn and practice relationships, and lay the groundwork for a mature adulthood.

Foster family care has both strengths and weaknesses. Consequently, the strengths of the specific foster family must be matched carefully with the needs of the specific foster child.

Chapter 16

GROUP CARE

For some children, even the most favorable foster family cannot provide the expert kind of environment which the child requires. Group care, then, is the placement of choice. Like foster family care, group living has both implicit strengths and weaknesses. Group care should be selected as a placement resource because its strengths can most adequately address the needs of the child, rather than as a placement of convenience.

GROUP CARE AND THE CHILD

For the child, some of the advantages in group living appear when he needs distance in interpersonal relationships, especially with parent figures, while at the same time he needs to feel protected by being with them. For example:

• In the group setting, the distance afforded interpersonal relationships provides a neutral setting for a child, which is sometimes necessary to permit healing from an acute shock.
• The demands for close interpersonal relationships implicit in his own family or a foster family, and which the disturbed child finds too stressful, can be avoided.
• The loyalties of the child to his parents can be relinquished at his own pace when he is not conflicted by too early close and emotional pulls to other parent figures, the demands of which might cause him to resist making new ties.
• Sometimes an anxious child gains support when he is constantly surrounded by the group. A child of a given character structure may serve as a catalyst for other children in the group; for example, the acting-out child may stimulate the withdrawn child.
• The group setting can also permit conflictual feelings not accessible to individual treatment to emerge and be handled, which is needed before the child is able to use foster home care.
• The neutral setting which the group home or the group in the institution can provide may serve the child who, in the course of being

prepared for adoption, requires a place where he is not too much reminded of his background before he goes to a permanent family.

• For the adolescent who is gradually moving away from the control of adults, a group setting is more consistent with his developmental stage than a foster family home.

GROUP CARE AND THE PARENTS

Placement of a child in a group setting is also advantageous from the point of view of its influence on the parents.

• The parent may not permit the child's placement in a foster home because of their inability to face their own failure (real or perceived) as parents, because of their narcissistic pride, or both. Although the child himself may yet not require the group setting, his parents' feelings would doom foster family placement to failure.

• Many parents fear the loss of their child's affections through attachments to a foster family. The threat of loss of the child's ties to them does not arise when the less personal interrelationships of group care are used.

• By placing the child in group care, the parents can believe that the child lacks something which foster parents could not give him either, which reduces their guilt.

• Parents who, out of their own need, tend to disturb the child in placement and to disrupt the placement itself, can be better tolerated and dealt with in their contacts with the child in a group facility than in a foster family.

GROUP HOME CARE

Group care is provided by community-based group homes and by institutions. These two types of facilities have both similarities and differences.

In most states, a group home serves ten or fewer children; however, several states license group homes for as many as twenty children, which blurs the distinction between group homes and institutions.

Perhaps the greatest difference between a group home and an institution is with reference to the community. The immediate community for the group home is the community in which the group home is located. Children in residence attend community schools, they swim in the community pool, they receive therapy from community professionals, and they associate with community children, as would be the case if they were living at home.

One of the decisions the worker has to make in selecting a group care facility, then, is whether or not the child is ready to participate in community life.

By contrast, an institution may replace not only the family and its societal functions, but also the immediate community. Historically, institutions were "total institutions," with school and church on the grounds, with shoe shop, broom shop, kitchen garden, dairy herd, and farm. The institution was the total community for residents, who had no need to leave the campus until they were discharged. Some of these characteristics of institutions still exist today, albeit in modified form. Other institutions, however, have blurred this distinction by becoming increasingly a part of the surrounding community.

The chief distinction between a group home and a large foster family home is that an agency owns or operates the group home, and in the group home, child care workers, i.e., the primary caregivers, are employees of the agency which operates the group home, whereas foster families are not. This is a crucial distinction, for in the group home control remains with the agency as to which child shall be admitted or discharged. Because a foster family home is operated in the family's own home, if the family demands that a child leave, he must leave. When there is doubt as to whether a facility is a group home or a family foster home, a simple test will provide the answer: In case of crisis, who leaves, the staff or the child?

The group home has some significant advantages over the institution, among them the following:

- The group home program can be changed easily to meet changing needs of referrals.
- A cohesive group may develop more easily in the informal setting of a group home.
- Rules and regulations can be fewer in number and can be modified with respect to an individual child's needs without engendering the hostility of a campus full of children.
- Because most group homes contain ten or fewer children, a resident is not likely to get lost in the crowd.
- Staff generally have time to monitor school progress and activities and to interact with school personnel.
- Spontaneous activities or ideas can be carried out with relative ease.

The flexibility of group home programming has a major appeal. The group home program may be designed for a wide variety of needs, from providing care for retarded children to providing care for emotionally disturbed children.

The group home seems particularly indicated for adolescents. Their capacity for intimate relationship with surrogate parental figures may be diminished, or they may simply be too close to independent living to require parental figures. Adolescence is a time of growing away from the control of adults, and forcing them into the necessarily close relationship of a foster family may be contra-indicated.

A community-based group home, then, is the next step in the continuum of services after foster family care. The group home has a unique mix of some of the strengths of a foster family and some of the strengths of an institution, while avoiding many of the weaknesses of both. This may be the placement of choice for many children.

INSTITUTIONAL CARE

Institutions have a valid and honorable place in today's child care. Institutions have a continuum of their own which ranges from the general institution through residential treatment to the psychiatric ward and closed facility for delinquents.

A responsible institutional program is a specially designed environment in which the events of daily living are used as formats for teaching competence in basic life skills. The living environment becomes both a means and a context for growth and change that stress learning through living. Every element of institutional life is tied into the development of each individual child and of the group. Getting-up time, school, meals, bedtime, work, recreation, interpersonal relationships, problem-solving, etc., all become part of treatment.

The purpose of the institution is to prepare the child for dealing with life after he leaves the front gate for the last time. How well he performs in the institution is less important than the fact that while he is in the institution he gathers the tools which will enable him to survive after he leaves.

The institution must provide:

- Structure;
- Orderliness and dependability of life;

• Outside parameters for behavior, but freedom within those parameters;

• Education in accordance with his abilities;

• Specialized treatment in accordance with his need;

• Individualized goals which will be changed as he achieves;

• An opportunity to learn and practice the decision-making process;

• Maturational experiences—a chance to test himself against the reality of his life, including a chance to succeed and a chance to fail successfully;

• Group process;

• Coordination of the child's individual goals with family goals which are spelled out in the family plan of care;

• For the adolescent, preparation for independent living.

As is to be expected in such a complex task which involves children with problems or children from families with problems, there are both strengths and weaknesses.

Strengths of Institutional Care

The following are some of the strengths of institutional care:

• The institution may be equipped to provide structure more effectively than other settings.

• Because of the variety of staff, almost every child can find someone he is comfortable in making his confidant, be it child care worker, social worker, secretary, janitor, or farmer.

• Observations of a child come from as many different perspectives as there are staff members. A teamwork approach may provide a more comprehensive and objective assessment of a child than is possible in a foster family home or group home.

• With many staff members, the stress of working with an acting-out resident can be shared.

• More acting-out behavior can be tolerated in an institution than in any other setting.

• The child can be permitted to live in an institution without developing a close relationship with anyone while he gathers strength after a series of negative experiences.

• A reciprocal relationship between child and staff is not necessary. If a child cannot enter a relationship with an adult, a one-way relationship is acceptable in an institution, pending the time the child can learn or acquire the emotional strength to interact. Institutional staff members may be required to give to the child without receiving any response.

• The group can be consciously composed in accordance with the needs of the child. The child can be assigned to a living group in which he is the youngest or oldest, most or least aggressive, smartest or least smart, or most or least of anything else in accordance with his needs.

• Specialized services can be provided more efficiently on a campus than in other settings.

• Parents may feel less competition with a large staff than with an individual or a couple.

Weaknesses of Institutional Care

The following are some of the weaknesses or limitations of institutional care:

• An institution is inherently dependency-producing. Lights always come on, food appears on the table, the vehicles always have gas, etc., and the child has no evidence of the effort that went into ensuring that these things happen.

• Unless the program is carefully designed, residents may not be permitted to make decisions, they may not have control over their own savings accounts, rules may be arbitrary, capricious, and designed more for the convenience of staff than for the good of the residents, etc.

• Residents may not have the right of self determination.

• The institution is apart from the world at large and constitutes a contrived, artificial environment.

• Adolescents may not have normal growth experiences, such as acquiring a driver's license and having driving experience. (In some states this is due to prohibitive insurance rates, rather than failure in the program.)

• In many communities, a stigma is attached to children who live in an institution, with resultant discrimination.

• The individuality of a child may be lost. Talents, skills, and interests of the child may not have an opportunity for expression.

• Staff may or may not be adequate for the task at hand, either in numbers, training, or supervision.

• Children in institutions typically have few opportunities to give to others; they tend always to be receiving. In long-term institutional care, children tend to expect always to be given to.

• Children in long-term institutional care have no opportunity to experience family living.

• Children may not be allowed to experience failure. Staff anticipate each assignment and appointment and ensure that each child is exactly where he is supposed to be at the time he is supposed to be there, thus depriving him of a learning experience.

Programming

All institutional programs contain many parts, many of them identical from one institution to another: food, shelter, school, work, etc. Two special program elements, however, are crucial in any progressive institutional program.

Incentive Program

The program must have an incentive system which will give the child some control over his own destiny. The days are long gone when the institution's superintendent could sit in his office and make the rules for the campus.

An incentive system is a program in which the child is rewarded for appropriate behavior by receiving expanded privileges. At the outset, the child can see the full range of expected behaviors and available privileges. He can decide for himself whether or not the privileges are sufficiently desirable as to warrant changing his behavior.

Behaviors to be included for a particular child are negotiated by child and staff—child care worker, social worker, or both. The incentive system is thus specific to each child in accordance with his needs. In the discussion of points, privileges, or levels, the child learns something of the art of negotiation and is provided a safe and structured experience in dealing with adults.

When the child has demonstrated his ability to meet and adhere to the standards of one level, he moves to the next higher level, where there are increased responsibilities and increased privileges. Gross violations of behavior on one level indicate that the child is not yet mature enough for that level, so he is returned to an earlier level where he has demonstrated his competence.

The child's performance in the incentive system is recorded on a daily basis—or more often, if needed; thus, the child has daily evidence of his progress. His scores over time can be charted so that he has visual evidence of the trends of his behavior. Ultimately, he should be able to work himself off the system and, for all practical purposes, function independently.

An incentive system essentially does away with concerns about discipline and punishment. The incentive program is impersonal, in the sense that verbal tugs of war between residents and staff are unnecessary. The child is not at war with the staff; he is not in competition with other residents; he alone controls whether or not he acquires increased privileges. In this construct, the child care worker serves as the facilitator of the system; she is no longer the imposer of penalties or punishments; she is not expected to "make" the child behave—that responsibility rests with the child.

Ideally, children in residence participate in developing the incentive system. By so doing, they have "ownership" of the program. Moreover, residents know better than adults what privileges are most meaningful to them.

The advantages of the incentive system include the following:

- Behavior is rapidly brought under control.
- Consistency among staff members in dealing with the same behavior is enhanced.
- Each child and each group has a clear understanding of what behavior is expected.
- Discipline emerges as an integral and natural part of the incentive system.
- The child has some control over his own life; responsibility for increasing his privileges and freedom clearly belong to the child.
- The child has a clearly visible, current measure of his progress.

The incentive system provides an excellent medium for teaching the most basic social skills, including the following:

- Self-care and hygiene;
- Personal responsibility;
- Care of property;
- Management of daily living routine;
- Skill of negotiation;
- Behavioral management;
- Interpersonal relationships; and
- Interpersonal communication.

Group Work

Every institution must use some sort of organized group work.

One of the unique characteristics of the institution is the living group, and group work is a method of using the strengths of the group in the service of treating individuals within the group.

It must be remembered that the cottage is not a place where children come just to live. The cottage is a place of healing, learning, unlearning, relearning; children come for a purpose, they have work to do, and they have goals to work on. All members of the group are engaged in this work.

Every group in time develops some sort of balance: some residents become leaders, others become followers, and still others are outcasts. In other words, each group has its own "pecking order." Whenever a child joins the group or leaves the group or because of the growing strength of an individual child or children, the balance of the group changes. A leader may be superseded, a new leader emerges, followers may change group roles, etc. Each child must find his place in the pecking order. Will he be a leader? Will he be a follower? Will he become a scapegoat or doormat for the rest of the group? Will he retain his initial role, or will his increasing self confidence enable him to change roles? Effective group work will ensure that every child is an active participant in cottage life.

In the context of the institutional living group, the word "group" takes on a specialized meaning. It means more than an aggregation of individuals; it refers to a specific quality of relationships among the members, a quality that is marked by the interdependence of group members.[1]

As "groupness" develops, i.e., as children perceive themselves and are perceived by others as belonging to a group, they share interests, goals, values, and rules, they work interdependently to solve problems, and they act as a unit toward the larger environment. As they work to facilitate group interests, their growing interdependence leads them to become concerned about each other as individuals, and the strengths of all individuals are brought to bear upon the problems of each individual.

Children are by nature and from experience—and often with good reason—suspicious of adults, so they listen to each other much more readily than they listen to even the most astute and sympathetic adult. Peers may say exactly what the adults have said, but children will hear what their peers say and ignore the adults' counsel. Group work capitalizes upon this by empowering the group members to listen to each other and to contribute to the welfare of each other.

The process of group functioning can and must be guided by the child care worker. An institutional cottage will have group process, whether the staff wants it or not. The question is whether the staff or residents will guide the group. Better that the staff refine its group work techniques so as to utilize the strengths of the group in the life of the cottage.

The child care worker serves as a facilitator in group work, guiding, suggesting, and integrating. She helps the group develop ground rules for group meetings and then ensures that the ground rules are followed.

After the group is well established, she can take an increasingly diminished role in the group give-and-take.

The nature and extent of group work varies widely from institution to institution, but if group work is not an integral part of the program, the institution has forfeited one of its strongest tools of treatment.

Group work literature is available in quantity to help child care workers design therapeutic group work in the cottage. Suggestions are available for how group work can be started, how group meetings can be structured most productively, when to meet (e.g., if the group meets before supper, rather than after, meetings will be shorter and more productive), what kind of chairs to use and how they are most effectively arranged, etc. Other findings from the very substantial experience of group work can enhance the effectiveness of group work in the institution.

The Residential Staff

The quality of residential care is inextricably bound up with the quality of residential staff. Residential work calls for high skills in making relationships at many different levels, from administrators, child care staff to the involvement with children and with visiting parents, however inadequate, bizarre, hostile, or destructive their behavior may be.

The child care role should be seen as pivotal in institutional life, with all other professionals acting as support staff. The child care worker actually lives with the child and sees him under every and all circumstances; therefore, the child care worker should provide the major treatment for the child.

The role of the institutional social worker should include less treatment of individual children and more in-service education, consultation to child care staff, family therapy, and community liaison work. Increasingly, the separation between family work and child care is difficult to justify.

Such a role shift will require accompanying changes in the educational preparation of social workers for residential treatment; they will need training in supervision, management, in-service education, and program evaluation as well as in clinical treatment.

Clinical authority for an individual child or for a group should not be given to an outside consultant who has little or no direct contact with the child and whose contacts with the agency consist of a once-a-week visit.

The clinician really needs to be an ongoing part of the institutional team.

In a related area, every staff member should receive training on a regular schedule. This means cooks, secretaries, janitors, groundsmen, and farmers. Everyone who is employed by a children's institutions is by that fact involved in child care and should receive sufficient training that all children are assured consistent treatment from all staff members. Adequate time and coverage should be provided so that all staff can attend training sessions.

Creative Programming with Families

The purpose of the institution's work with families should be to create a bridge between the group living environment and the child's family. Institutions have found that many parents of children in care can be utilized in the agency program. Family involvement will take many forms, each of which should constitute a linkage between the family culture and the culture of group life. The following are only some examples of the ways in which families have been involved:

• Family support groups. Families of children in care meet at the facility under the guidance of a worker to share experiences and problems, to learn from each other, and, perhaps most important, to learn that they are not the only family with a child in care.

• Parent education. Classes in parenting skills, in childhood growth and development, or in other pertinent subjects, are held under the auspices of the facility staff.

• Parent involvement in the life space. Parents have painted walls, given music lessons; they have done construction, shared in the discipline of their child, refereed ball games. Using any of their talents for the benefit of the agency gives the parent some "ownership" in the agency and its program.

• Home visiting by the child care staff. Child care workers who lived with the child have visited in the family home instead of—or in addition to—having the institutional social worker visit. By visiting in the child's home, the child care workers gain insight into the child's background; the parents have an opportunity to develop a relationship with their child's direct caregivers on their own "turf."

• Participation in school programs. After a history of seeing their child in negative terms, the parents have an opportunity to see their child perform positively with his peers. Parents may be involved in painting backdrops, running the lights, or in any other way compatible with their talents.

• Parents have free access to their children in person or by phone. The agency pays for telephone calls if the parents cannot afford it.

• Parents shop with children for clothes, accompanied by a worker in special situations.

• Education planning. A common characteristic of placed children is poor academic performance. The most successful programs of remediation have involved parents.

• Board participation. Consumer membership on a board of directors has been found to be productive in bringing reality into board meetings.

• Advisory Committee. In one institution, a parent advisory committee was organized, based on the premise that parent participation would provide a boost to their egos, that their acceptance by the staff and administration would facilitate their treatment and that parental involvement would be supportive to the children.

• Parents as legislative advocates. Children's concerns historically have had low priority on both the state and federal levels. Articulate parents have been used to advocate for increased funding for all children's concerns.

Another purpose of family work should be to identify any natural helping networks that exist in the child's family constellation which could be called upon to support and maintain growth achieved in the group living environment.

Such networks might contain the following:

• Extended family members;
• Friends;
• Clergy;
• Natural neighbors;
• Other indigenous helpers.

The program should be open to involving these persons actively whenever this is appropriate. Such a network may be especially important for the child whose family has minimal involvement with him.

Special Concerns for Children

Several special concerns for children deserve attention.

Life Book

The "Life Book" has been found to be helpful for many children. The social worker (or a foster parent or a child care worker) helps the child retrieve a sense of his own past by taking him to visit and photograph foster homes or other places where he has lived, his own home, the hospital where he was born, the schools he attended, and foster parents, teachers, or other persons who have had meaning to him in the past. Parents can be helpful in this project.

The Life Book can be not only a photograph album, but a scrapbook which contains report cards, programs of school activities (especially those in which the child participated), copies of a birth certificate, court orders, school papers bearing favorable comments, and anything else which may have meaning to the child.

In the context of the family, such scrapbooks are an embellishment of family living; for the child in placement, scrapbooks may constitute a replacement for family living, inadequate at best, but perhaps crucial in helping the child feel a bit less that he exists in a vacuum.

Visiting Resource

If no one in the child's family is able or willing to be involved with the child (despite casework and financial support), someone needs to be found who is prepared to take a continuing interest in the child on a long-term basis. Many institutions have been creative in developing visiting resources for children in care so that they have some exposure to family life. Children in residence visit these family homes on weekends, vacations, and at other times when it is appropriate to get away from campus life.

Record-Sharing

A long-standing controversy has centered upon whether or not to share records with the child. More and more agencies are opting to be open and above-board with the children and open the children's own files for them to see. Opening the files removes the mystique from the files and from the office and tends to reduce anxiety of the child about what is being written about him. Some children, in reading their record for the first time, have found great reassurance that so many different people have tried to help them over the years.

WHO SHOULD BE REFERRED TO AN INSTITUTION?

Some of those for whom a stay in residential institutions can be helpful are:

- Children who have a satisfactory tie to an own parent, a tie which both the child and the parent want to keep close;
- Children of recently divorced parents, children who have become confused and torn in their loyalties, who require a rest away from relatives and who need the more diluted or impersonal relationships possible in an institution;
- Children who have experienced many moves and replacements, who need more than anything else to stay in one place long enough to put down physical roots, and to make emotional ties with an adult or two;
- Children who, for one reason or another, cannot accept foster care, or whose behavior is such that they are not acceptable to foster parents. For many children it is a favorable factor that the institution is entirely different from a family home. In the institution, the child can make a completely fresh start, whereas if placed in a foster home, directly or too soon, he may find too many associations with the home life he has left;
- Children whose parents cannot tolerate seeing another individual or couple take over the parenting function for their child and would undermine any foster family placement or group home placement;
- Children abruptly snatched from their own homes. Children who face placement still smarting from the wounds of an emergency separation, may do best if they work through some of their feelings before attempting to relate to foster parents;
- Children whose behavior requires more structure and controls than would be available in a foster home or group home;
- Children who have a psychiatrically diagnosable condition which few foster parents are equipped to handle;
- Children whose stay in alternate care is specifically for the purpose of clarifying the family situation, the result of which may be return of the child to his own home, termination of parental rights and release of the child for adoption, or professionally-prescribed long-term foster care.

THE INSTITUTION AND THE PLACING WORKER

The placing worker should be able to expect the following of the institution:

- Some philosophy of behavioral change which can be described;
- Realistic plans of care;

• Incentive program;
• Training for staff;
• Group work;
• Education in accordance with the needs of the child;
• A program designed for the needs of the child rather than for the convenience of the staff;
• Accurate reporting on the child's progress at agreed-upon intervals;
• Involvement of the parents by the facility in accordance with the agency/family plan of care.

The institutional staff should be able to expect at least the following from the placing worker:

• Referral material will be honest and accurate;
• Records, including school records, will be complete when the child is placed;
• The worker will keep in touch with the child by personal visits, mail, and telephone;
• The worker will keep in touch with the family and periodically report to the institutional staff the status of the family;
• The worker will be available to the institutional staff when they have questions or concerns about the child or his family. She will keep her supervisor informed about the case so that the supervisor can take action in the worker's absence;
• She will arrange for the child home to visit as often as possible. Even if he cannot return home to live, he needs to see for himself what the family is;
• The worker will not let siblings get lost;
• If the worker leaves her job, she will take her successor to meet the child personally.

WHEN USING AN INSTITUTION FOR THE FIRST TIME

Many institutions are highly professional and operate effective programs for children, youth and their families. However, institutions across the country have a wide range of program effectiveness and professionalism; therefore, the worker should be proceed carefully when using an institution for the first time.

The worker must bear in mind the fact that an institution is licensed does not indicate adequacy of program. This is not a failure of the licensing process; licensing does not purport to enforce program quality. Only minimum standards, which are established in the law or in departmental regulations, are enforceable. Many licensors do make recommendations for improving the quality of a program, but recommendations are not enforceable. Thus, the placing worker is responsible for doing her own research to make sure that the institution can do what is needed for the child she must place.

The worker should have more information about the institution, its staff, program, and philosophy than appears in the agency brochure or is given by the institutional representative. The following questions suggest some of the areas about which she will want to have information.

1) For what kinds of problems is the program designed?

2) What is the size of living groups?

3) What is the average length of stay—documented, not guessed at?

4) What is the function of the institutional social worker—to give therapy to individual residents or to provide consultation and training to staff and to do case planning?

5) Are goals set for residents? If so, who sets those goals?

6) What mechanism is there for residents to grow and have self determination? Is there an incentive system? What kinds of privileges can be earned?

7) What records are kept of residents' goal attainment? How is residents' progress documented?

8) What structure is built into the program?

9) To what degree is group work utilized, and in what form?

10) For what reasons are residents moved from cottage to cottage?

11) What recreation is available? Are residents permitted to take advantage of recreational facilities? Are they taught productive recreational activities?

12) What is the spiritual content of the program?

13) How much free time do the residents have?

14) To what degree is the program related to the community?

15) To what degree are parents recognized, accepted, utilized?

16) Are visiting arrangements made in terms of the need and potential of the family and child, or for the convenience of the agency?

17) For older residents, what preparation is made for life outside the institution?

18) What disciplinary procedures are used? (Residents can give this information.)

19) How are residents helped to learn to handle responsibility? Can they have part-time jobs? What control do they have over their own funds?

20) What provisions are made for preparation for independent living?
21) What provision is made for aftercare?

SUMMARY

Institutions have an honored place in the continuum of child care, but too often they pretend to be or are believed to be what they are not, and cannot be. The oft-repeated, well-intentioned boast of the inexperienced child care worker that "We're just one big, happy family" is manifestly untrue, no matter how much the child care worker would like to think it, and irrespective of how smoothly the cottage operates.

One of the trickiest problems in interpreting institutional care is differentiating between a group which has familylike characteristics and a group which is actually a family. Cottages (or a living group, irrespective of the physical structure) do, indeed, have familylike characteristics—children eat at the same table, live under the same roof, share various parts of their lives, etc.—but that does not make them a family.

One cannot put 10–16 troubled, unrelated children under one roof with paid staff members who are unrelated to the residents, who work regular shifts, take regular time off, and have vacations apart from the children, and call them a family. To pretend that the cottage is a family denies the reality, which is entirely honorable, that this is a placement of treatment.

Group care is the treatment of choice for some children at one point in their lives. Group care is an authentic, constructive primary life experience for some children whose needs cannot be met adequately and appropriately in family care[2]. Group care should be used because its distinctive strengths serve a child and his family better than any other kind of care.

Institutional care is at the opposite end of the continuum from family care; therefore, it is to be used only for as long as the child needs its unique environment. As soon as the child has derived maximum benefit from the institutional program, he should start back up the continuum in the direction of family living.

The overburdened worker may find it easier to overlook a child in an institutional placement than in foster family care or group home care because of the numbers of staff members available to the child. With an institutional placement, perhaps more intensely than with other types of placements, steps must be taken to ensure that the child remains only as long as necessary.

The negative effects of inappropriate, long-term placement in an institution are at least as severe as inappropriate placements in other settings. Too often the child being discharged from an institution past the formative years of his life may be clinically improved but quite empty in personality and unrelated to the real world in which he must live all the rest of his life. His previous reality, the institution, was artificially contrived and hence too protected, so that he is ill prepared to meet life's true realities.

Where treatment institutions are not available to some placing agencies for treating the needs of the emotionally disturbed child and of his parents, or when other community resources, such as homemaker services or day care, are lacking, by default the general institution is sometimes used to meet these needs in part, if a foster home cannot.

It is regrettable that this happens, because the institution then becomes a dumping ground where the child with respect to his special needs is abandoned, and the institution's usual program is hampered by the difficulties presented by the child with whom it is not equipped to cope.

It cannot be too much stressed that the type of placement facility to be used first be determined by the diagnostic indications of each individual child and his parents. Once these are established, the resources available must be assessed as to which will most closely meet the needs indicated.

Endnote

[1] Henley, H. Carl, and Plumer, Erwin H. (Eds.). *The Residential Child Care Worker: Concepts and Functions.* Chapel Hill, NC:Group Child Care Consultant Services, 1978, p. 149.

[2] Ibid., p. 147.

ADDITIONAL READINGS

Bryce, Marvin and Lloyd, June (Eds.) *Treating Families in the Home.* Springfield, IL: Charles C Thomas, 1981.

Bryce, Marvin and Maybanks, Sheila (Eds.) *Home-Based Services for Children and Families.* Springfield, IL: Charles C Thomas, 1979.

Chase, Naomi. *A Child Is Being Beaten.* New York: McGraw Hill, 1975.

Children in Foster Care Institutions—Steps Government Can Take to Improve Their Care. Report to the Congress by the Comptroller General of the United States, HRD-77-40, February 22, 1977.

Glickman, Esther. *Child Placement Through Clinically Oriented Casework.* New York: Columbia University Press, 1957.

Gruber, Alan R. *Children in Foster Care.* New York: Human Sciences Press, 1978.

Jenkins, Shirley and Norman, Elaine. *Filial Deprivation and Foster Care.* New York: Columbia University Press, 1972.

Katz, Sanford N. *When Parents Fail: The Law's Response to Family Breakdown.* Boston: Beacon Press, 1971.

Kline, Draza and Overstreet, Helen-Mary. *Foster Care of Children.* New York: Columbia University Press, 1972.

Knitzer, Jane, Allen, Mary Lee, and McGowan, Brenda. *Children Without Homes.* Washington, D.C.: Children's Defense Fund, 1978.

Mandell, Betty. *Where Are the Children?* Lexington, MA: Lexington Books, 1973.

Mayer, Morris and Blum, Arthur. *Healing Through Living.* Springfield, IL: Charles C Thomas, 1971.

Mayer, Morris, Richmond, Leon, and Balcerzak, Edwin. *Group Care of Children: Crossroads and Transitions.* New York: Child Welfare League of America, 1977.

Mnookin, Robert H. "Foster Care—In Whose Best Interest?" *Harvard Educational Review,* Vol.43, No. 4, November 1976.

More Can Be Learned and Done About the Well-Being of Children. Report to the Congress by the Comptroller General of the United States, MWD-76-23, April 9, 1976.

Peck, M. Scott. *The Road Less Traveled.* New York: Simon and Schuster, 1978.

Redl, Fritz. *When We Deal With Children.* New York: Free Press, 1966.

Wald, Michael S. "State Intervention on Behalf of 'Neglected' Children. Standards for Removal of Children from Their Homes, Monitoring the Status of Children in Foster Care, and Termination of Parental Rights." *Stanford Law Review,* Vol. 28, April, 1976.

Whittaker, James K. *Caring for Troubled Children.* San Francisco: Jossey-Bass, 1979.